THE HIGHLA

THE HIGHLANDS
OF SCOTLAND

W. DOUGLAS SIMPSON

**ILLUSTRATED
AND WITH A MAP**

ROBERT HALE · LONDON

© W. Douglas Simpson 1969 and 1976
First published 1969 as Portrait of the Highlands
Reprinted 1970, 1972 and 1975

This edition first published 1976

ISBN 0 7091 0415 4 (hardcover)
ISBN 0 7091 5887 4 (paperback)

Robert Hale & Company
Clerkenwell House
Clerkenwell Green
London EC1R 0HT

Reproduced by Photolitho by
Jarrold and Sons Ltd, Norwich

CONTENTS

ILLUSTRATIONS

INTRODUCTION

Anyone who glances at a relief map of Scotland will perceive at once that the country is divided into three parts by well-marked demarcation lines trending all from north-east to south-west. These natural divisions may be labelled: the Southern Uplands; the Central Lowlands; and the Highlands. In their turn the Highlands are subdivided by the deep narrow depression, likewise trending from north-east to south-west, which contains the great chain of freshwater lakes, Loch Ness, Loch Oich and Loch Lochy, and the marine fiord of Loch Linnhe—all now linked together by the Caledonian Canal. The line which separates the Southern Uplands from the Central Lowlands runs, roughly speaking, from Dunbar on the east to Girvan in the south-west. The 'Highland Line' is formed—again to speak in very broad terms—by a line extending from Stonehaven in the north-east through Dunkeld, Comrie and Aberfoyle to Helensburgh on the Firth of Clyde. Nevertheless, the area north of this line is not all of Highland character. It includes the coastal plain extending round the north-eastern knuckle of Aberdeenshire and both shores of the Moray Firth as far as the extreme north of Scotland, in the county of Caithness.

The four great dividing lines that I have indicated are formed by very ancient geological fractures or 'faults', each of which has been accompanied by profound down-slipping and dislocation of the rock formations. Below the Southern Boundary Fault we find a tangled area of barren mountains, yet by no means equal in height or ruggedness to the Highlands properly so called. The rocks of the Southern Uplands are sedimentary in origin, and belong to an early stage in the geological history of our globe. To a large extent they are composed of coarse, hard grits, with many intruded or extruded igneous masses. Aeons of weathering, culminating in glacial scouring during the last Ice Age, have reduced the Southern

Uplands to bare rounded summits, nowhere exceeding a height of 3,000 feet, and altogether lacking the bold peaks that characterize the Highlands.

The Central Lowlands, or Middle Basin, offer a striking contrast both to the Southern Uplands and to the Highlands. They are composed of relatively soft sandstones and shales, mostly belonging to the Old Red Sandstone and Carboniferous periods of the geological record. As in the Southern Uplands, they include much igneous material. These rocks of the Central Lowlands contain the chief mineral resources of Scotland, her coal measures, oil shales and iron ores. Moreover, most of the best agricultural soil is here. Hence the Central Lowlands, though comprising less than one-fifth of the total area of Scotland,[1] contain about three-quarters of her population, and certainly an overwhelming proportion of the national wealth.

The geological feature which delimits the Highland area from the Central Lowlands is known as the Highland Boundary Fault. The Northern Highlands are similarly marked off by the Caledonian Fault, extending, practically in a straight line, from Inverness to Oban. In Gaelic speech it is known as Glen More nan Albin, the Great Glen of Alba—Alba being the ancient Celtic name of Scotland north of the Forth and Clyde. But the rocks on either side of the Great Glen are broadly similar in character. They consist of hard and ancient metamorphic rocks, belonging to two great systems, the Moine Series and the Dalradian Series, whose exact relation to each other, and respective positions in the geological time scale, are still imperfectly understood. These metamorphic rocks have been invaded, on at least two occasions, by masses of granite and other igneous rocks, which form the principal mountain areas of the Central Highlands. It is the resistant qualities of all these varied but stubborn rocks that have led to their surviving the agents of denudation so as to form today the chief mountain complex of the British Islands. In the Cairngorm group on the east, and in the isolated Ben Nevis on the west (the highest mountain in Britain) the Central Highlands of Scotland possess all the five British summits which attain a height of over 4,000 feet.

[1] In round figures, the total area is 30,000 square miles—not 30,000 acres, as stated, by an absurd blunder, in the first edition of my former work, *The Ancient Stones of Scotland* (1963), p. 17!

With their superb scenery of mountain, moorland, glen and loch; with the scientific interest of their geology and natural history; with their unrivalled facilities for winter and summer sport and recreation; with their distinctive racial and social characteristics and their historical and antiquarian appeal; and with the romantic literary glamour cast around them by the genius of Sir Walter Scott—offering all these varied attractions, small wonder that year after year our Scottish Highlands draw visitors in increasing thousands from far and near. 'Tourism'—to use the ugly word by which all this may be summed up—is being deliberately fostered upon an increasing scale—the more so because the Highlands are otherwise poor in natural resources, and constantly menaced by the creeping spectre of depopulation. In particular, since the last war the development of the Highland area for winter sport is being pushed with remarkable vigour and no small measure of success. Thus we have now ski-ing centres in the Ben Lawers area, in Glencoe, in Glenshee, and on both sides of the Cairngorms. But also, vigorous efforts are being made to build a more solid economic basis for the future of the Highlands. We need here mention only the development of forestry, of hydro-electric schemes, of distilling, and of isolated ventures such as the aluminium and paper-making industries at Fort William. Of all these, and of other such hopeful projects, more will be said in due course.

It is the purpose of the first part of the present volume to offer a portrait of what may loosely be described as the Central Highlands of Scotland. That is to say, we shall be examining the area of mountain land between the Midland Basin and the Great Glen, excluding the Northern Highlands, the eastern plains, and the Atlantic coast with its fiords and islands. The second part of this work will deal, in more summary fashion, with the Northern Highlands, including their western and northern sea-fronts, but omitting the eastern coastal plains.

Following a policy the short-sightedness of which will become apparent long before this present century is out, the British Government is avidly engaged in dismantling the Highland railway system. Within the Central Highlands we are now left with little more than the main lines between Perth and Inverness, between Glasgow and Fort William, and, on its eastern margin, between Aberdeen and Inverness. The result of this purblindness is to cast an intolerable burden of motor traffic upon an inadequate road system—though it is fair to say that much has been done, and still is doing, to improve our Highland roads and bridges. Air services connect Edinburgh, Glasgow and Aberdeen with Inverness. Public motor-bus transport, though at present far from adequate for the area, is improving steadily; and during the season comprehensive bus tours, with hotel accommodation thrown in, are available to cover most districts. Camping facilities and 'bed and breakfast' lodgings are increasing with every season. The general standard of our Highland hotels is steadily improving, though still apt to leave Americans discontented. Inflexibility of meal hours, lack of variety in cooking, and the absence of baths attached to bedrooms, have been the principal sources of complaint; and of course our absurd British licensing laws are a constant annoyance to visitors. Under the prevailing penal taxation, not a few owners of stately homes or historic castles now eke out their dwindling budgets by taking in 'paying guests'. All in all, the traveller, whatever his purse, has gone a long way, in his prospects of comfort, since, in the earliest systematic handbook to the Highlands, published in 1834, guidance and warning was given him for his adventurous journey. It is sufficiently amusing to permit abbreviation as follows:[1]

Neither scientific nor pleasure tours should in general be undertaken by a party consisting of more than four persons, as well from the difficulty of procuring accommodations at night as provisions by the way. If a carriage is used, it should be one which opens from the top, or a low four-wheeled gig, with two seats and a boot for luggage, and drawn by one good hardy horse, or two small ponies; and the latter vehicle should have a large umbrella or canvas aprons. Pedestrians should have their wardrobe as light and scanty as possible; but in every case we would recommend woollen clothing to be used. . . . A walking umbrella should always be carried, to protect one from the sun as much as from the rain, together with a compass, a pocket spy-glass, and a travelling map wrapped in an oil-skin, which will also serve to carry a few sheets of writing paper and sketch book, with pen and ink and drawing materials. Forget not a few buttons,

[1] George and Peter Anderson, *Guide to the Highlands and Islands of Scotland* (1834), pp. 730-1. This, the first edition of this remarkable book, is emphatically the one to read. Later issues, stitched and darned and interpolated and expanded to unmanageable dimensions, have in large measure lost their usefulness and charm.

pins, thread and needles, and soap and shaving materials, with a piece of linen rag and fine shoe-leather for bruises and sores, and a little medicine, chiefly laxative and sedative. Be not over nice in requiring sheets for your bed . . . and when obliged to sleep in a shepherd's or labourer's cot, endeavour to get straw or ferns as your mattress, and next to them heather, which, however, requires some art to arrange, but on all occasions avoid sleeping on hay, unless you wish to be reduced to jockey size. Accustom yourself to living on two meals a day, which are quite enough; but never leave your inn in the morning, without taking with you at least a piece of bread, to prevent faintishness by the way. Eat it along with the water you will feel disposed to drink on your journey, but use spirits of all kinds in great moderation, especially during the early parts of the day. If on a botanical or geological excursion of some endurance, carry but one pair of strong, large-sized shoes, one pair of trousers, one cloth waistcoat with leather pockets, one square short coat, provided with six large pockets, two out and two inside, and two in the breasts, two pair of coarse worsted socks, two shirts, one black silk neckcloth, and a cap. . . . Knapsacks are always tearing and going wrong, and letting in the rain where it is not wanted; so that, if the appearance of a light wicker basket so woven as to be watertight is disregarded, it will be found the best general receptacle for all sorts of stores and comforts. But for the most part, the pedestrian should make his wardrobe so portable as to be easily contained in his coat pockets. Water-proof capes will be found of great service by all travellers, though perhaps a little burdensome on a walking excursion.

All of which adds up to a portrait of our early nineteenth-century wayfarer in the Highlands as something much resembling (less the tin armour!) the White Knight in *Through the Looking-glass*: "You see", said that famous warrior to Alice, "it's as well to be provided for *everything*." But the modern traveller in the Highlands does not require to be so encumbered. He can throw all his luggage into the back of his car: and if he be a scientist whose quest requires him to forsake the beaten paths, then a shooting-brake or a jeep will take him almost everywhere he wants to go. And the time may not be so far distant when the hoverplane will be called in as an aid to survey work among the mountains.

Though the roads on either side of the Great Glen now form the main communication between Inverness and Oban, the Caledonian Canal itself is still in limited use. In the heyday of sailing vessels, it was much favoured, particularly by the fishing fleets, since it

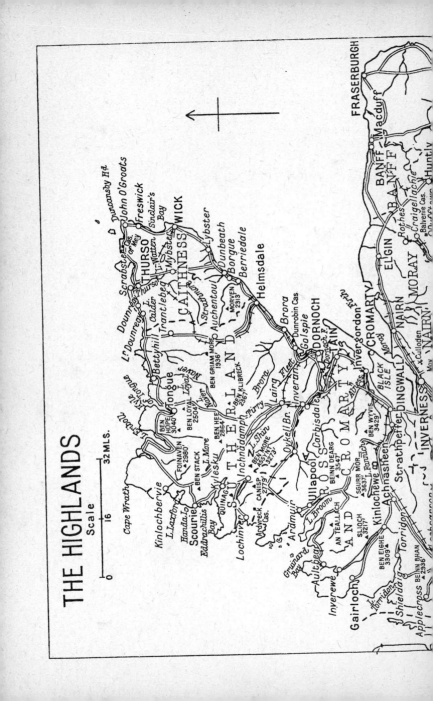

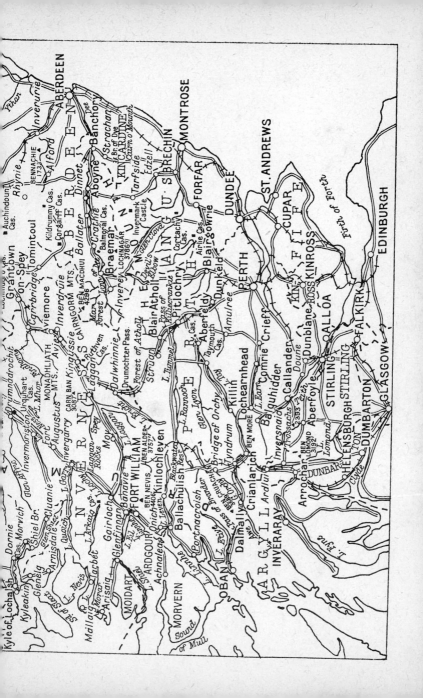

avoided the stormy passage of some four hundred miles round Cape Wrath and through the treacherous waters of the Pentland Firth. But large modern steam or motor powered trawlers prefer to avoid the Canal, with its small capacity and its twenty-eight locks.

The first survey for the projected canal was made by James Watt in 1773. Impelled by the strategic needs of the war against Napoleon, when French privateers haunted our coastal waters, work upon the Canal was commenced in earnest in 1803, under the over-all direction of Telford. But the victory of Trafalgar lessened the urgency of the project, and the Canal was not opened for use until October, 1822. At the inaugural ceremony about seventy gentlemen traversed the Canal "in a steam barge, the first vessel that passed from sea to sea". Originally the Canal was designed to admit the passage of a 32-gun frigate; but in 1847 it was much improved, with a view to capturing a greater proportion of the trade between America and the Baltic, as well as for the transport of Highland timber to the collieries of the Midland Basin, and for the benefit of the herring fishery. Before the general use of steam power, the passage of the canal, in fair weather, took a couple of days. The summit level, at the entrance to Loch Oich, reaches a height of 105 feet O.D. The ultimate cost of the Canal, as completed in 1849, was over £1,300,000; and at the maximum effort some 3,000 men, mostly Highlanders, were employed. Thus the Canal played its part in relieving the unemployment that followed upon the termination of the Napoleonic wars. Perhaps the most remarkable feature of the Canal is the series of eight locks, known as Neptune's Staircase, between Banavie and Corpach, some three miles above Fort William. The total length of the Canal is about 60 miles, of which 22 miles are canal proper, the rest being the chain of lochs. The water depth is about 20 feet; the Canal is 123 feet wide at surface level, and 50 feet wide at bottom.

During the two World Wars there was a considerable increase in the use made of the Canal, mostly by naval vessels. In 1966 a pulp and paper mill was opened at Corpach. Bulk supplies of wood chips are brought from Canada to Loch Linnhe and blown through a 1,500-foot pipe to the mill. In the summer season, pleasure craft cruise along the Canal, affording hundreds of tourists their best view of the magnificent scenery of Glen More nan Albin.

PART ONE

THE CENTRAL HIGHLANDS

CHAPTER I

THE GEOLOGICAL FOUNDATIONS

We have said that the Central Highlands are composed in the main of metamorphic rocks belonging to the Moine and Dalradian series. The Dalradian rocks occupy most of the eastern part of our area: roughly speaking, to the south-east of a sinuous line running from the Moray Firth at Buckie to the lower end of Loch Lomond. Beyond the limits of our study, the Dalradian sequence continues across Loch Fyne into the peninsula of Kintyre. To the north-west of the Dalradians, up to our limit in the Great Glen, the Moine series forms the Central Highland Granulites, extending south-westward in the Great Glen as far as the alcove of Loch Linnhe, and as far eastward as Strathspey and the headwaters of the Dee, the Garry, and the Tummel. Beyond the Great Glen, Moine rocks occupy a vast tract of country in the Northern Highlands; but with this we are not at the moment concerned.

The Dalradian rocks consist of an enormous assemblage of different types—gneisses, schists, limestones, shales, grits, quartzites and serpentines—which possess only this feature in common, that they have all been metamorphosed, or altered from their original condition, by the combined agencies of pressure, heat, chemical changes and vast tectonic movements. As to their former state, and their place in the geological sequence, no agreement has so far been reached. In some cases, it is even doubtful whether the original rock was of sedimentary or igneous character. It is, however, cogently argued now that the metamorphosis of the Dalradian rocks is likely to have taken place at least as early as the Cambrian epoch —that is to say, as metamorphosed they are about equal in age to the most ancient stratified rocks which contain a regular assemblage of fossils. According to the latest chronology, the Cambrian epoch dates from between five hundred and six hundred millions of years ago. Imagination boggles at the contemplation of so vast a lapse of time: yet how much older than the Cambrian rocks are our Dalradians *before they were metamorphosed*, no one can venture even to guess.[1]

Intruded among the Dalradians are great masses of granitic rocks compact and for the most part stubbornly resistant to the forces of denudation, so that today they form the principal mountain masses of the Central Highlands—the Cairngorms, Lochnagar, Mount Keen, Mount Battock, and Ben Rinnes. All these belong to what are known as the Younger Granites; and it is thought that they were introduced among the Dalradians at the end of Silurian times, when the great mountain building movement in our own area, known to geologists as the Caledonian Orogeny (but affecting all Britain, as well as Scandinavia) appears to have taken place. By it what is today represented by the Scottish Highlands was uplifted into a mountain complex of Himalayan proportions. Our present Highlands are no more than the worn down and dissected roots of their gigantic predecessors. Geologists have given to these ancient mountains the name of the 'Caledonides'.

Probably more or less of the same date as the Newer Granites are certain broad intrusions of basic matter—i.e., rocks which contain less silica than the granites, which are termed acid rocks, whereas basic rocks are richer in metallic oxides. One of the most important basic rocks is gabbro. Within our area it forms the upland of the Cabrach, but excluding the graceful summit of the Buck, which is formed out of knotted schist.

These Younger Granites, of presumed Silurian or Lower Old Red Sandstone date, must be carefully distinguished from the Older Granites, which are now ascertained to have been intruded during the regional metamorphism of the Dalradian rocks. In terms of landscape relief, the Older Granites, which are much mixed up with the Dalradians so as sometimes to form a hybrid rock to which the term migmatite ('mixed rock') has been given, do not bulk large in our area; but they form significant masses at Ben Vuroch, north of Pitlochry, as also in Glen Doll, Glen Tilt and Glen Shee.

The Moine series of metamorphic rocks are represented in our area by the Central Highland Granulites. Mostly these are pale grey quartzite rocks, doubtless the product of intense and pro-

---

[1] See J. A. Miller and P. E. Brown, "How old is Scotland?" in *The Advancement of Science* (British Association) vol. XX, No. 88 (March 1964), pp. 527–39.

longed metamorphosis among sandstones, mudstones and shales, now thereby converted into flags and grits. Limestones and horn-blende schists are also present, though the former rock is much rarer than in the Dalradian series. All these former sediments have now become thoroughly crystalline.

These rocks of the Moine and Dalradian systems may be grouped together under the convenient, because non-committal, name of the Highland Schists. The whole complex presents some of the most difficult geological problems in the world. It may well be many years before even a broad measure of agreement is reached as to the origins, geological horizons, and inter-relationships of these two great suites of metamorphic rocks. In the Central Highlands the Moines seem to underly the Dalradians, but the precise relationship between the two systems remains undetermined. In-evitably, therefore, this is no field for the amateur investigator. But when we turn to the sedimentary formations in our area, we find ourselves presented with some fascinating glimpses into the geological history of Scotland, to a large extent free from the per-plexities of the older and highly altered rocks which we have grouped together under the general term of Highland Schists.

One of the most famous of such localities is the Rhynie-Kil-drummy basin, on the north-eastern margin of our area. It is formed by an outlier of Middle Old Red Sandstone deposits, faul-ted down between the knotted schists of the Correen Hills and the gabbro intrusion (above mentioned) of the Cabrach. The pass so formed provided one of the principal routes from Mar into Moray; and in the days when the latter province was sturdily resisting in-corporation into the expanding realm of Scotland, the importance of the breach in the northern mountain barrier of Mar was recog-nized by the building of an important castle at either end of the gap: Kildrummy, "noblest of northern castles", on the south; and Strathbogie (later known as Huntly Castle) on the north, where the great road into Moray crossed the River Deveron.

If the reader will forgive a homely comparison, we may liken our Kildrummy-Rhynie basin to an elongated shallow dish with a crinkled rim. This dish is half filled with porridge, the surface of which, *more Scotico*, has been sprinkled over, freely and irregularly, with oatmeal—here heaped up in little piles, there spread out—to form a thin cover or dusting.

The sides of our basin are formed out of Dalradian Schists. I have described them above as perdurable rock masses which, resisting unsummed aeons of denudation, yet slowly and stubbornly yielding on storm-swept summit and in stream-furrowed glen, stand up today, scarred yet defiant, to form the crinkled rim of our imagined dish.

The porridge with which the dish is half-filled consists of sandstones, conglomerates and shales. These were brought down and spread out in thick beds by torrential rivers that, some three and a half millions of years ago, cascaded roaring down the rugged sides of a mighty mountain system of which, as I have said above, the Highlands that we know are but the wasted roots.

The oatmeal scattering in our dish represents those thick deposits of pebbles, gravel and sand with which the sandstones have been covered by the glaciers of the Ice Age, and the surging floods that overswept the country during the long years when the ice sheet was slowly melting.

We have seen above how wrapt in the obscurity of an unimaginable past are the natural conditions under which the Highland schists were formed. About the Old Red sediments we know a great deal more, for since the days of Hugh Miller this must be accounted the classical geological system of Scotland; and it has been studied, by a long succession of able investigators, with the zeal and thoroughness which the stratigraphic interest of these beds and the importance of their fossil remains deserve. Upon the rugged, uneven floor made by the ancient gneisses and schists, our conglomerates were accumulated out of the enormous loads of pebbles and boulders brought down from the Caledonides by impetuous torrents fed by a heavy seasonal rainfall. In shallow brackish pools, frequently swept by storms or agitated by inpouring streams, were laid down the sandstones, flags and shales. It is a great law of our planet that every orogeny, or mountain-building movement, culminates in a volcanic paroxysm. The Old Red Sandstone period accordingly was marked by much Phlegrean activity: and that our basin contained an active volcano, or volcanoes, we know from the presence among the sandstones of a couple of lava flows. Recently, indeed, the site of an explosive vent has been identified at Contlach in the parish of Auchindoir.

In Old Red times fishes were the lords of creation. But of all the varied animal life of that ancient time the sandstones of our basin have yielded but the scantiest traces—here the track of some burrowing crustacean, there the trail of an annelid, or perhaps the blurred scrape of a fin across a ridge of sand; and in two cases, remains of the *Pterygotus*, a kind of extinct scorpion. But the ancient plant-life of our basin has now been made famous throughout the scientific world by the discovery in 1913 near Rhynie of a petrified peat bog crowded with the remains of lowly plants in such perfect preservation that their minutest cells and tissues can be examined under the microscope. These very primitive plant forms, among the most ancient so far known in the world, seem to be the remote ancestors of our present club-mosses. Amid the rotting vegetation fungi flourished; and these also have been splendidly preserved. Along with the plants were found the remains of certain mite-like and spider-like creatures, as well as what seems to be a very small variety of *Pterygotus*. It appears that the siliceous water by which this ancient peat-moss was first drowned, and then so thoroughly petrified, was poured out boiling from a near-by geyser during the final stages of the volcanic activity of which I have spoken.[1]

We have still to speak of the oatmeal sprinkled over our porridge plate. No visitor to the Kildrummy basin can fail to be struck by the extraordinarily stony nature of the fields. Their soil is simply crowded with stones, of all sizes from the smallest pebble to boulders as big as a football. They are all smooth and well-rounded, and the majority consist of quartzite. The presence of so many stones in the soil is due to the fact that our basin is overspread with a vast series of glacial or fluvio-glacial gravels[2]—the deposits left by a gigantic precursor of the present River Don, drawing its turbulent water from the decaying ice-field of the Cairngorms. How tremendous was the carrying power of this ancient river is shown by the fact that the gravel beds are found as much as 900 feet above sea-level on the western margin of our basin, and up to 750 feet on the opposite side!

[1] Vegetation in the Rhynie basin on a much larger scale than these lowly plants of the fossil peat-bog is vouched by the cast of a stem now in the Geological Museum of Aberdeen University. It is 5 inches thick and survives to a length of 4 feet. It seems to represent a gigantic version of our present 'mare's tails'.

[2] In geological parlance, the word 'gravel' is applied to any loose deposit of water-borne materials coarser than a sand—even when the deposit contains as many large stones as in the Kildrummy gravels.

For a second vignette of the geological history of the Central Highlands we betake ourselves to their northern margin—to an area famous not only for its geology but for its historical and antiquarian interests. At the point where Strathnairn debouches upon the plainlands that border the Moray Firth, and over against dolorous Culloden Moor, is Clava, a place renowned among archaeologists for its group of chambered cairns, burial monuments of the neolithic period. These are the family vaults of a race of long-skulled wanderers who, coming up from the Mediterranean along the Atlantic coasts, entered Scotland by the western seaboard, and slowly overspread the west and north of the country—one of their main avenues of infiltration being, naturally, the Great Glen. But our concern here is with geology. The bedrock of the Clava area belongs to the Middle Old Red Sandstone, and is, therefore, roughly contemporary with the Rhynie outlier. From its flagstones have been recovered the fossil remains of some of those bizarre fishes, or fish-like creatures, which at that early stage in the life-history of our globe, were, as I have already mentioned, the lords of creation. These extraordinary creatures have never been more vividly described than in the classic language of Hugh Miller:[1]

Certainly a stranger assemblage of forms have rarely been grouped together—creatures whose very type is lost, fantastic and uncouth, and which puzzle the naturalist to assign them even their class; boat-like animals, furnished with oars and a rudder; fish plated over, like the tortoise, above and below, with a strong armour of bone, and furnished with but one solitary rudder-like fin; other fish less equivocal in their form, but with the membranes of their fins thickly covered with scales; creatures bristling over with thorns; others glistening in an enamelled coat, as if beautifully japanned; the tail, in every instance among the less equivocal shapes, formed not equally, as in existing fishes, on each side the vertebral column, but chiefly on the lower side—the column sending out its diminished vertebrae to the extreme termination of the fin. All the forms testify of a remote antiquity—of a period whose fashions have passed away. The figures on a Chinese vase or an Egyptian obelisk are scarce more unlike what now exists in nature than are the fossils of the Lower Old Red Sandstone.

But Clava is less renowned among the geologists of today for its Old Red fishes than for its Arctic shell-bed of the Great Ice Age

[1] *The Old Red Sandstone*, ed. 1869, pp. 60-1.

Looking towards the Bridge of Feugh near Banchory
The 'Three Sisters of Glencoe'
(overleaf) Loch Kinnord by the Moor of Dinnet

—a deposit which has aroused much discussion, and the true nature of which is still unsettled.

During the period of maximum cold, our Central Highlands were covered by a vast *mer-de-glace* or ice sheet, from which probably only the highest summits emerged like the 'nunataks' of Greenland today. Of this ice-sheet the 'till', or boulder clay, which ascends in some places to a height of nearly 1,800 feet, is the principal memento. In many a gravel pit and water course it may be studied upon the lower grounds of our area. It is a stiff clay, grey or tawny or reddish in hue, crowded with boulders, great and small, which are all of them smoothened and partly rounded by ice-action, and often show beautiful 'striae' or scratchings. Intermingled with the clay are sands and gravels, brought down and sorted out by the turbulent streams that coursed through and escaped from the slowly melting ice.

Great oscillations in the respective levels of land and sea took place during the Ice Age, as seems to be shown by the Clava bed of Arctic marine shells, which is now at a level of 500 feet above the shore of the Moray Firth. This bed is older than the boulder clay, which overlies it to a depth, as preserved, of 45 feet; while between the boulder clay and the shell-bed is a thickness of 20 feet of finely stratified brown sand. The shells themselves are embalmed in a bluish-grey silt. The shell-bed is known to extend for a length of at least 190 yards: its breadth has not been ascertained. Below the shell-bed are more glacial gravels and clays, different in character from those above; and the whole series rests upon the Old Red Sandstone. If this evidence has been correctly interpreted, it would thus seem that, at the time when the shells accumulated, Culloden Moor and the plain of Clava must have been drowned beneath the waves of an Arctic main.

The alternative view is that the shelly clay has been transported body-bulk, like a gigantic raft, into its present position by glacial action. But the undisturbed condition of the clay, the absence of trituration in the shells, and the almost complete freedom of the whole deposit from striated boulders, all seem to tell against this hypothesis. Nor, having regard to the known direction of the ice-stream, from south-west to north-east, is it easy to imagine where any glacier could have picked up such a shell-bed. The land-ice that traversed Clava had not previously passed over the Moray or the Beauly Firth. It is true that at Leavad in Caithness, at a height

The 'Vat', a famous pot-hole

Strathglass, Inverness-shire

of some 325 feet above sea-level, there occurs a glacially transported raft of disintegrated Cretaceous sandstone, measuring some 240 yards in length and 150 yards in breadth, and as much as 25 feet thick, which has been moved to its present position from beds of that formation which are known to occupy parts of what is now the basin of the Moray Firth. But this movement, colossal as it must seem, lies in the ascertained path of the ice stream across Caithness from south-east to north-west—the out-flowing *mer-de-glace* from the Northern Highlands having been diverted in this direction by the Scandinavian ice barrier. Yet, even on the assumption that at one time in the Glacial Period Loch Ness was open to the sea, it is difficult to imagine how such a plainly littoral deposit as our Clava shell-bed, where the shells have lived and died quietly in tranquil waters on a flat sea-bottom, apparently about 15 or 20 fathoms deep,[1] could have accumulated in a deep narrow chasm like Loch Ness. And, while the shelly clay of Clava might conceivably, in its frozen state, have been coherent enough to be capable of transportation, as a huge erratic raft, like the Leavad sandstone, could a glacier or ice-sheet possibly lift it out of the trough of Loch Ness, over the Drumossie Ridge to a height of at least 500 feet in Strathnairn? And, after such an adventurous voyage, could it be thought that the finely bedded marine silt should come to rest, horizontally and all uncrumpled, with even the vertical annelid burrows undisturbed, and the shells in position as they grew, many of them retaining their delicate epidermis unrubbed and unscratched—in marked contrast to what one finds in the shelly boulder clays of Caithness and Orkney?[2]

In 1893 the Clava shell-bed was investigated by a Committee of the British Association for the Advancement of Science. Unfortunately, owing to lack of money and technical difficulties, the excavations were incomplete. Since then the British Association has twice met in Aberdeen—in 1934 and 1963. It is regrettable that neither of these occasions was taken to clear up, once for all, the important and fascinating problem of the Clava Shell-bed. In particular, it still remains an open challenge to the Geological

---

[1] The depth at which shells of the same species flourish in more northern waters today.

[2] Or in the contorted masses of sedimentary rocks left stranded in the glacial deposits of the Laich o'Moray.

Department of Aberdeen University.[1] Meantime the problem has here been presented, simply as an intriguing facet of this present brief sketch of the geology of the Central Highlands.

The northern boundary of this area is defined, as my readers understand, by the Caledonian Fault, represented as a surface feature by Glen More. This is a crack of long standing in the tough old hide of Mother Scotland. It dates back at least as far as Middle Old Red Sandstone times, as we may infer from the way in which deposits of that period, which occupy the basin formed by the inner alcove of the Moray Firth, are prolonged down into the cleft of the Great Glen. It is a cleft of great depth. The deepest sounding in Loch Ness gives a measurement of 129 fathoms; while the fine mountain of Mealfuarvonie, which is wholly composed of Old Red Conglomerate, rises above the loch to a height of 2,284 feet— and who can say how much material has been stripped from its beetling crest by aeons of denudation? The Great Glen is one of the major faults in the geological structure of the British Isles. And though at least three hundred million years, according to the latest computation, have elapsed since it was first formed, it has not yet achieved stability. Frequent earth tremors at Inverness attest continued movement along the line of fracture; and in an eloquent description of the "Caledonian Valley", Hugh Miller has recalled how "the profound depths of Loch Ness undulated in strange sympathy with the reeling towers and crashing walls of Lisbon during the great earthquake of 1775", and how "the impulse, true to its ancient direction, sent the waves in huge furrows to the north-east and the south-west".

Equally majestic, as a geological feature, is the Highland Boundary Fault, which delimits our area on the south. This is a highly complex structure—a fault-zone rather than a simple fracture. It has been calculated that the sedimentary rocks on the down-throw side of the fault have subsided to a depth of at least 20,000 feet. On this line, also, earthquake shocks are frequent—more than four hundred, for example, have been recorded at Comrie. One of these, on 23rd October, 1839, cracked numerous buildings in the town, and opened a fissure two hundred yards in length.

Geology is the womb of history, so I have remarked in another

[1] Perhaps some day a Highland University will take up the gauntlet so long left lying by the University of Aberdeen!

volume of this series. Some may think it part of man's conceit if the unsummed aeons and slow majestic processes of geological time are regarded but as a prelude to the short and turbulent record of humanity. Compared with the stupendous chronologies which I have set before you in this outline sketch of Highland geology, the whole tale of man's activities upon our globe may well seem as insignificant as the dance of midges on a summer eve. Yet if we view philosophically the slow unfolding of life's drama upon this planet, and its steadfast evolution from lower to higher forms, as a planned process, culminating (thus far) in the appearance of our race, we are surely warranted in believing that mere time is not the true yardstick of assessment, and that the gradual preparation of Mother Earth may in a real sense be regarded as the prelude to the emergence of a being for whom, with all his imperfections, the psalmist of old could boldly claim that his Creator had made him a little lower than the angels, and crowned him with glory and honour. Any other view surely condemns us to a merely mechanistic conception of life, such as must bring all our moral purposes to blank frustration, and quench our best endeavours in the cold grey ashes of an ineluctable extinction. A philosophy of this sort may serve to lighten fools the way to dusty death. But the geological record offers no ground for any such pessimism. On the contrary, it is the most heartening and inspiring chronicle that a man may read. As recorded in the archives of the rocks, the testimony of the Lord is sure, making wise the simple.

CHAPTER II

THE HIGHLAND SCENE:
DRUMALBAN AND THE MOUNTH

If the reader of this book climbs to the top of Ben Nevis, or one of the Cairngorm group, or Ben Lomond or Schiehallion—or indeed any summit of the Central Highlands reaching a height of above 3,000 feet—he will be struck, as he surveys the mountain panorama spread forth in majesty around him, by the fact that, broadly speaking, no outstanding mass appears to overtop the general level. The reason for this is that the Central Highlands, geologically considered, are a dissected plateau. Before the onset of the last Ice Age, aeons of denudation had reduced the ancient Caledonides to a more or less uniform level. The processes of grinding down were continued, no doubt at a much accelerated pace, in the main period of the Ice Age, when the whole of Scotland was buried beneath a *mer-de-glace*, moving in general slowly outwards over what is now the basin of the North Sea. During the later period of 'valley glaciation', when ice fields persisting on the main mountain masses sent their glaciers down each glen, the principal features of our Highland landscape were established. Since then, in the course of the ten thousand years, or thereby, that have probably elapsed since the disappearance of the glaciers, frost and snow and rain and wind have combined in carrying on the ceaseless work of carving the worn-down roots of the ancient Caledonides into the Highland scenery that we know today, with its mountain masses, its broad uplands, its cols, its corries and its glens.

In the northern part of our area, between the headwaters of the Spey, Don and Dee on the east, and the Great Glen on the west, considerable areas of the pre-glacial plateau survive in a relatively undissected condition. South and west of this area the scalpel of Dame Nature's surgery has been much more fully used. Here accordingly are found the principal glens and lochs. This difference is due to a complexity of causes, of which it is sufficient to mention here the difference in resisting capacity between the Moines and the Dalradians, combined with local conditions induced by cross-folding and faulting. Weak strata and shattered rocks have been exploited by the agents of erosion, so as in large measure to dictate the position of the lakes and the course of the rivers. Though in most cases the water system of the Central Highlands dates back to before the Ice Age, the depths of the lochs and the courses of the rivers have been profoundly influenced by the glacial epoch.

Upon most of our maps of Scotland the topography of the Central Highlands continues to be bedevilled by the words 'Grampian Mountains' printed more or less vaguely across our area, roughly from Ben Lomond in the south-west along the margin of Strathmore towards the Cairngorms in the north-east. It is greatly to be wished that the word 'Grampian' should disappear from our atlases, and from books dealing with the Central Highlands. To begin with, the name is bogus—like that of the Hebrides, discussed in my former volume of this series. It arose from a blundered transcript of the place-name, *Mons Graupius* or *Craupius*, where the Roman general, Julius Agricola, defeated the Caledonian confederacy under Calgācus—the first Highlander whose name we know—in the year A.D. 84. The earliest printers of the *Life of Agricola*, written by his son-in-law, the great historian Tacitus, misread a *u* for an *m* in their manuscripts. Where *Mons Craupius* was is still unknown: but all the evidence seems now to point to the innermost alcove of the Moray Firth, somewhere in the neighbourhood of Inverness. It would indeed be one of the supreme ironies of history if the scene of the first great attempt to tame the Scottish Highlands should turn out to be at or near that of the last and successful effort—on "bleak Culloden's heath"! This possibility is by no means so unlikely as my readers might at first imagine.

In Latin, *mons* may signify either a single summit or a mountain range. Thus in their own homeland the Romans called the Apennines *Mons Apenninus*. There is therefore no reason, in seeking the place of Agricola's famous victory, to look around for a single, isolated summit. Indeed the narrative of Tacitus gives us no hint of any such outstanding feature. *Mons* in fact may signify little more than an upland moor, in the present case with slope sufficient for an army to array itself in tiers. According to Tacitus, the Caledonians occupied *adclive iugum*, a sloping ridge. I quote from the first and most splendid English translation, published by Sir Henry Saville in 1591: "The Britons were marshalled in the higher ground, fitly both to the show and to terrify, the first battalion standing on the plain, the rest in the ascent of the hill, knit and rising as it were one over another: the middle of the field was filled with the clattering and running of chariots and horsemen."

The real topography of the Central Highlands allows no place for a Grampian chain. It was well understood in early Celtic times, when we read of two mountain systems, *Drumalban* and the *Monadh* or *Mounth*. Drumalban, the *Dorsum Britanniae* or "Backbone of Britain" in Adamnan's book on St. Columba, is the central mountain ridge extending in a sinuous line from Ben Lomond to Ben Hope in Sutherland. This is the wind and water shear that sends our Highland streams to the Atlantic or the North Sea. From the central point of Drumalban, more or less about the Drumochter Pass, extends the transverse ridge of the Mounth, along the south side of the Dee valley, forming the well known chain of summits—Lochnagar (properly the 'White Mounth'), Mount Keen, Mount Battock,[1] Clochnaben, Mount Shade, Cairnmonearn—dwindling eastward in height till the Mounth runs out upon the North Sea at Tullos Hill, opposite Aberdeen—where the last of its summits is marked by a prehistoric burial cairn. These two ranges, Drumalban and the Mounth, constitute the real geographical and historic structure of the Central Highlands.

In the course of the dissection of the Highland plateau as noted above, the eastern and southern flanks of Drumalban and the Mounth have been carved up into a series of valleys—from south to north, Strathardle, Glen Shee, Glen Isla, Glen Prosen, Glen Clova and Glen Esk. Due to the Highland Boundary Fault, the ridges between them terminate, more or less abreast, on a line

---

[1] These names are not English substitutes for the native Gaelic word *Ben*. They are properly Mounth Keen and Mounth Battock, and Mounth Shade, all signifying their prominence in the Mounth. Some of the passes over this great barrier, leading from Atholl and Strathmore across into Mar, similarly preserve the ancient name: the Tolmounth, the Capel Mounth, the Fir Mounth, the Forest of Birse Mounth, the Cairnamounth, the Cryne Corse Mounth, and the Cowie Mounth. See my *The Province of Mar*, p. 132. It is indeed a pity that this ancient and historic name of The Mounth should have disappeared from our atlases.

along the west side of Strathmore. This is the entirely deceptive lore of mountains along which the words 'Grampian Mountains' in 'Grampian Highlands' are so diligently inscribed, year after year, by our cartographers. It is as if I were to present to you, at the level of your eyes, my outstretched hand with the fingers close together. You get the impression of a continuous line, but of course you know that it is composed of separate members. The appearance of continuity is false. So in this book there will be no further mention of 'the Grampians'. If use and wont are to be regarded as endowing the name with any survival value, then it should be restricted to a purely general descriptive label denoting 'he Central Highlands. But what is wrong with talking about tthe Central Highlands'?

Having thus clarified our mind about the topography of our area, how shall we summarize the general character of its scenery?

It would be easy to compile a conventional summary of Highland picturesqueness, on the lines of the prose writings of Sir Walter Scott or Dorothy Wordsworth. That, however, I do not conceive to be the purpose of this chapter: though something will be attempted, in their proper place, to portray descriptively some of the most famous or most typical aspects of the Highland scene. For the moment, my desire is to help the reader to recognize those features of the landscape which are special to the Central Highlands, and to understand how they have come to be. We shall deal both with the geographical and the human conditions of our area: with the land itself and with the use made of it.

One feature that must strike every visitor to the Highlands, at an early stage in his exploration, is the fact that many of the glens are of broad U-shaped section, and that the streams which now flow down them are puny in relation to their valley. They are what the geographer calls 'misfits'. Such phenomena are a product of the closing phase of the Ice Age—the period of 'valley glaciation'. The scouring effect of a glacier, prolonged for thousands of years, produced a U-shaped valley, whereas a valley cut out by a stream offers us a V-shaped section. The U-shaped valley is thus the achievement of an extinct glacier, and the relatively tiny stream that now flows down it is but the shrunken remnant of a much larger and more forceful torrent that, while the ice stream still occupied the upper part of the glen, poured out in summer tumult from its melting front.

Another characteristic feature of the Highlands, likewise a product of former glaciation, is the 'hanging valley'. In many a Highland strath or glen you will note that the valleys of the tributary streams open at a high level upon the flank of the main valley, so that the lateral stream descends towards its confluence in a series of rapids or cascades. This can be studied all over the Highlands. A notable instance is provided by the side streams which fall into Loch Awe, in the Pass of Brander. U-shaped valleys, 'misfits' and hanging valleys can also be found almost everywhere: to give only one locality, in the Lochnagar area there are fine examples of all three phenomena. Hanging valleys with their cataracts and rapids, have in many cases been dammed so as to provide hydro-electric power. The valley of the Feugh, the principal tributary of the Aberdeenshire Dee, provides an excellent and easily accessible example of a 'misfit' stream occupying a broad U-shaped valley out of all proportion to the present size of the river, and with hanging valleys on the side of the Mounth. A notable Feughside instance of a hanging valley in reverse is provided by the famous 'Devil's Bite' that forms so striking a skyline feature between Clochnaben and Mount Shade, two summits of the lower Mounth. The 'Devil's Bite' now forms a 'wind gap', at a height of some 1,300 feet. It slopes *southward* towards the Water of Dye, a tributary of the Feugh, and its lower or southern end is half-filled with fluvio-glacial detritus. Evidently it originated when the Feugh valley was still choked with ice, whereas in the valley of the Dye, on the sunward side of the Mounth, the melting ice had shrunk to a lower level. With its Devil's Bite and its great granitic tor, 95 feet in height, Clochnaben is one of the most conspicuous, as it is one of the most rewarding hills within easy reach of Aberdeen.

Before leaving Feughside, we may point out that it forms an admirable illustration of the tripartite use of a Highland valley. On the haughs alongside the river is fertile farmland; the lower slopes are clad in wood; the bare uplands are consecrated to hill sheep, grouse and deer. Today this disposition is typical of the Highlands: but it was not always so. In olden times the haughs were undrained swamp, and farming clung to the lower slopes. Cultivation has moved down into the bottoms, leaving on the upper slopes, in many cases, the rigs of the 'twal 'ousen' plough to mislead the uninstructed visitor that more land was under culti- vation in 'the good old days'. This is one of the reasons why, in traversing the Highlands, you often find the farmsteads at a lower level than the old roads, with which they are connected by steep cart tracks. The main roads remain where they have always been, but the steadings have moved down the brae. Generally in the Central Highlands the farm steadings, and therefore the roads that link them, are to be found on the sunward side of the glens. This characteristic is well illustrated upon Feughside.

Above the level of the boulder clay, the higher hills are barren, stripped alike of loose rock and soil by the ice of long ago. Large areas, however, now form moorland of peat and heather, afford- ing sustenance to blackfaced sheep, deer and grouse. So that the heather does not grow coarse and so high as to prevent the young birds getting at the tender shoots, a regular programme of muir- burn is carried out on all sporting estates. This is usually done in the early days of spring, when the glow of fires and the drifting smoke become a picturesque and characteristic feature of the land- scape. Muirburn is performed according to a definite rotation, usually about once in every eight or ten years, and the strips of heather in their various stages of recovery form a patchwork of colour, black and brown, tawny and green, which arouses the puzzled admiration of strangers unaccustomed to the economy of a Highland moor.

Amid the highest summits two physical features of great majesty present themselves to the climber. These are the screes and the corries. Nothing gives a more awesome picture of the effects of intense frost and violent rainfall upon the rocky summits of the Highlands than the tremendous screes, or slopes of fallen fragments, which spread out fanwise from the base of a mountain crag. They are by no means confined to high altitudes: perhaps the most im- posing screes in our area are found in the Pass of Brander, already mentioned. On either side of this awesome gorge the precipices rise to a height of over 1,300 feet, while the River Awe in between is no more than 115 feet above sea-level, at the point where it emerges from the Loch. For two thirds of their height the crags are blanketed with huge screes, which between them allow barely enough room for river, road and railway to force their way through to the western seaboard.[1] This famous pass, perhaps the most fearsome in all Britain, was the scene of a notable victory gained in August, 1308, by King Robert Bruce over his inveterate foe, John of Lorne. A full account of this action is given by Barbour in his great national epic, *The Brus*: and it is surprising to learn that already, at so early a date and in so remote a locality, the river was spanned by a bridge—evidently of timber, since the men of Lorne had hoped in vain to destroy it on their flight. Barbour provides us with a vivid sketch of the tremendous scenery of the Pass: and as it is one of the earliest descriptions of a Highland landscape I venture to present it to my readers, using the modernized version of the fine old black letter edition of 1758. The scene of the battle is described as:

> an evil place
> That so strait and so narrow was,
> That two-some samen might not ride
> In some place of the hill its side.
> The nether half was perilous
> For a schore[2] craig high and hideous,
> Raught[3] to the see[4] down fra the pass.
> In either half the mountain was
> So cumbersome and high and stay[5]
> That it was hard to pass that way.
> Crethinben[6] heght that mountain
> I know that not in all Britain
> An higher hill may founden be.

Cruachan Ben, as it is still always called in the Highlands, is not the highest mountain in Britain, but it is certainly among the noblest. It rises sheer from the north end of Loch Awe and the Pass of Brander; and its huge mass, reckoned to cover an area of some twenty miles in girth, fills up the entire country between the River Awe and Loch Etive. In outline it is wondrously graceful, culminating in twin cone-like peaks—like 'Sheba's Breasts' in *King Solomon's Mines*. The beauty of the mountain is best enjoyed from the west, from the neighbourhood of Connel Ferry and

---

[1] One of the most remarkable things about the geology of the Pass of Brander is the survival, near the Bridge of Awe, of a small patch of sandstones, marls and shales belonging to the Carboniferous period, with some characteristic plant remains of that ancient time.

[2] sheer [3] Reached [4] See—lake: cf. German *See* [5] Steep [6] Cruachan-ben.

Dunstaffnage, or from the Sound of Mull. The heights of the two peaks are 3,689 feet and 3,611 feet. The lower slopes are beautifully clad in natural wood and copse, while the upper part is in general smooth, rounded and grassy, but with numerous rocky outcrops. The summits are bare rock, with lofty and rifted precipices facing north. From the tops a magnificent prospect is enjoyed, said to be equalled only by the views from Ben Lawers and Ben Lomond. To the south and west, the freshwater Loch Awe, and the marine fiords Loch Etive and Loch Linnhe, are seen to great advantage, as well as the Inner Hebrides from Rum to Jura, including, directly opposite us, a full and noble profile of Mull. In clear weather, a glimpse is obtained of Goatfell in Arran, far away to the south. Northward and eastward is displayed a grand panorama of the Central Highlands, extending from Ben Nevis in the north to Ben Lawers in the east, and Ben Lomond more towards the south.

This splendid mountain is composed of Younger Granite. In recent years, it became famous by reason of the huge hydroelectric generating plant which has been contrived literally within the bowels of Cruachan Ben, in one of the greatest quarrying operations ever conducted in the British Islands. Some account of this vast and complex undertaking will be given subsequently (p. 277).

Cruachan Ben also provides us with magnificent examples of the second feature which I have noted as characteristic of the high and haggard Highland mountains. In its beetling northern front are three superb corries. Corries, known to the Welsh as *cwms*, are somewhat puzzling features in our British mountains. They are found also in the Eastern Alps, where they are known as *cirques*. A corrie may be described as a kind of arm-chair basin in the upper flank of a high rocky mountain, or like a gigantic cauldron with one side knocked away. Very often corries contain lochans or tarns, as in the famous corrie on Lochnagar, where the tarn has given its name, which is said to signify the loch of the rocks, to the whole mountain, properly called the White Mounth; or, in Gaelic, Mon'gheall. The origin of corries is not fully understood, but they are evidently a product of glacial action. This can be seen at a glance in the great corrie of Lochnagar. Its rim is formed by a brow-beating crest of vertical, frost-shivered granite. The effect of the weather at this height is shown by the fact that this crescent of sheer cliffs is clad below by a huge apron of screes, as steep as a bastion. Thus far described, the phenomena are plainly due to post-glacial erosion. But all round the still, dark waters of the loch itself are mounds of morainic detritus, clearly showing that the corrie, in spite of all subsequent disintegration, is fundamentally the product of glacial action, intense and prolonged. The height from the surface of the loch to the crest of the precipice is no less than 1,200 feet, of which half is formed by scree and half by cliff. The chord of the corrie, reckoned at summit level, must be three-quarters of a mile across. Every mountaineer who surveys this astounding scene, as viewed for example from the Meikle Pap, will have on his lips Byron's famous poem in praise of "the steep frowning glories of dark Lochnagar". Truly Sir Henry Alexander was right when he claimed that "this great corrie of Lochnagar is, in its combination of all the features of corrie scenery, without a rival in this country".

Among the Ben Nevis group and in the Cairngorms snow may linger all summer in the corries, although there is, strictly speaking, no 'eternal snow' in the Scottish Highlands. One of the corries on the east front of Beinn a'Bhuird is said to retain a patch of snow all the year round. This used to be known as 'the King's Table-cloth'—the yarn being that Finla Mhor, the chief of Clan Farquhar, was confirmed in his lands in the Braes of Mar by James V, so long as the Table cloth should be spread on Beinn a' Bhuird. I remember during the fine summer of 1925 standing outside Invercauld talking to the laird, the late Colonel A. H. Farquharson. I pointed out that he had lost his estate, for there was no patch of snow on Beinn a' Bhuird. He laughed and replied: "Go up and see!" His claim was that in the late summer the dwindling snow patch becomes so blackened with detritus shot down upon it from the overhanging crags, that it is no longer visible!

Bens and glens, corries and screes, do not exhaust the variety of the Highland landscape. Something must also be said about the moorlands.

By far the largest area of moor in the Central Highlands is the celebrated Muir of Rannoch, a peaty desolation, overlying granite, and covering some twenty square miles, at a mean height of about 1,000 feet. It lies in western Perthshire, and has a place in literature for the part it plays in R. L. Stevenson's *Kidnapped* and Neil

Munro's *John Splendid*. Stevenson describes the Muir as follows:

> The mist rose and died away, and showed us that country lying as
> waste as the sea: only the moorfowl and the peewees crying upon it,
> and far over to the east, a herd of deer, moving like dots. Much of it
> was red with heather; much of the rest broken up with bogs and hags
> and peaty pools; some had been burnt black in a heath fire; and in
> another place there was quite a forest of dead firs, standing like skele-
> tons. A wearier looking desert man never saw.

Most people think of the Muir of Rannoch only as a black desolation of sour peat, treacherous bog and heather, intersected by
ditches of stagnant water and marshy pools, and relieved in its lack
of feature only by a couple of lakes, Loch Ba and Loch Lydoch,
and by the distant prospect of grand mountains all around, including Ben Lawers, Ben Alder, Ben Nevis and Cruachan Ben.
Loch Lydoch is some five miles or more in length, with a number
of islets, and teems with trout. The northern margin of the Muir
is now defined by the Blackwater Reservoir, which serves the
British Aluminium Company's plant at Kinlochleven. At the time
when this was inaugurated in 1909, the dam of the Blackwater
Reservoir was the largest in Britain. On the east the Muir of Rannoch is traversed by the West Highland Railway, and on the west
by the new road from Tyndrum to Glencoe. The Muir of Rannoch was not always a treeless waste. In every ditch you will find
the roots and trunks of pine trees, preserved and blackened like
ebony by the peat—as have also been the bundles of faggots which
the railway engineers in 1889–94 laid down to provide a firm
foundation for their sleepers.

Very different in character is the Moor of Dinnet, on the southern verge of the Howe of Cromar, in Aberdeenshire. This stretch
of moorland covers a large spread of fluvio-glacial gravels and
terminal moraines, at a height of over 500 feet above sea-level.
These deposits represent a long pause of the shrinking Dee valley
ice-stream towards the end of the glacial period. The Moor contains two beautiful lakes, Loch Kinnord and Loch Davan. These
are fine examples of 'kettle-holes'—that is to say, basins left by
masses of 'dead ice' long lingering in the same position until
finally they vanished.

The Moor of Dinnet is one of the outstanding attractions of
Deeside. It is a grandly beautiful expanse of rock surface, boulders

and heather, whose purple glories must be seen to be believed. Here the dwarf birch vies with the whin, broom, blaeberry and bracken in relieving the gorgeous monotony of the heather. Unfortunately the heather is losing the battle with the bracken and the birches, which have now got completely out of hand.

The Moor of Dinnet was not always uninhabited. It is extremely rich in vestiges of prehistoric occupation; and on Loch Kinnord is a crannog, or lake dwelling, as well as an island—perhaps likewise artificial—which once supported a medieval castle that played no minor part in Scottish history. On the eastern margin of the Loch are important deposits of diatomite, but these are, alas! no longer worked.

Overlooking the Moor of Dinnet from the west is one of the great natural curiosities of the Highlands. This is the 'Vat', a famous pot-hole, which has been described as "probably unique in Britain". It measures about 60 feet in diameter and 20 feet in depth to the surface of the rock fragments with which it is probably now about half filled up. A tall slender cascade now falls into the 'Vat', and screens a cleft in the rock known as Rob Roy's Cave, but more probably a retreat of Gilderoy, a notorious local freebooter early in the seventeenth century.

We have already noted some of the evidence that in olden times the Central Highlands were far more rich in natural woodland than is the case today. The indigenous forest communities were composed mainly of oak, birch and pine. Of these the birch has rarely been planted, and is now, as we saw in the case of Dinnet Moor, actively propagating itself, so that it now forms one of the most graceful and best loved adornments of the Highland scene, where it flourishes up to a height of 2,000 feet. In the days when scientists possessed both the will and the ability to express themselves with literary skill, a famous Scottish naturalist, William Macgillivray, wrote a beautiful description of our Highland birches which surely deserves high place in the select catalogue of scientific eloquence:[1]

What tree is more graceful than the slender Birch, which, springing from a rift in the rugged and lichen-patched crag that overhangs

[1] W. Macgillivray, *The Natural History of Deeside*, pp. 166–7. This fascinating work was privately printed for Queen Victoria in 1855, and is now not easy to come by.

the mountain torrent, rears its white stem aloft, and spreads all around its brown branches, dividing into countless twigs, which become more and more delicate, until at last they almost resemble slender cords, hanging in separate groups, as if drawn down by the weight of the numberless tiny and glancing leaves that flutter in the breeze. . . . If it be associated with other trees of native growth, it will appear the more beautiful by contrast. There it stands in its simple beauty, pre-eminent among the dark-leaved Alders, and light green bushy Hazels. When the sun shines upon it after rain, its leaves reflect the light like gems, and its delicious fragrance fills the air around. When the fitful blast sweeps along the valley, its long drooping twigs gracefully sway, and its slender top yields, to resume its stately grace when the calm succeeds. In gloomy weather, when the mists have gathered on the hills, and the rains have soaked the ground, its dripping twigs hang gleaming in beauty; and in winter, when the hills and valleys are clothed with snow, tufts of which rest on the more robust trees, it projects into the cold atmosphere, unencumbered, to endure with impunity the most biting frosts. Gladness, and patient endurance, and quiet sorrow, find sympathy in the Birch, or emanate from it. The Pine is a gloomy and stubborn tree, but the Birch responds in its graces to the gentler emotions.

The native oakwoods of the Highlands seem to have for the most part perished, though the tree has been freely planted, particularly in the neighbourhood of lairds' houses, since the early seventeenth century. In our area, however, there still remain communities of oak which appear to be natural. One of these is on Craigendarroch, a prominent isolated granite hill at Ballater, on Deeside. The name of the hill, which reaches a height of 1,300 feet, signifies the rock of the oaks. It appears that the trees were cut some time after 1850, and have now regenerated themselves from coppice. Such a Gaelic place-name as Doire Darach, meaning oak copse, beside Loch Tulla south of Muir of Rannoch, must indicate the former presence of natural oakwood.

Much more significant are the remains of the native pine forests of the Highlands.[1] Within our area, the following sites may be listed: Glen Falloch, Tyndrum, Glen Orchy, and Black Mount, all in the mountain country east of Firth of Lorne and Loch Linnhe; the Black Wood of Rannoch; Meggernie in Glen Lyon; Glen

[1] See H. M. Steven and A. Carlisle, *The Native Pinewoods of Scotland*, 1959— a work of which no more need be said than that its manner is worthy of its matter.

A block of the Rynie Chert, showing fossil plant stems
(overleaf) The dissected plateau of the Cairngorms

Nevis; Glentanar, Ballochbuie and Mar, all on upper Deeside; Abernethy, Rothiemurchus, Glenmore, Glen Feshie, Dulnan and Glen Avon, all in Strathspey. The Forest of Rothiemurchus may serve as an example. Now much reduced in size, it is carefully protected, and survives by natural regeneration. One of the trees when cut was found to be as much as 310 years old, but the commonest age group appears to be 120–180 years. The tallest measured tree was 70 feet in height. The Forest of Rothiemurchus is the haunt of the red deer, the wild cat, the fox and the red squirrel, the capercailzie, the black grouse, the buzzard, the kestrel, the sparrowhawk, the peregrine falcon, and the golden eagle. In the heart of the Forest is one of Scotland's famous beauty spots, Loch an Eilean, which was the last resting place in Britain of the osprey, until this interesting bird was reintroduced, as everyone knows, and guarded by the most stringent precautions, at Loch Garten in the Abernethy Forest.

The highest altitude at which a living pine tree has been recorded in Scotland is on the Sron Riach of Ben Macdhui, in the Cairngorm Mountains, 2,800 feet. This was not more than a stunted shrub, about a foot in height!

From at least the eighteenth century, Highland lairds began to interest themselves in afforestation, and in the introduction of exotic trees. The principal species thus planted, for aesthetic purposes, as shelter belts or as a long term investment, have been the larch, the Douglas Fir, and the Sitka spruce.

Finally, a word or two as to the climate of the Central Highlands.

In spite of anything that the pundits may say, it appears likely that the climate of our country is at present deteriorating. My own recollection, extending back over sixty years in Aberdeen, is quite clear that in my schooldays the winters, though colder, were harder and more healthy, and that the summers were brighter and warmer. It may well be that we are passing through a minor cycle of climatic stress, such as are well authenticated in history—for example in the first quarter of the fourteenth century. At present we seem to be enduring a sequence of long and depressing winters, cold, damp, dark, and stormy, succeeded by short dubious summers with a surfeit of rain and a dearth of warmth and sunshine.

Be this as it may, it cannot be claimed that Scotland today en-

Loch Awe and the Pass of Brander

Ben Alligin, showing Torridonian sandstone

joys a kindly climate. So far as the Central Highlands are concerned, the main disadvantage is not so much our winter weather as the absence of a really long, hot and sunny summer. This deficiency creates difficulties alike for the farmer, the fruit grower, and the tourist. One of the worst faults of our Scottish weather is its fickleness. An American officer once remarked to me during the First World War: "You ain't got a climate, you've only got samples!"

The governing climatic factor in our area is undoubtedly the weather over the Atlantic Ocean, from which come our prevailing winds. In winter these blow mainly from the south-west, that is, over the warmer areas of the Ocean, across which they reach us. Not only, therefore, are our Highland winters mild, but wet, since the ocean-borne winds come to us water-laden, and discharge their rain upon our mountains. Of course this helps the forester: but on the reverse of the medal, it is hurtful to crops and favours an excessive growth of peat bogs and wet moorland—land, that is, of little use.

The effect of the warm Atlantic winds, blowing over the Central Highlands from the south-west during winter-time, is strikingly revealed by the fact that west of Drumalban, the January isotherms show a mean temperature of 40° F., whereas in Labrador, in the same latitude, the isotherms are below 10°.

On the western side of Drumalban, the annual rainfall varies from 60 to 80 inches, but on the mountain summits reaches a much higher figure—as much as 160 inches on top of Ben Nevis. In 1898, no less than 240 inches was recorded here! All over the Central Highlands, wind is probably the chief obstacle to the exploitation of the soil, whether by the farmer, the fruitgrower, or the forester. A curious inversion of conditions sometimes occurs, forming what the forester calls 'frost-hollows'. Since warm air rises and cold air sinks, it can happen that the mountain summits may in the absence of wind or for other causes, become warmer than the valleys. There is a case on record when the temperature on the top of Ben Nevis was 17.6° F. warmer than that at Fort William, 4,350 feet beneath. Thus 'frost-hollows' may form in the valleys, and these of course are avoided by the tree planter. For this reason, and of course, for purposes of drainage, the forests are placed mainly on the hill slopes, as we noted in considering the valley of the Feugh.

Generally, it may be stated that the climate of the Central Highlands varies not only from day to day, but from place to place, due to variations in the topographical conditions, particularly in relation to the prevailing winds. To quote from a recent study, "in a region such as this, relief and climate march hand in hand; one must speak more of the micro-climates of the Highlands than of the climate, if the environmental conditions are to be fully understood."[1] Thus Deeside and Strathspey tend to enjoy a better summer than other Highland valleys, since in both the western mountains catch the Atlantic rains, and clear skies give full effect to the sunshine. Owing to the governance of the Atlantic winds, the overall average snow fall in the Central Highlands is no higher than twenty-five days per year.

An unpleasant feature of the climate in our area is its proneness to torrential downpours, particularly in the country which is drained by the Dee, the Don and the Spey. The reason for these visitations is obscure. Such downpours lead to serious flooding in the lower valleys of these three rivers. They are much more than what are popularly termed 'cloudbursts', since the deluge can continue for days. By far the worst of these calamities, so far as our records go, was the famous Muckle Spate of 1829, which is the subject of a classic contribution to Highland literature.[2]

[1] A. C. O'Dell and K. Walton, *The Highlands and Islands of Scotland* (1961), p. 37.
[2] Sir Thomas Dick Lauder, *The Great Floods of August, 1829*, 3rd ed., 1873.

CHAPTER III

ABOUT THE HIGHLAND FOLK

Who are the Scottish Highlanders?

The question is by no means so easy to answer as might at first be imagined. Mere residence in the Highlands of course counts for nothing. Nor can we restrict the term to those who still 'have the Gaelic'; for their number, alas! is dwindling year by year, and is becoming ever more restricted to those who dwell on the west side of Drumalban and in the Hebrides. In the Central Highlands, and in the upper valleys of the Tay, the Dee, the Don, the Spey, the Findhorn and the Nairn, dwell thousands of folk whose ancestors, within a century ago, used the ancient tongue as their daily speech. Nowadays they speak only English, though with a well-marked Gaelic accent and intonation. Surely they have not ceased to be Highlanders. Anyhow, language is no criterion of race. In Stornoway today, you will find Pakistanis who speak Gaelic.[1]

Many good people form in their mind's eye a picture of the Highlander as someone who wears a kilt, and sports his own favourite tartan—or the one which his tailor assures him he is entitled to wear. But kilt and tartan are today no possible means of distinguishing a Scottish Highlander. Today, Highland costume is to be seen in all parts of Scotland, especially among young folk; and rightly so, since—given suitable legs!—it is at once a comely, a convenient, and a healthy garb. Young Scots going overseas for a holiday tend to affect the kilt because it is popular abroad, and helps to secure for the wearer, particularly if he be a 'hitch-hiker', consideration and help which he might otherwise lack. Nor, less happily, is Highland dress today without its political undertones; for it is favoured by Scottish Nationalists—as if they were claiming Scotland's right to be recognized not only as an independent

[1] See on this my *Portrait of Skye and the Outer Hebrides*, p. 106.

but also as a Celtic nation. Yet the fact remains that the modern Highland dress is of comparatively recent origin. It cannot be claimed as the garb of the ancient Gael. In an early nineteenth-century history book, I remember to have seen a picture of the Battle of Harlaw (1411) in which the Highland host are depicted all in kilts, and their chiefs in full evening dress, with lace at neck and wrists! But there are no convincing grounds for asserting that the kilt, as worn today, is older than the eighteenth century. Previous to that time, a Highlander of quality wore *trews*—that is to say, close-fitting hose covering both calf and thigh; a short, close jacket; and over this the 'belted plaid', a voluminous wrapping which was folded round the body in such a way as to leave free the arms, and the legs below the knee. So ample was the plaid that it could be used as a wrap if the wearer had perforce to sleep beneath the canopy of heaven.[1] As worn by day, it was secured round the waist by a belt, while the upper part was kept in position by a brooch, worn upon the left shoulder. Much care was bestowed upon the decoration of these plaid-brooches, which among the wealthy classes were usually of silver; but even the brass ones worn by lesser folk are often tastefully patterned. The trews were worn mainly by the upper folk, particularly on horseback. The common people went bare-legged—hence the term 'Red-shanks', often applied to the Highlanders. Apart from the plaid, their only garment was usually an ample shirt, reaching to the knees; and contrary to modern ideas, worn as an outer garment. Those who could afford it had their shirts of Irish linen dyed a saffron colour. Shoes of raw hide protected the feet.

The ancient form of the plaid which I have tried to describe was called the *filleadh mor* (filamor), or 'great kilt'. In the modern Highland dress, which seems to have come into fashion early in the eighteenth century, the *filleadh mor* has been divided into two, namely the *filleadh beg* (filabeg) or little kilt—that is to say, the kilt as now worn, and the modern plaid, an overmantle secured by a brooch upon the left shoulder.

De rigeur, nothing should be worn under the kilt. The shorts,

---

[1] In a note to Chapter XIX of *Waverley*, Sir Walter Scott tells us that there were "different modes of disposing the plaid, one when on a peaceful journey, another when danger was apprehended; one way of enveloping themselves in it when expecting undisturbed repose, and another which enabled them to start up with sword and pistol in hand on the slightest alarm."

often of tartan stuff, which modern convention usually demands, are in no sense descended from the ancient trews, and should not properly be so called.

John Taylor, the London 'Water Poet', who made his celebrated visit to the Central Highlands in 1618, has left us a clear picture of the hunting costume then worn in the Braes of Mar:

> The habite is shooes with but one sole apiece; stockings (which they call short hose) made of a warm stuffe of divers colours which they call Tartane: as for breeches, many of them, nor their forefathers, never wore any, but a jerkin of the same stuffe that their hose is of, their garters being bands or wreathes of hay or straw, with a plead about their shoulders, which is a mantle of divers colours, much finer and lighter stuffe than their hose, with blue flat caps on their heads, a handkerchiefe knit with two knots about their necke; and thus they are attyred. Now, their weapons are long bowes and forked arrowes,[1] swords and targets, harquebusses, muskets, durks, and Loquhabor-axes. With these armes I found many of them armed for the hunting. As for their attire, any man of what degree so ever that comes amonst them, must not disdaine to wear it: for if they doe, then they will disdaine to hunt, or willingly to bring in their dogges; but if men are kind unto them, and be in their habit, then are they conquered with kindnesse, and the sport will be plentifull. This was the reason that found so many noblemen and gentlemen in those shapes.

Into this 'shape', accordingly, the Cockney poet was put by his host, "my good Lord of Marr". Good sport, good food and good drink—of which last there is a surprising catalogue—so enraptured the guest that he recorded his zest in a couple of sonnets. The second of these may be reproduced here as an early appreciation of Highland scenery, at a time when mountains were generally regarded with fear and horror:

> If sport like this can on the mountaines be,
> Where Phoebus flames can never melt the snow,
> Then let who list delight in vales below,
> Skie-kissing mountaines pleasure are for me:
> What braver object can man's eye-sight see,
> Than noble, worshipfull, and worthy wights.

---

[1] Such 'forked arrows' had specially large barbed heads for hunting. One with barbs no less than 2½ inches long was dug up in 1926 during the excavation of Kindrochit Castle, Braemar—already a ruin when Taylor visited it in 1618.

As if they were prepared for sundry fights
Yet all in sweet society agree?
Through heather, mosse, 'mongst frogs, bogs, and fogs,
'Mongst craggy cliffes and thunder battered hills
Harts, Hindes, Bucks, Roes are chas'd by men and dogs
Where two houres hunting fourscore fat deere kills.
Lowland, your sports are low as is your seate,
The High-land games and minds are high and great.

From the Water Poet's narrative it is clear that tartan in some form was in general use in the Central Highlands by the early seventeenth century. Indeed there are earlier references. For example, in 1538 James V had a Highland costume made for himself, which included "3 ells of Heland tertane to be hoiss at four shillings and four pence to the ell". At what time the various clans adopted each a peculiar 'sett', or pattern of tartan, is a matter which has occasioned hot dispute. One thing is certain, that the prevailing multiplicity of tartans now offered in our shops is of comparatively recent origin. In fact the whole thing has become something of a racket. The vendors of Highland tartans stick up in their windows lists of almost every conceivable surname, each accompanied by the tartan to which it is pretended that the owner of the name is entitled. Thus, in the case of my own surname, a Simpson is entitled to sport the Fraser tartan, simply because Simpson signifies the son of Simon, and the Christian name Simon is frequent among the Chiefs of Clan Fraser!

As is well known, the Highland dress was proscribed by Act of Parliament after the 'Forty-five'. The operative part of this measure is as follows:

From and after the first day of August, One thousand, seven hundred and forty-seven, no man or boy within that part of Great Britain called Scotland, other than such as shall be employed as Officers and Soldiers in His Majesty's Forces, shall, on any pretext whatever, wear or put on the clothes commonly called Highland clothes (that is to say, the Plaid, Philabeg, or little Kilt, Trowse, Shoulder-belts), or any part whatever of what peculiarly belongs to the Highland Garb; and that no tartan or party-coloured plaid or stuff shall be used for Great Coats or upper coats.

The penalty for disobeying this Act was seven years' transportation! In 1782 it was repealed. But the general revival of Highland dress dates only from the visit of George IV to Edinburgh in 1822, when the monarch—regardless of his figure!—appeared in a kilt of Royal Stewart tartan, and Sir Walter Scott turned out resplendent in Campbell trews. At first the Highland dress, owing to its heavy cost, was restricted to the upper classes, and so tended to acquire a certain snob value.

It should be unnecessary to conclude this brief disquisition upon Highland costume by insisting that the kilt is a man's dress. For women, a tartan skirt is both proper and comely. But nothing is more distasteful than to watch those wretched kilted girls who figure upon dancing platforms at some of our Highland Gatherings, their breasts bespangled with medals. Equally unseemly is a pipe-band of kilted women.

Upon all counts it is clear, then, that Highland garb is nowadays no criterion of a Highlander. So, once again, we are brought back to our question, but with a change of emphasis: who *were* the ancient Highlanders?

In Ptolemy's famous map of Britain, compiled in the second century of our era, the Central Highlands are shown as occupied by a tribe, or probably a confederacy of tribes, known as the *Calēdŏnii*. Their name survives in Dunkeld, the Dun or fort of the Caledonians; in Rohallion, the Rath or fort of the Caledonians; and in Schiehallion, the Fairy Hill of the Caledonians. East of the Caledonii Ptolemy places the *Vacomagi*. These people occupied Strathmore and the country between it and the North Sea, extending from the Tay to the Mounth, and including, as it would seem, East Perthshire and Strathspey. The country between the Mounth and the Spey is occupied by the *Taixali*: Kinnaird Head, at the north-eastern point of the knuckle of Buchan, is the *Promontorium Taixalorum*. Needless to add, the boundaries between these three tribes, or confederacies, are quite loosely defined.

By the time when the Roman garrisons were withdrawn from Britain, early in the fifth century, the Central Highlands were occupied by the Picts, who were divided into two groups, the Dicalydones, presumably the former Caledonii, and the Verturiones, whose name later appears in the district or province called Fortriu—i.e., roughly, the area east of Drumalban and between the Tay and the Mounth. The principal stronghold of the Verturiones is thought to be the hill fort of Dundurn, near the lower end of Loch Earn in Perthshire. This imposing fortress, well adapted it would seem to be a tribal capital, is recorded to have undergone a siege in 683; but it is doubtless much older, and indeed the Roman fort at Dealginross appears to have been planted to watch it.

Our problem therefore seems to be narrowing itself down to a still more dubious question: who were the Picts? Unfortunately, Pict is a name without racial content. The latest Roman writers, to whom the word meant simply 'painted folk', from their custom of tattoing, apply it generally to all the inhabitants of the country formerly known to them as Caledonia. From all the evidence available to us, it is likely that these inhabitants were little less mixed in racial texture than are their successors of today. Obviously the upper classes were of Celtic stock, and the place names of the Central Highlands are overwhelmingly Gaelic. It is equally probable that older strains, going back to the infiltration of the vigorous Beaker Folk at the dawn of the Bronze Age, roughly about 2000 B.C., have persisted in the Highland population. Unfortunately, the introduction of burning the dead in the High Bronze Age destroys, to a large extent, the evidence available from skeletal remains. Nevertheless, there are sufficient proofs, from other sources, of continuous additions to the ethnic stock of the Central Highlands, alike from east and west. Red hair has long been regarded as a characteristic of the Highlander; and in the first century Tacitus speaks of the red hair and large limbs of the Caledonians, which in his view pointed clearly to a German origin. Yet it has long been noted that western Argyllshire and the Inverness-shire Highlands contain a substantial proportion of people with dark hair and eyes.

From the dawn of historical records our picture becomes much clearer. There is ample proof that the Scots, immigrants from Ulster who in the sixth century founded their kingdom of Dalriada in what is now Argyllshire and the adjacent islands, were soon infiltrating across Drumalbàn towards the Eastern Lowlands. Of course this process would be accelerated after 843, when Pictland and Dalriada were united under a Scotic King, Kenneth MacAlpin. On the other hand there is, so far as I am aware, no evidence of any settlement in the Central Highlands of Angles from Northumbria: though it is worth remembering, by way of caution, that in remote Iona, in St. Columba's time, there were at least two 'Saxons' among his monastic community. The Norse occupation of the Hebrides and the western seaboard cannot have been devoid of influence upon the Central Highlands; though, of course, no significant conclusion can be drawn from the chance find of a tenth-century Norse oval brooch near Perth. But it is well to remember that in the period of the maximum Norse influence upon Scotland, in the eleventh century, Thorfinn the Mighty, Jarl of the Nordereys (the Orkney and Shetland Islands) seems in effect to have shared Scotland between himself and Macbeth—with whom, in 1050, he went on pilgrimage to Rome. Jarl Thorfinn seems to have controlled all Scotland north of the Tay; though how far his influence affected the racial composition of the Central Highlands it is impossible to say. His widow, Ingebjorg, became the first wife of Malcolm Canmore—a lady whose memory has long been dimmed by the brilliant halo of his second Queen, St. Margaret.

With the formation of the feudal kingdom of Scotland, under the auspices of the strong kings of the House of Canmore, in the twelfth and thirteenth centuries, and the complex series of processes summed up under the general term of 'Anglo-Norman penetration', a much stronger extraneous influence was brought to bear upon the Central Highlands. Anglo-Norman barons obtained a foothold among the mountains, or in the borderlands of the mountains, and were thus enabled to push their way up into the glens. Often this happened when a magnate of Anglo-Norman stock married a Celtic heiress: as in 1210, when William Comyn married the heiress of the last Mormaer or High Chief of the old Celtic Province of Buchan. This union gave that great Norman family a footing on the north-eastern *glaçis* of the Highlands; and in due course we find the Comyns established in a strong castle (Balvenie) at Mortlach in Glenfiddich. A son of this William Comyn, named Walter, married his way into the great Celtic district of Menteith, one of the two subdivisions of Fortriu. Thereafter Menteith appears in our records as a feudal Earldom. In 1229 this same Walter obtained a charter from Alexander II of the great Highland lordship of Badenoch and Lochaber. Thus within a quarter of a century the powerful Norman family of Comyn had obtained a vast territorial holding in the Central Highlands, with castles at Balvenie, Lochindorb, Ruthven, Inverlochy, and elsewhere. By marriage, likewise, the ancient Celtic

Province of Atholl, already transformed into a feudal Earldom, passed from its old Celtic lords into the Anglo-Norman family of Hastings. So also the old Province of Angus was acquired by the Umphravilles.

We cannot doubt that these great Anglo-Norman magnates brought into their new territories followers of their own—Norman, English, and Flemings. Such, in the first instance, would certainly be the garrisons of the Comyn castles, noted above. It is also clear that in many cases the newcomers adapted themselves to the Celtic society around them, just as the Anglo-Norman settlers in Ireland became *Hibernicis ipsis Hiberniores*. In other cases, leading Celtic magnates accepted the new order, took crown charters of their lands, and adopted feudal customs. The outstanding case is that of the Campbells, who built up their vast power in the Central Highlands upon steadfast allegiance to the Crown; whereas their rivals, the Macdonalds, foundered on their persistent endeavours to restore the semi-independent Lordship of the Isles.

What may be an interesting glimpse of the blending of Celtic with feudal institutions during the Anglo-Norman infiltration seems to be discernible in the great Highland lordship of the Comyns in Badenoch. The Gaelic name for the Mackintosh clan is *Clann an Toisich*, 'the toshach's children'. A toshach (Gaelic *toisech*) signifies a steward. If the *eponymus* of Clan Mackintosh held such a position, then (it has been most plausibly suggested) he may have been the Gaelic steward of Badenoch under its Comyn lords—who no doubt would be styled *mormaers* by the Celtic population.[1]

At no time is there evidence of a dispossession, of any magnitude, of the Celtic inhabitants of the Lowlands, and of their being driven up into the mountains. The plain truth is that there was much more racial affinity between the population of Lowlands and Highlands than is usually imagined. What was really important was the difference in language, customs and institutions. The famous battle of the 'Red Harlaw' has often been portrayed as a struggle *à outrance* between Celt and Teuton for the mastery of Scotland: yet in our next chapter we shall see how false is this conception. It is certain that there must have been many Gaelic speaking Celts, and men of Celtic ancestry, in the army of the Earl of Mar; while not all the followers of his antagonist, the Earl

[1] W. R. Kermack, *The Scottish Highlands* (1957), p. 33.

of Ross, were "wild Scots", or "pestiferous cateran"—as the Celtic Highlanders were politely styled by their Lowland neighbours. Throughout Scottish history, the importance of the so-called 'Highland line' has been much exaggerated.

Historically, the distinctive Highland institution has been the clan system. Today it survives mainly in tradition and sentiment. Yet beyond doubt it has exerted much influence in moulding the Highland *ethos* and character. Therefore we must look for a little at the clans.

The theory of a Highland clan would seem to be that it is an association of people all claiming descent from the *eponymus* of the clan, and therefore kinship with its chief, whose patronymic they bear. This idea of a Highland clan has been romanticised in Aytoun's lay of "The Old Scottish Cavalier":

> He kept his castle in the north,
> Hard by the thundering Spey;
> And a thousand vassals dwelt around,
> *All of his kindred they.*

The practice of the clan was somewhat different. Every clan was constantly recruiting itself by refugees from other clans, either because their clan was being broken up by punitive action on the part of the Government—as in the well-known case of the Macgregors—or was in process of destruction by more powerful neighbours, or, in individual cases, where the fugitive had incurred peril of the law—'broken men' as such were termed. Naturally the chiefs, always anxious to increase their power by enlarging the numbers of their following, welcomed such refugees, who on being accepted into the clan, adopted its patronymic. Thus the clan came, in course of time, to mean nothing else than the aggregate of men who adhered to a particular chief.[1] As in process

---

[1] Sir Walter Scott, who never allowed his sense of the romantic to overcome his knowledge of the realities of Highland life, has made the hard facts about the clán system crystal clear in his account of Fergus MacIvor (*Waverley*, Chap. XIX):

"He crowded his estate with a tenantry, hardy indeed, and fit for the purposes of war, but greatly outnumbering what the soil was calculated to maintain. These consisted chiefly of his own clan, not one of whom he suffered to quit his lands if he could possibly prevent it. But he maintained, besides, many adventurers from the mother sept, who deserted a less warlike, though more wealthy chief, to do homage to Fergus MacIvor. Other individuals, too, who had not

of time, more and more Highland chiefs adopted the feudal system, and accepted charters either from the Crown or from a more powerful chief, the normal relationship of lord and vassal, as existing in the Lowlands, came to apply also among the clans. Under the prevailing conditions of life in the Highlands—the mountainous country; the lack of towns, which are always the focus of orderly government and the arts and crafts of sober industry; the distance of the Highlands from the seat of authority, and therefore their immunity from the long arm of the State, imperfectly as this was everywhere exercised in medieval Scotland; and the chronic inability of the Highland population to support themselves on the meagre resources of their glens—all these things, added to the natural proneness of the Celt to internecine strife, combined to provoke and sustain the endemic warfare which gave the clans a bad name among their Lowland neighbours, and have earned them less than justice at the bar of history. The whole system was fully developed in Gaul and Britain at the period of the Roman conquest, and is clearly set before us in the writings of Caesar and Tacitus. If the latter is correct, among the Britons the growth of the clan system had already, by the time when the Romans appeared upon the scene, gone far to disrupt the tribal kingdoms of which we read in Caesar. To quote again from our Elizabethan translation:

> Heretofore they were governed by kings, now they are drawn by petty princes into partialities and factions: and that is the greatest help we have against those puissant nations, that they have no common counsel together: seldom it chanceth that two or three states meet and concur to repulse the common danger: so that whilst one by one fighteth, all are subdued.

Thus the clan system must be regarded as something characteristic of the Celtic race. What gave a peculiar twist to it, in medieval Scotland, was the superimposition upon the clans of Anglo-Norman feudalism. Each clan came thereby to be essentially a military organization; while, on the legal side, heritable jurisdiction was added to the more informal patriarchal authority

---

even that apology, were nevertheless received into his allegience, which indeed was refused to none who were, like Poins, proper men of their hands, and were willing to assume the name of MacIvor." No one will even begin to understand Highland history until he has grasped the constant state of flux among the clans.

immemorially vested in the chief. Yet it is a great mistake to imagine that a clan chief was a despot. However great the blind devotion of the clansmen to their chief—as portrayed for example, in "the Dougal creature" of Scott's *Rob Roy*—the chief had in practice to respect the opinion and sentiment of his clansmen. Excessive or capricious despotism on the part of a chief might result in his following transferring to another clan. To quote again from a remarkable gloss in Macpherson's Ossian, reproduced in full in my former volume:[1]

> The fear of this desertion no doubt made the chiefs cautious in their government. As their consequence, in the eyes of others, was in proportion to the numbers of their people, they took care to avoid everything that tended to diminish it.

As to the chronic disorder of the Highlands, it is well to remember how disorderly was life in the Scottish Lowlands during the later Middle Ages. On both sides of the so-called 'Highland line', burnings, slaughterings, reivings and harryings were rife, as every student of the Privy Council Registers will know. Both in Highlands and in Lowlands the same malpractices coincidental to the feudal system were assiduously employed by the magnates to enhance their power. One of the most inveterate of these was the system of indenture by 'bonds of manrent', to use the Scottish term for a practice characteristic, all over Europe, of the 'bastard feudalism' that marked the later Middle Ages. What this meant in the Lowlands, so often favourably contrasted to the alleged anarchy of the Highlands, is frankly revealed by a Scottish chronicler, writing of the state of matters in the fifteenth century:

> Schortlie murther and slaughter was come in sic delayance among the pepill and the kingis articles come in sic contemptioun that no man wist quhair to seik refuge wnles he had sworne him self ane servant to sum common murtherar or bludie tyrant to mantaine him contrair the invation of wtheris or ellis had given largelie of his geir to saif his lyfe and gif him sum peace and rest.

By such a 'bond of manrent' a lesser baron or chief pledged himself and his following to support his new overlord against 'all deadly'—i.e., against all other mortals—saving usually his allegiance to the Crown, in exchange for his new superior's backing, if need be in arms, in any quarrel in which he might be involved.

[1] *Portrait of Skye and the Outer Hebrides*, p. 133.

How completely this vicious Lowland practice had spread into the Highlands may be gathered from the large numbers of bonds of manrent in the Breadalbane charters. Perhaps I may be pardoned for quoting the wise remarks of a Chief of one of the greatest Highland clans, whose own charter-chest contains many such bonds of manrent:[1]

> I have already hinted at the probability that if we could now fully trace the history of the population on many of the great territorial estates of the Celtic chiefs and landlords, we should find that no small part of them had been recruited almost as soldiers are recruited, or adopted in groups and families of 'broken' septs, who came to seek protection, and were selected and planted on the land in substitution for disloyal or predatory septs who were driven out. This suspicion is amply confirmed by the remarkable collection of bonds of manrent which are published in the *Book of Taymouth*. For here we have every variety of circumstance which can show the absolute powers of disposal over the land, which were exercised by the chartered owners, and which it was absolutely necessary to exercise, for the peaceable settlement and improvement of the country. Moreover, we have in these bonds of manrent a very clear explanation of the language which has suggested to many writers a hazy notion that the Celtic chiefs were chosen or elected by their people. For in these bonds we see that 'broken men' coming in to settle in the Lord of Glenorchy's country, were said to 'elect him to be their Chief', exactly in the same sense in which a recruit may be said to elect the commanding officer of the regiment in which he chooses to enlist. Yet the Colonel of the 91st Highlanders would be very much astonished if he were said to be elected by his men.

The broad fact is that the distinction between 'Celtic' Highlands and 'Saxon' Lowlands in medieval Scotland has been grossly exaggerated. James I, James II, James IV and James V, as also James VI after he had the power of England behind him, all exerted their authority with decision far beyond the 'Highland line'. And in other and more subtle ways the Celtic areas were being slowly linked with indissoluble bonds to their Lowland neighbours. At no period was there a hard and fast frontier between them. Gradually but steadily, Anglo-Norman feudalism and institutions penetrated into the remotest glens of west and north. The leading Highland chiefs obtained Crown grants of their lands as personal property under feudal law, and thus secured

[1] The Duke of Argyll, *Scotland as it was and as it is*, 2nd ed., 1887, p. 206.

them to their descendants in perpetuity—violating any lingering Celtic notions, if such existed, of the land as belonging to the clan —a system under which the Chief would have enjoyed only a life-rent. Once this step was taken, the Chiefs were forced to admit the superiority and invite the protection of the Crown, and to recognize and submit themselves to the restraints of feudal law, the feudal system of proprietorship, and all the consequences that flowed therefrom. The steady rise in power of the Campbells was due to the consistency with which they followed this course. During the Civil War it was deserted by the first Marquis of Argyll—with disastrous consequences for his clan, and a fatal result for himself.

Another factor tending to the blurring of the distinction between Highlands and Lowlands was the influence of the Church, which brought all the weight of her spiritual and secular authority to bear upon the side of what old writers term 'civility'. The general uniformity of ecclesiastical architecture, all over the Central Highlands, with that which prevailed in the Lowlands, is itself a proof of the accessibility of the Celtic area to 'Saxon' civilization; and (as we shall find) precisely the same inference may be drawn from baronial architecture. Except that they are, in general, smaller and sometimes ruder, the churches and castles in the Highlands do not materially differ from their contemporaries outside the 'Highland line'. During the later Middle Ages, indeed, the cleavage between Highlands and Lowlands was, on a broad view, racial and linguistic rather than political or cultural. Nor was it nearly as accentuated as it became after the Reformation, which set the English-speaking population of Scotland upon a path not at once explored by their Celtic neighbours. Yet the very fact that the Highlanders, unlike their kinsmen in Ireland did, in the end and for the most part, embrace not only Protestantism but also Presbyterianism, is yet another proof of the prevalence and strength among them of Lowland influences.

The reader who has accepted the evidence and arguments marshalled in the foregoing paragraphs, will not be surprised when he is asked to believe that the 'barbarism' of the Highlanders has been much exaggerated. Upon this subject there is no need for me here to repeat what I have said elsewhere.[1] Endemic strife and

[1] *The Ancient Stones of Scotland*, pp. 28–31.

political insecurity are not necessarily inimical to the finer arts, as the history of ancient Greece, or of Italy in the later Middle Ages, should remind us. Also we must remember that culture and literacy are two quite different things, and that there is such a thing as an oral culture, which may attain high quality. The Emperor Karl the Great learned to read, and only with great difficulty, towards the end of his life: yet he was a master of German and Latin, and could understand Greek. Moreover he was a notable patron of learning and the arts—so much so that we speak today of the 'Carolingian Renaissance'. He may be described as illiterate, but he was certainly neither uneducated nor uncultured. The great heroic epics of early European literature were recited or sung in the halls of kings and nobles, long before they were reduced to writing. There is no certain mention of writing in the *Iliad* or the *Odyssey*; and for all we know, Homer, or whoever was the original author or authors of these immortal poems, may have been unable to write them down. Perhaps the tradition which makes the poet blind may be a dim recollection that he could not commit his compositions to writing. More than likely the same holds good for the unknown poet of *Beowulf*. So far as the Celtic peoples are concerned, it is certain that a great deal of their early history and poetry was handed down orally by the bards, who "sat at the tables of the great; accompanied them with their harps to festivals; sang their praises and satirized their enemies; and recited poems in honour of valiant warriors who had fallen in battle."[1] By such agencies a great deal of what may truly be described as literature was handed down from generation to generation among the Scottish Highlanders. It is pertinent here to quote some wise observations of the greatest authority on Celtic Scotland, William Forbes Skene:[2]

Among savage nations poetry is always the first vehicle of history; before any regular means are taken for perpetuating a knowledge of the early history of their tribes, they are usually in the habit of reciting in verse the deeds of their forefathers, and their early traditions are thus handed down from the most remote antiquity. This custom, although common to all nations in a primitive state of society, was peculiarly so to the Highlanders. The natural disposition of a hunt-

[1] T. Rice Holmes, *Ancient Britain* (1907), p. 266.
[2] *The Highlanders of Scotland* (1837), vol. I, p. 206.

ing and pastoral people for poetry and hyperbole was increased in them by the peculiar and imaginative nature of their character, by their secluded situation, and the romantic aspect of their country; and thus poetry was from the earliest period almost the only medium by which a knowledge of the great events of their early history, the achievements of their forefathers, and the illustrious examples presented for their emulation was conveyed to the Highlanders, and the warlike and somewhat chivalrous character of the nation preserved.

Nevertheless, it is not to be supposed that the medieval Highlanders were wholly unlettered. The earliest known example of a Scottish medieval charter, signed personally by the granter, exhibits to us the fair hand of Donald, Lord of the Isles, the Highland hero of the 'Red Harlaw'. From a much earlier period we have the precious *notitiae* of the Book of Deer, dating from the eleventh and twelfth centuries—the oldest known specimens of Scottish Gaelic. To the early sixteenth century belongs that charming *mélange* of Gaelic poetry, *The Book of the Dean of Lismore*. The compiler, James Macgregor, was a native of Fortingall, a large parish of central Perthshire, partly in Atholl and partly in Breadalbane, with its church at the Clachan of Fortingall, in romantic Glen Lyon. Of this church the good Dean was vicar; and it seems to have been at Fortingall, with the aid of his brother Duncan, that he made his wonderful collection of Highland poetry. Duncan, incidentally, was himself a poet; and it is interesting to find that one of the authors whose pieces are preserved in the Dean's Book was "Duncan Mor from Lennox", while another is no less a person than Sir Duncan Campbell, "the good knight" of Glenorchy, whose stronghold of Kilchurn is one of the most imposing examples of castellar construction in the Central Highlands. His poem is a caustic satire on a stingy person who has just died. Among the proofs of the deceased's parsimony it is told that he "would beg a book to read". This scarcely suggests an illiterate society. In fact references to writing are frequent in these poems. A third piece in the collection is ascribed to a Countess of Argyll. It is of course quite impossible to give any idea of the varied charm of these delightful poems, even if they can be read only in an English version; or of the light which they cast on that picturesque tapestry, society in the Highlands during the later Middle Ages. Only a brief extract from three poems can be permitted here. The first contains a description of Glen Shee, which today has acquired fame as one of the principal ski-ing centres in our area:

> Glen Shee, the vale that close beside me lies,
> Where sweetest sounds are heard of deer and elk,
> And where the Feinn[1] did oft pursue the chase.
> Following the hounds along the lengthening vale,
> Below the great Ben Gulbin's grassy height
> Of fairest knolls that lie beneath the sun
> The valley winds.

Another poem from which I present an extract is of high historic interest. It is a passionately patriotic address to Archibald, second Earl of Argyll, on the eve of his departure, at the head of his clansmen, to join the army which James IV would lead to disaster at Flodden. On that fatal field, when "the flowers o' the forest were a' weed awa'", Earl Archibald fell by the side of his gallant sovereign. Here is how the unknown author addresses his departing chief:

> Now that thou risest 'gainst the Saxon,[2]
> Let not thy rising be a soft one
> Have your swords with sharpened blades,
> Let your spears stand by your sides,
> Let us not forsake our country,
> Let us fiercely, bravely fight.
>
> Earl of Argyll, I thee beseech,
> Be as a hero in the conflict;
> A hero who shall reign supreme
> O'er Gael from the famous land,
> Noble, high-born prince of the Gael,
> Thou'lt in apportioned Albin reign.

Note the combination of ardent Scottish patriotism with the proud conviction of the exalted destiny of the Chiefs of Clan Campbell, then steadily climbing, up the ladder of loyalty to the Crown, to a dominant position in Albin, or Alban—the ancient name for Scotland.

[1] The Fingalians, Ossianic heroes.
[2] The English, not the Lowland Scots, are clearly meant.

Most remarkable of all things in the Dean of Lismore's collection is the knowledge which these medieval Highland poets reveal of the geography of the world, and of its ancient history. Take for example this extract from a fine poem on the death of Alexander the Great, written by an author, otherwise unknown, named Duncan McPherson:

> Four men met at the grave,
> The grave of Alexander the Great:
> They spoke the words of truth
> Over the hero of Greece the fair.
> The first man of them said,
> "There were yesterday with the King
> The world's great hosts, sad the tale,
> Though today he lonely lies."

The second man speaks

> "Yesterday the world's great king
> Proudly rode upon the earth;
> But today it is the earth
> That rides upon the top of him."
> Then did the third wise speaker say,
> "Yesterday Philip's son owned the world
> But today he only owns
> Of it all not seven feet."
> "Alexander, brave and great,
> Who won and treasured gold and silver,
> Today", the fourth man wisely said,
> "The gold it is that treasures him."[1]

A fifteenth-century Lowland Scotch version of the medieval *Romance of Alexander* is extant; and the above striking poem indicates that this medieval epic was not unknown also in the Gaelic Highlands.

Of the numerous other remains of early Gaelic literature in Scotland, space allows us but a bare mention of the vivid and valuable prose narrative of Montrose's campaign, preserved in the *Black Book of Clanranald*. It will at all events be clear to my readers how far we have travelled today from the bigoted ignorance of honest old Dr. Johnson in 1773:

[1] The point made is that Alexander the Great was said to have been buried in a coffin or urn made of gold.

Of the Earse language, as I understand nothing, I cannot say more than I have been told. It is the rude speech of a barbarous people, who had few thoughts to express, and were content, as they conceived grossly, to be grossly understood. After what has been lately talked of Highland bards and Highlands genius, many will startle when they are told that the Earse never was a written language; that there is not in the world an Earse manuscript a hundred years old; and that the sounds of the Highlanders were never expressed by letters, till some little books of piety were translated, and a metrical version of the Psalms was made by the Synod of Argyle.

In more modern times, the Scottish Highlands have produced two great Gaelic poets—Rob Donn and Duncan Ban Macintyre. Of these, the latter was as truly the poet of the Central Highlands, as Rob Donn was that of the country to the north of the Great Glen. "Both were uneducated men, but their productions bear the stamp of vigorous genius." Only Duncan Ban, "Duncan the Fair", concerns us at the moment. He was born, of crofting parents, at Drumliaghart in Glenorchy, on 20th March, 1724, and died in Edinburgh on 14th May, 1812. The nearest school and church were at Dalmally, fifteen miles down the glen, and it appears that of formal education the lad had none. Certainly his signature, on his certificate of discharge from the Breadalbane Fencibles in 1799, is that of an illiterate man. Dwelling in the Campbell country, he could not do otherwise than support the Hanoverian interest during the Forty-five; yet it is clear from his famous poem on the battle of.Falkirk (17th January, 1746) that he served against the Jacobites from conviction—though the circumstances which led him to bear arms on the losing side in the last victory of Prince Charles Edward are both comic in themselves and characteristic of the times. One of the Breadalbane tacksmen, called up for service under the Militia and Fencible Acts, was Archibald Fletcher of the Crannach. Not having any liking for the perils of war, Fletcher engaged Duncan MacIntyre as a substitute, for a fee of 300 merks and the use of his sword. The poet bolted as fast as every one else before the Jacobite charge; and in the headlong flight he lost his employer's sword. After the end of the campaign, when he returned, apparently quite unabashed, to his native glen, Fletcher refused to pay him his hire, because he had failed to bring back his sword. In revenge Duncan composed his first poem, a vivid account of the battle, in which he lampooned Fletcher and derided the quality of his sword; "mickle iron with edge full little . . . the notched broadsword of ill-luck." This bold and effective piece of satire, passed eagerly around from mouth to mouth, was like to have cost the budding poet dear: but the Earl of Breadalbane intervened, and forced Fletcher to pay the 300 merks. Thus, says Duncan's biographer, the poet "had his cash in hand, and his revenge beforehand".

In his later days, doubtless under the influence of the savage treatment of the Highlands after the rising, the poet appears to have changed his mind; and other poems, including a second one upon the battle of Falkirk, betray much more Jacobite feeling. So far as they have been preserved, the poems of Duncan Ban Macintyre are considerable in bulk and varied in theme and mood. No one who can read them only in an English garb can form any judgment upon them; but amongst those who 'have the Gaelic' he is accounted as their greatest poet, and his songs are repeated, all the world round. For our present purpose, the point to be enforced is that Duncan Ban Macintyre is a cogent proof of the fact that culture is something wholly different from literacy or education.

Not that opportunities of formal education were wholly lacking in the Highlands—at least for the better-off classes. This will have been apparent from what has been said about the Dean of Lismore's Book. That doughty champion of the Highland cause, the late Dr. Evan Macleod Barron, has produced ample evidence, not only that Highland gentlemen sent their sons to the grammar schools in the burghs adjoining their mountain fastnesses, but that there were also schools within the 'Highland line': for example, during the seventeenth century, at Inveraven, Boharm and Mortlach, all within the Banffshire Highlands; at Kingussie in Strathspey; and even in far Lochaber. At Fortrose, the ancient cathedral city of Ross, it was reported in 1661 that "there has always been a flourishing school in that place, where children from all places of that country and especially from the Highlands and Isles of Scotland did resort, the same being the next adjacent school to them."

In 1661, Macdonald of Glengarry "had a house near Inverness, and he brought to live with him there and sent to the Grammar School the two young Macdonalds of Keppoch, whose subsequent murder at the hands of their kinsmen is so tragic an episode in Highland history."[1] Upon all accounts, it seems reasonably clear that the famous Education Act of James IV, enacted in 1496, whereby barons and freeholders of sufficient substance were held bound to send their sons and heirs to school "till they be competently founded and have perfect Latin", was not without effect in the Highlands as in the Lowlands.

To those who may have been accustomed to think of the Highlanders and Lowlanders as in effect two separate peoples, whose contacts were, more often than not, as Baillie Nicol Jarvie phrased it, "on the north side o' friendly", attention may be called to a memorable episode in the life of that redoubtable freebooter, Rob Roy Macgregor. This notable robber, who may with justice be termed the last of the cateran, had a kinsman, no less a person than Dr. James Gregory, Professor of Medicine and Regent in King's College, Old Aberdeen, a distinguished physician and man of letters, and member of the brilliant family that produced, among other men of learning, the inventor of the reflecting telescope. During the 'Fifteen' Rob Roy was sent by the Earl of Mar down to Aberdeen in order to gather recruits for the Jacobite army. The University don invited the outlaw to stay with him in his manse, and had much difficulty in restraining his formidable kinsman from carrying off his host's young son to the hills, "in order to make a man of him". It is related that on a second visit of Rob Roy to his kinsman in Aberdeen, long after the failure of the rising, the professor and the cateran were walking arm in arm along a street when a body of redcoats appeared. "It is time for me to look after my safety", said Rob Roy; and disengaging from the academic arm, he promptly dived down a close! Sir Walter Scott not untruly describes these incidents, related to him by members of the Gregory family, as bringing "the highest pitch of civilization so closely in contact with the half-savage state of society."

Our enquiry has shown that the Highlander today, no less than the Lowlander, is the complex product of many blended races and cultural influences. The factors by which both were moulded differed, perhaps, less in kind than in degree. What distinguishing

[1] For all this see at length the evidence in the Introduction to the second edition (1934) to Dr. Barron's well-known book on *The Scottish War of Independence*.

characteristics of mind and character may have been inherited by the modern Highlander from his ancestry and environment?

A characteristic that has often been remarked among the Highland population is a certain tendency to melancholy, which at its best might be termed a subdued disposition, and at its worst may amount to something not far removed from morosity. This tendency to *tristesse* is the more remarkable by contrast with the sprightly humour of the Irish and the flamboyant ebullience of the Welsh. Is it due, perhaps, to the inward sorrow of a gifted race that might think itself pushed to the wall—to the memory of the gross ill-treatment, neglect and ridicule to which the Scottish Celts were subjected for so many years after the Forty-five? Or has Highland melancholy been partly induced by the sore battle for existence amid an unsympathetic environment, by the mountains so often darkly forbidding, if not veiled in dreary mist or beaten by furious storms? Certainly this is the aura that pervades much of Macpherson's *Ossian*:

"The wind was abroad in the oaks; the spirit of the mountain shrieked ·The blast came rustling through the hall, and gently touched my harp. The sound was mournful and low, like the song of the tomb." "Arise, winds of autumn, arise; blow upon the dark heaths! Streams of the mountain, roar! Howl, ye tempests, in the top of the oak! Walk through broken clouds, O moon; show by intervals thy pale face!" "Often are the steps of the dead in the dark-eddying blasts; when the moon, a dun shield, from the east is rolled along the sky." "From hill to hill bend the skirted clouds. Far and grey, on the hills, the dreadful strides of ghosts are seen." "The stream murmurs long. The old tree groans in the wind. The lake is troubled before thee; dark are the clouds of the sky." "Thou hast seen the sun retire, red and slow behind the cloud; night gathering round on the mountain, while the unfrequent blast roared in the narrow vales. At length the rain beats hard: thunder rolls in peals. Lightning glances on the rocks. Spirits ride on beams of fire. The strength of the mountain streams comes roaring down the hills." "Like the voice of a summer breeze, when it lifts the heads of flowers, and curls the lakes and streams. The rustling sound gently spreads o'er the vale, softly-pleasing as it saddens the soul."

Fine similes of this sort abound in Macpherson's measured prose. By contrast, in the poems of the Dean of Lismore's Book, the attitude towards nature is altogether more cheerful. If, therefore,

The great corrie on Lochnagar

Macpherson's sombre similes be regarded as a product of his own time, may they not reflect a change of attitude in the later eighteenth century—due, it could be, to the sense of oppression and foreboding under which the Highland population then was living?

Other faults which outside observers, not always charitably disposed, have attributed to the Scottish Highlanders are inordinate pride, and its concomitant, touchiness; quarrelsomeness,[1] and inability to combine; a tendency to extremism, notably in religious affairs; intemperance; and a certain slyness, particularly in monetary matters. On this matter, it is not impertinent to note that these same failings have often been imputed to the Scottish nation as a whole. In so far, therefore, as there may be truth in all this, it might seem to bear out the contention, advanced above, that the racial distinction between Highlander and Lowlander has been greatly exaggerated. A failing more special to the Highlanders is perhaps a tendency to indolence and procrastination. This indeed some have thought to be a general weakness of the Celtic races. It is expressed in the Highland wisecrack: "When God made time, He made any amount of it." One thinks, inevitably, of the use which another gifted nation of Celtic stock are said to have made of the word *mañana*!

On the other side of the medal, the gleaming virtues of the Scottish Highlanders are fully recognized by all who know them, and therefore need no elaboration here. First of all comes their splendid courage in warfare, which in 1766 earned them a famous tribute in Parliament from the Earl of Chatham, who first on a large scale enrolled Highlandmen in the British regular army:

> I sought for merit wherever it was to be found: it is my boast that I was the first minister who looked for it and found it in the mountains of the north. I called for it, and drew into your service a hardy and intrepid race of men. They served with fidelity, as they fought with valour, and they conquered for you in every part of the globe.

Then again, we think of the courtesy shown by the Highlander towards strangers—a courtesy which gains in charm because it is

[1] John Splendid in Neil Munro's novel makes the intriguing suggestion that Highland quarrelsomeness is due to the Highland scene: "I am aye thinking the Almighty put us into this land of rocks and holds, and scalloped coast, cold, hunger, and the chase, just to keep ourselves warm by quarrelling with each other."

The Moor of Rannoch and the Black Mount

often accompanied by a certain initial and dignified reserve. Hand in hand with courtesy goes the grand Highland quality of hospitality. No one who has accepted this—be it in castle or in cottage—can deny that the Highlander as host is indeed, like St. Columba "an abounding benefit of guests". Equally striking is the kindness and helpfulness of the Highland crofters towards each other. Doubtless this is partly owing to the uncertainty and accidents attendant upon life in the glens, where such calamities as clan warfare, famine, the loss of cattle by theft, disease or other causes, the high mortality among the people themselves, and the utter absence of any kind of 'welfare services', created conditions of recurrent distress which could be relieved only by the succour of kindly neighbours. Of such instances the Highland annals are full, though naturally they have aroused much less attention than the bloodstained records of internecine strife. Nor should we underestimate the softening influence exerted by the universal practice of 'summering', whereby in the warm season the cattle were taken up to 'sheilings' among the hills, there to enjoy fresh pasturing under the care of the younger members of the community—the lads and lasses of the clachans.[1] Summering provided the occasion for countless little courtesies between the family groups in their annual journey to and sojourn in the 'sheilings'—just as, in the long winter nights, neighbourliness and community feeling were fostered by song and music around the blazing peat fires. It is easy to romanticise the *ceilidh* and the sheilings; but it is just as easy to forget their undoubted and beneficent influence upon Highland society.

Among the upper classes the characteristic Celtic custom of fosterage must have done much to spread abroad kindly feelings and to strengthen the bonds of kindred. By this pleasing practice the son of a chief was placed for his upbringing in the family of one of the chief's tacksmen or tenants, or sometimes a more distant friend. An inviolable bond of affection and fidelity was thus forged between the foster father and his *dalt*. Every lover of Scott will recall the devoted self-sacrifice of Torquil of the Oak towards the young chief of Clan Quhele at the fatal conflict on the North Inch of Perth.[2] In the Breadalbane muniments are a number of cases of fosterage, of which one may be selected to

[1] See on this matter my *Portrait of Skye and the Outer Hebrides*, pp. 114–15.
[2] For a similar case, but in historic fact, see below, p. 85.

show how the institution worked in practice. In 1580 Sir Duncan Campbell of Glenorchy—of whom more will be said in the next chapter—agrees that two of his tenants, husband and wife, "shall have his son Duncan in fostering, they sustaining him in meat, drink and nourishment, till he be sent to the schools, and afterwards at the schools." The foster parents pledge themselves to provide the lad with "reasonable support" at the schools. For all this the Chief and the foster-father make the necessary provision in cattle and horses; but the milk is to be the perquisite of the foster-parents, less a quantity sufficient to pay the Chief a rent for the pasturage.

One trait the Scottish Highlander shares with his kinsmen of the Isles. If he leaves his native glen or mountain side, he retains, wherever he may settle and however long his exile, a haunting, affectionate memory of the scenes of his childhood. At home he may seem indifferent to the beauty or grandeur of his surroundings: elsewhere his nostalgia often displays itself in a vigorous championship of his own district or shire as the most beautiful in all the Highlands. In the first chapter of *The Fair Maid of Perth*, Sir Walter Scott observed that in such a discussion, "a native of any other district of Caledonia, though his partialities might lead him to prefer his native country in the first instance, would certainly class that of Perth in the second, and thus give its inhabitants a fair right to plead that—prejudice part—Perthshire forms the fairest portion of the northern kingdom." In what might be called a stated case, Sir Walter goes on to indicate, pretty clearly, that such, at the end of his life (*The Fair Maid* was published in 1828, four years before his death), was his own considered opinion. It is an opinion that will find many supporters.

CHAPTER IV

A SKETCH OF CENTRAL HIGHLAND HISTORY

In his brilliant introduction to the Ordnance Survey Dark Age Map of North Britain, the late Dr. O. G. S. Crawford alludes to

> that struggle between west and east which is a recurrent feature of Scottish history, and probably also of Scottish prehistory. It has been perverted by popular romance into a struggle between Highlanders and Lowlanders; but in actual fact the attacks came not from the barren and sparsely inhabited valleys of the central Highlands, but *through* them from the western coast. These valleys could never have raised armies large enough to overrun the relatively populous plains of the east. Essentially the struggle was dictated by the land; the westerners needed something better than the rugged cliffs and wind-swept islands of Argyll to provide food for their increasing population.

In these sentences Dr. Crawford has set forth a historical truth of cardinal importance, which has been little understood by Scottish historians. His theme will form the guide-line of the present brief summary of Central Highland history.

Dr. Crawford goes on to point out that in the sixth century the Britonic kingdom of Strathclyde, with its capital at Altclut (Dumbarton, the *dun* or fortress of the Britons) barred the direct approach from the west to the Forth and Tay regions. Back doors, however, into Pictland were provided by the mountain passes over Drumalban, and all of them were used by the intrusive Scots of Dalriada. Dr. Crawford lists these gaps in the *Dorsum Britanniae* as follows:

> One such corridor starts on the Firth of Lorne near Dunolly and passes along the southern shore of Loch Etive to the modern places of Dalmally, Tyndrum and Crianlarich, thence up Glen Dochart to Loch Tay and so by Dull (an ancient site) down the Tay valley to Dunkeld and out into Strathmore. . . . The route is joined at Dal-

mally by another which starts at Dunadd[1] and proceeds along the eastern shores of Loch Awe. . . . At Crianlarich it is joined by a route from Dumbarton along Loch Lomond. At Killin Junction a route opens south-eastward and divides into two branches, one leading down past St. Fillans and Dundurn (both old sites) into Strathearn and the other down Strathyre to Callander and Menteith. These branches meet the main eastern thoroughfare of Scotland at Dunblane, Rottearns, near Ardoch, and Scone. All are ancient sites, Rottearns, according to Watson, meaning Ireland's *rath* or fortress (Rath Erenn).[2]

By a remarkable omission, Crawford has naught to say about the most important route of all—Glenmore-nan-Albin, the Great Glen, which we have already described as forming the northern margin of our area. From remote prehistoric times—and this fact gives Crawford the case which he left doubtful—there is ample evidence of the important influence that this great natural avenue has exerted upon Scotland's national development. In neolithic days it was the route by which the chambered cairn builders of Argyll reached the north-eastern and northern plains. In the sixth century of our era, it afforded an easy path for the two great saints of the west, Columba from Iona and Moluag from Lismore, to the Pictish capital at Inverness. And in the critical formative period of the twelfth and thirteenth centuries, the Great Glen acquired a special significance because it afforded a convenient lateral communication between the two provinces of Ergadia in the south-west and Moravia in the north-east,[3] in both of which irreconcilable Celticism made its last, its longest and its sternest stand against the feudalizing and unifying policy so resolutely enforced by the Normanizing kings of the Canmore dynasty.

For the purposes of the present sketch, the history of the Central Highlands may be taken as commencing with the Anglo-Norman penetration. Of this and its consequences, political and social, sufficient has been said in the foregoing chapter. It is, however,

[1] On the Crinan Canal; the chief *oppidum* of Dalriada, and therefore the first capital of the Scots in Scotland. See my *The Historical Saint Columba*, ed. 1963, pp. 26–9. W.D.S.

[2] W. J. Watson, *The Celtic Place Names of Scotland*, pp. 227, 285. Rath Erenn is on record *circa* 500. If the identification be correct, this is an instance of early Scotic penetration from Dalriada into Pictland. W.D.S.

[3] Ergadia is the ancient Latin name for modern Argyll; but the Celtic province so called included the entire western seaboard as far north as Loch Broom.

necessary for us now to look at the ecclesiastical reorganization which followed in the wake of the newcomers. This was even more far-reaching in its results than the superimposition of Norman feudalism upon the Celtic clan system. To understand what happened, we must provide ourselves with some understanding of that most remarkable institution, the Celtic Church.

Inevitably, the early Christian Church, growing up in the bosom of the Roman Empire, adapted herself to the political organization amid which she developed. We have an interesting proof of this in the survival of certain terms which, used nowadays almost entirely in an ecclesiastical connotation, are in fact derived from late Roman provincial administration. The words 'rector' and 'vicar' originally denoted different grades of Roman governor—though it is curious that in the Roman Empire a vicar was superior to a rector, just as a count (*comes*) stood higher in the military hierarchy than a duke (*dux*). So also a diocese in the later Empire was a group of provinces. What happened was that the early Church organized herself territorially, adapting herself to the administrative subdivisions of the Empire. Thus the Christian communities, in town and country, gradually came to be organized in parishes, each under the charge of a priest, while the parishes in course of time were grouped together into dioceses, each controlled by an *episkopos*, overseer, or bishop. In the fourth century the Christian Church in Britain, which sent forth St. Ninian to convert the Picts, is known to have comprised at least three dioceses, York, London, and probably Lincoln.

But in the fifth, sixth and seventh centuries, when the Celtic lands in the west—Wales, Scotland and Ireland—were sundered from the Roman world by the intrusion of a great wedge of Teutonic paganism caused by the Anglo-Saxon conquest of England, the Churches in these lands developed in a manner markedly different from the rest of Latin Christendom. No territorial framework of parishes and dioceses emerged. Instead, the Church adapted herself to the tribal organization of the Celts. The ecclesiastical unit was neither the parish nor the diocese, but the monastery. Monasteries tended to become attached to tribes or clans; and the abbot was usually chosen from the ruling family of the tribe. Bishops, of course, there were. But their duties were mainly restricted to ordination, and they were attached to the monasteries, in which, in all respects other than their episcopal functions, they were subordinate to the abbot—somewhat as in a British regiment the chaplain, while his precedence is recognized in all that pertains to his spiritual functions, is in other respects subordinate to his commanding officer.

What has given the Celtic Churches a place of imperishable glory in the Christian record is their astounding missionary enterprise. Unlike the medieval abbeys, in which men shut themselves up in small communities apart from the world, the Celtic monasteries, numbering in many cases hundreds, nay even thousands of monks, became vast beehives of evangelism. By them was accomplished the conversion of the West. From Iceland to the Apennines, and far eastward into the plains of Hungary, these dauntless missionaries wandered, preached and taught. It is a record without parallel in the history of the world. Yet, ineluctably, came the time when the fires of missionary zeal would burn low, when sloth and secularism would sap the vigour of the monasteries, when their patrimony would be usurped by lay abbots for worldly uses, and the far-flung chains of clachan churches and preaching stations would be neither manned nor maintained. And it was in this epoch of decline that the cardinal weakness of the Celtic Church, her lack of a sound territorial organization, made itself fatally apparent. For all ecclesiastical history teaches us that the only basis for an enduring Church is a solid framework of parishes, each served by a priest or minister, whether the parishes be grouped into dioceses or presbyteries. Such a firm territorial framework, supported by adequate endowments, can keep the Church in being even during a period when the evangelical spirit is feeble—as was the case both in Scotland and in England during the eighteenth century. When a new period dawns of fervour and enterprise, the resources and the organization are there to meet the need.

Therefore it was not only inevitable, but absolutely necessary and desirable, that in the course of the twelfth and thirteenth centuries, the Celtic Church, by this time far spent in decay, should yield to the highly disciplined, strongly organized Church of Rome, administratively based on the parochial system, and founded economically on the institution of tithes. This great revolution, which played a cardinal part in the emergence of our Scottish nation, was the achievement of the powerful, far-seeing and large-minded kings of the Canmore dynasty. Let us now see how the change came about in the Central Highlands.

Our area contained three Celtic monasteries of special note: Dunkeld, Dull, and Glendochart. By far the most important one was Dunkeld. Let us look first at it.

As an ecclesiastical centre, Dunkeld first appears in history in the year 850, when Kenneth MacAlpin, King of the united realm of Picts and Scots, transferred the relics, or some of the relics, of St. Columba, to Dunkeld from Iona, which had been repeatedly sacked and burnt by the pagan Norse. At Dunkeld he established a monastery, and planted therein a diocesan bishop, with the intention of giving him the primacy over the ancient province of Fortriu—that is to say, more or less, the modern districts of Menteith and Strathearn. It does not, however, appear that this diocese of Fortriu (if indeed we may properly call it a diocese) was of long duration. On the other hand the abbey continued to survive; but in this declining period of the Celtic Church it very soon passed under the control of hereditary lay abbots, who claimed to be the *co-arbs* or successors of St. Columba, appropriated the monastic revenues, married and begat children, and became, in the fullest sense, secular proprietors of the monastic patrimony. One of these, Crinan, married a daughter of King Malcolm II; and their son was Duncan I, Shakespeare's "gracious Duncan"—the victim of Macbeth. Duncan's son and avenger, Malcolm Canmore, who married the saintly Margaret, gives his name to the Canmore dynasty, as it is usually termed; though some scholars prefer to call it the House of Atholl, since it originated from Crinan, the lay abbot of Dunkeld. At all events it is clear that our Central Highlands gave to the Scottish kingdom its most powerful, successful and creative dynasty. With the death in 1098 of Ethelred, a son of Malcolm and Margaret, who held the titular post of Abbot of Dunkeld, the lay abbacy there finally disappears from the record, and the way was cleared for the foundation of the diocese and cathedral in 1107 by King Alexander I.

The Celtic monastery at Dull, near Aberfeldy, was founded by the famous St. Adamnan, the biographer of Columba. From 679 until 704 he presided over Iona, and presumably during his tenure of office the daughter house of Dull was founded. It likewise, with its great territories, which extended as far as Drumalban, passed into the hands of lay abbots, and in the eleventh century was held by our old friend Crinan, who as the *co-arb* both of Columba and Adamnan, thus possessed, as a secular magnate, the patronymies of Dunkeld and Dull. What wonder, therefore, that he seemed a fit match for the King's daughter! Unlike Dunkeld, after Crinan's death the monastery at Dull declined into a parish church, which Malcolm, Earl of Atholl, before 1198, granted to the Augustinian Priory of St. Andrews.

Lastly, a word about Glendochart. This monastery was founded by St. Fillan, but which this was of the sixteen saints of that name recorded in the Calendars, is quite uncertain. At all events, it became a wealthy house, and, like the other two, passed, during the decline of the Celtic Church, into the control of lay abbots. By William the Lion's time the Abbot of Glendochart had become a great lay magnate, ranking as an equal with the Earls of Atholl and Menteith in feudal jurisdiction over his territories in Perthshire and Argyll. In 1296 Malcolm and Patrick of Glendochart, presumably descendants of the former lay abbots, did homage as feudal barons to Edward I. In the War of Independence the lordship of Glendochart disappears—perhaps forfeited by Bruce, who, to replace it, founded in Strathfillan a small priory of Austin canons, a cell of Inchaffray. Of the old Celtic monastery there still remain two splendid relics, St. Fillan's Bell and the head of his *bachuill*, or pastoral staff—both now among the treasures of the National Museum of Antiquities of Scotland. The bell of bronze remains in its simple original form, but later piety has adorned the *bachuill* with a richly fashioned silver casing.

Of early Highland history something has been said in the foregoing chapter. In so far as it is proper to speak of a purely Celtic period in the Central Highlands, this may be thought to have been terminated by the Anglo-Norman infiltration in the twelfth and thirteenth centuries, the result of which was the over-laying—if indeed that be the correct term—of the Celtic tribal or clanship polity by a Highland variant of feudalism. It is with the War of Independence that we first get a clear picture of the Central Highlands under their new dispensation. Scottish history during this critical period will never be understood until it is grasped that King Robert Bruce, who will forever and rightly be honoured as the liberator of his country from English thraldom, was nevertheless at no time, even till his death, the accepted ruler of a united realm. The whole weight of the Balliol and Comyn interests was consistently cast into the scales against him; and after his death, against his successor, David II. The proud language of the famous Declaration of Independence, addressed to Pope John XXI from Arbroath Abbey on 6th April, 1320, claims to speak on behalf of a united nation; yet, within four months of its despatch to Rome, three of the magnates whose seals are appended were found condemned as being art and part in a dangerous conspiracy against the King, which was crushed by Bruce, with what was regarded by many as undue severity, in the 'Black Parliament' of Scone; while at least two more of those whose names appear in the Declaration, came under grave suspicion. It does not appear that the Balliol interest bulked large in the Central Highlands. On the other hand, the Comyns, as we have seen, were lords of Badenoch and Lochaber, and were allied by marriage with the powerful West Highland Clan Macdougall of Lorne, whose inveterate hostility to Bruce twice involved the Central Highlands in military operations: in 1306 and in 1308. In the former year King Robert, defeated at Methven on 19th June, fled through Strathfillan across Drumalban towards the Atlantic seaboard, but was intercepted at Dalry, near Tyndrum, by John Macdougall of Lorne, and defeated in the famous skirmish in which he is said, by an ancient tradition, to have lost the 'Brooch of Lorne', now a prized possession of John of Lorne's descendant at Dunollie Castle. On the second occasion (August, 1308), Bruce reappeared in Lorne upon vengeance bent, and defeated his old antagonist in the battle of the Pass of Brander, with which I have dealt in a previous chapter.

After the great King Robert's death in 1329, Edward Balliol, with the backing of the young and vigorous English King, Edward III, renewed in arms his claim to the Scottish throne; and in this, the second War of Independence, the English king secured a grip upon the northern realm greater than his mighty grandfather had ever achieved. "None but children in their games," says Andrew of Wyntoun, "dared call David Bruce their king." Salvation came to the afflicted realm mainly through the exertions of a great Highland magnate, Sir Andrew de Moray, Warden of Scotland. In addition to his rich barony of Bothwell in Lanarkshire, with its peerless castle, Sir Andrew was lord of Avoch in Easter Ross; and as the husband of Christian Bruce, King Robert's sister, was in effective control of the Earldom of Mar, with its strong castle of Kildrummy. One of the leading supporters of the Balliol cause was David de Strathbogie, titular Earl of Atholl and Steward of

Scotland, whose father had been forfeited by Bruce for adherence to the English cause. Him the Warden of Scotland eliminated in the decisive battle of Culblean, (30th November, 1335), at the eastern gateway of the Deeside Highlands; whereupon Atholl's widow, an English lady, Katherine de Beaumont, fled to her late husband's stronghold, the old Comyn castle of Lochindorb. Here she was closely besieged by the victorious Warden, but was rescued, when the garrison, blockaded in their island fortress, were at their last gasp, by Edward III in person. The English king's forced march from Perth through Atholl and Badenoch, by Blair Castle, the Drumochter Pass and Ruthven to Lochindorb, accomplished in four days (12th–15th July, 1336), is one of the most romantic episodes of fourteenth-century history. The beleaguered garrison, as we learn from the lady's own account, had been reduced to four bushels of rye and a single jar of wine!

The combination of power based upon feudal seigneury and clan allegiance reached its climax in the Central Highlands in the tremendous career of Alexander Stewart, Earl of Buchan and Lord of Badenoch, a son of Robert II. This royal ruffian is better known in history as the 'Wolf of Badenoch'. A brilliant portrayal of the man and his times, and of the state of the Highlands about the end of the fourteenth century, is given in Sir Thomas Dick Lauder's romance, *The Wolfe of Badenoch*—a work which, ever since it was first published in 1827, has been unduly overshadowed by the superior renown of the *Waverley Novels*. Even more spectacular was the career of the 'Wolf's' natural son, also Alexander Stewart. His seizure of Kildrummy Castle, his rape of its owner, Isabella, Countess of Mar, and his consequent establishment in that ancient Celtic Earldom, transformed the leader of caterans into a powerful feudal magnate, a warrior and statesman of international reputation, and certainly the greatest of all who have borne the proud titles of Earl of Mar and Lord of the Garioch. In Scottish history, he is celebrated as the Victor of Harlaw: and to that renowned conflict, in some degree to be regarded as the watershed of Central Highland history, it is necessary that we should now bestow particular attention.

In 1398 the Scottish Parliament enacted that Castle Urquhart, near the northern outlet of the Great Glen, should be taken into the hands of the King, "who shall entrust the keeping of it to good and sufficient captains, until the kingdom be pacified, when it shall be returned to its owners". About the same time, the Regent Albany was building for himself at Doune in Perthshire a mighty fortalice, which elsewhere I have described as "the highest achievement of perfected castellar construction in Scotland". No doubt it was intended by the Duke of Albany in the first instance to be the chief seat of his Earldom of Menteith. Yet it seems likely that larger considerations played their part in his choice of this site. In the Middle Ages two great routes through the Central Highlands, from Edinburgh to Inverlochy, and from Glasgow to Perth and Inverness, intersected at Doune. Whoever controlled these routes might be considered in a good posture to bridle the Highlands. Since Roman times the Teith valley has been regarded as a gateway to the mountains, and therefore by the Romans was secured by a fort at Bochastle, close west of Callander:

> On Bochastle the mouldering lines
> Where Rome, the Empress of the world,
> Of yore her eagle wings unfurled.

Now in Albany's day the principal military problem confronting the Scottish government was the hostile power of the Lord of the Isles, who inherited ancient memories of Celto-Norse independence, and moreover was deep in secret league with England. Hill Burton has pointed out that

> in the great truce between France and England in 1389, in which the allies of the high contracting powers were included, Scotland was a party as the ally of France, and the Lord of the Isles was a party as the ally of England.

Formidable enough in itself, this peril was intensified by the claim of the Lord of the Isles to the Earldom of Ross, a claim resisted by Albany on behalf of his own son, the Earl of Buchan. So it may well have been that the special circumstances in which the Duke of Albany stood towards the threatening power of the Lord of the Isles could have helped to induce him to plant a powerful castle on the main route from Edinburgh or Stirling *via* the Teith, Strathyre, Lochearnhead, Glendochart, Tyndrum and the Pass of Brander, to the key western fortalices of Dunstaffnage and Inverlochy.

The preoccupation, thus revealed in the government of Albany with the need to control, whether in Glenmore or in the Drumalban passes, the routes from the Western Highlands and Islands to the eastern plains, was rooted in an urgent political problem which became ever more menacing throughout the fourteenth and fifteenth centuries. Historians have hardly grasped the full import of the conflict between the Scottish Crown and the Macdonalds, Lords of the Isles, which bulks so large in Highland history during these turbulent centuries. In their aggressive policy towards the House of Stewart, the island Chiefs drew upon all those proud memories of the once independent kingdom of the Hebrides, the realm of Somerled and his masterful successors, whose dominions had been forcibly incorporated in the kingdom of Scotland after the victory of Largs in 1263. As independent princes, John of the Isles in the reign of Robert II, and his descendants for a century thereafter, comported themselves in their dealings with the Scottish Crown. With no consciousness of treason, but rather as one sovereign negotiating with another, they bargained with English kings; and, in the extraordinary Treaty of Ardtornish-Westminster (1461) actually concluded with Edward IV a pact for the dismembering of Scotland. It is idle to explain away such things as irresponsible sedition. Rather should we understand them as a contest between the Crown and an insular kingdom not yet organically assimilated into the realm of Scotland.

In 1411 the quarrel came to a head in the 'brim battle' of the Red Harlaw. This renowned conflict, which has left an imprint on the memory of Scotland only second to those of Bannockburn and Flodden, is properly to be understood as an episode in that "struggle between west and east" of which O. G. S. Crawford has written. In the preceding chapter I have pointed out that it was in no real sense a conflict between Celt and Saxon. Still less are we to think of it as a case of 'civilization' *versus* 'barbarism'. Equally vain is the view which depicts the Red Harlaw as the critical and cardinal contest that decided for ever the supremacy of Teuton over Celt in Scotland. This was the idea expounded by John Richard Green in his *Short History of the English People*:

> So pitiable seemed the state of the kingdom that the clans of the Highlands drew together at last to swoop upon it as a certain prey; but the common peril united the factions of the nobles, and the victory of Harlaw saved the Lowlands from the rule of the Celt.

As we have seen, the battle had its origin in a purely feudal dispute about an earldom—a dispute, moreover, in which the Lord of the Isles was juridically in the right. His quarrel with Albany was turned to good account by Henry IV, so that in one aspect the battle of Harlaw may be regarded as "an incident in the uneasy relations between England and Scotland". Yet behind the quarrel about the Earldom of Ross loomed the vast though vague pretensions of the *quondam* kingdom of the Isles. What left an enduring memory in the minds of Lowland Scotland was the heavy loss among gentle and simple, serving under the Earl of Mar:

> Gin ony body speir at you
>   For them ye took awa'
> Ye may tell their wives and bairnies
>   They're sleepin' at Harlaw.

From the time of Harlaw onwards the governing factor in Central Highland history is the rise to dominance of the great confederacy comprised under the name of Clan Campbell. This may fairly be regarded as another instance of Crawford's drive of West against East. Only it was more successful than that of the Macdonalds; for, although Alexander, Lord of the Isles, despite his father's check at Harlaw, succeeded in obtaining recognition from James I of his claim to the Earldom of Ross, the insular potentates failed to maintain themselves on the eastern seaboard, the Earldom being forfeited to the Crown in 1476. By contrast, early in the next century Campbells reached the Moray Firth, through the marriage of Sir John Campbell, son of the second Earl of Argyll, to Muriel, daughter of the Thane of Cawdor. Where the Macdonalds had failed the Campbells succeeded, because of the greater consistency and adroitness with which they pursued their policy of aggrandisement. This was firmly based upon steadfast loyalty to the Crown. Moreover, the Campbells, like the Hapsburgs, understood perfectly the art of contracting deft marriages, as in the case of the Cawdor heiress. In the pursuit of their ambitions they were not only skilful but ruthless. Inevitably they incurred the mortal hatred of their neighbours, and in particular of their worsted rivals, the Macdonalds: yet, after all, they were acting in just the same way as Clan Donald had done. The only difference was that they were successful.

Clan Campbell have always called themselves the 'Sons of

Diarmid', from their mythical ancestor who slew the Boar of Caledon, it is said in Glenshee—a legend which will be considered when we come to deal with that interesting locality. The real founder of their fortunes was Sir Neil Campbell, whose constant support of Bruce, from the days when the King's fortunes were at their lowest ebb, was rewarded by a grant of territories formerly belonging to the forfeited Macdougalls, Lords of Lorne. Sir Neil Campbell's father was named Colin, in Gaelic Cailein. He was known as Big Colin (Cailein Mor). Hence, in Gaelic fashion, the succeeding chiefs of the Clan all bore the soubriquet of Mac Cailein Mor—or, in Saxon mouths, MacCallum Mor. It is unnecessary, in the present sketch, to pursue the proliferation and expansive progress of Clan Diarmaid. Suffice it to say that by the close of the Middle Ages they had obtained substantial control over Argyll below the Great Glen (but excluding Kintyre and the southern islands), as well as the vast Central Highland territories of Glenorchy and Breadalbane. Their principal seat was at Inveraray, near the head of Loch Fyne, where the little town that grew up under the shelter of their castle became a burgh of barony in 1472, and a royal burgh in 1648.

During the ecclesiastical revolution of the sixteenth century, the Earls of Argyll, true to the family characteristic of choosing the winning side, emerged as pillars of the Reformation. Only the seventh Earl relapsed into Catholicism, an act of conscience that cost him his estates. For the Central Highlands, as indeed for Scotland generally, the Reformation proved initially a religious and cultural catastrophe. For generations there was a desperate shortage of ordained ministers, and several parishes had often to be served by a single lay 'reader', who could do little more than read to his congregation a makeshift service based upon the Book of Common Order. Similarly, John Knox's noble ideal of a school in every parish remained a dead letter. The lairds and chiefs who had acquired Church lands were in no mood to spend their new wealth upon schools and schoolmasters. All honour is due to the Presbyterian Church for the strenuous efforts that she made to overcome these formidable difficulties. They were complicated by the fact that it was not until after the Forty-five that the Presbyterian form of church government became firmly established in the Central Highlands. A further difficulty was that education was then largely in the hands of the Kirk, and few teachers were available who were competent in the Gaelic tongue. Add to this the political instability, not finally resolved—and then at what a price!—until after the Forty-five, and it is not surprising to find that, as late as the early years of the nineteenth century, half of the Highland population was unable to read. Imperfect as it doubtless was, the old Gaelic culture, largely based upon oral transmission, had faded, and nothing had been put in its place.

Through the fortunate preservation of *The Black Book of Taymouth*, we are presented with an admirable picture of the mode of life of a great Central Highland Chief at the turn of the sixteenth century. A portrait of Black Duncan Campbell of Glenorchy, in the possession of his descendant, the Earl of Breadalbane, shows him with as sinister an expression as ever a Macdonald could think appropriate to a Campbell visage. Incidentally, he is shown in Lowland armour, as are all the Chiefs of his line, from the fifteenth century onwards, whose pictures, done in colour, are found in *The Black Book*. Black Duncan (*Donnachadh Dhu*) appears to have derived his nickname from his swarthy complexion. In the *Black Book* he appears as a man of culture and a most enlightened landowner. In his prime of life he was familiar with foreign camps and courts. He was an avid book lover, and had a Scotch version of the French *Roman d'Alexandre*[1] transcribed for himself. In true Campbell fashion, he added greatly to his estates, and spared no pains in improving them. He built three castles, extended and adorned others, and built a bridge over the Lochy "to the great contentment and weal of the country". Round his various seats he laid out parks, and was a pioneer in afforestation, putting down plantations of oak, fir and birch. He also took steps to improve the breed of horses on his domains—for this purpose obtaining a stallion from Prince Henry's stable in London. His household books show with what exactitude his financial affairs were managed, and the inventories of his 'plenishing' reveal the luxury in which he lived. When he died in 1631, at the ripe old age of eighty-three, Donnachadh Dhu was succeeded by his son, Sir Colin, a man of equally refined tastes, a good scholar in Latin, French, and Italian, a lover of gracious living, who imported foreign furniture and commissioned no less than sixteen portraits by George Jamesone, the Aberdeen-born father of Scottish painting.

[1] See above, p. 60.

A relic of the old Caledonian Forest on the shore of Loch Morlich

The great Civil War of the seventeenth century found the clans of the Central Highlands more or less established within distinct territorial boundaries. In the south-west was the vast territorial interest of Clan Campbell, dedicated to support of the Covenant, and therefore opposed to the policy of Charles I. North-east of the Campbells was a solid block of clans opposed in the first instance to the Campbells, and therefore royalist in sympathy. These were the Camerons of Locheil, the Macdonalds of Keppoch (staunch Catholics), the Macphersons and Mackintoshes of upper Strathspey and Strathdearn, the Farquharsons of Braemar, the Struan Robertsons in Rannoch, the Stewarts of Atholl, and the Clan Menzies—all of them Royalists, and to a large extent crypto-Catholics. On the eastern margin of our area were the Gordons, a powerful group whose chief, 'Cock o' the North', was the Marquis of Huntly. His loyalty to Charles I was never in question: "You may take my head from my shoulders, but not my heart from my King," so he declared, and nobly he redeemed that proud pledge upon the scaffold. Yet he could never bring himself to co-operate heartily with the King's great lieutenant, Montrose, from natural resentment at the latter's shabby kidnapping of him in 1639, during Montrose's Covenanting days. It is possible that the lack of consistent Gordon support was fatal to the Royalist cause in Scotland; for only from this clan was it possible for Montrose to obtain the large force of 'Gentleman' cavalry which were necessary for a descent upon the Lowlands. In Strathdon were the Forbeses, hereditary rivals of the Gordons, and therefore supporters of the Covenant. In mid-Strathspey the Grants, always jealous of the Gordons, along the east side of Loch Ness the Frasers, and in Glen Esk the Lindsays, were all Covenanters.

From what has just been said it is obvious that at no time, in the course of his astonishing intervention on behalf of King Charles, did the Great Marquis enjoy the united support of Gaeldom. Even among those Chiefs with royalist sympathies, many held aloof, either through fear of the Campbells, or simply waiting to see which way the cat would jump. Neither were the 'Irishes', brought over from Antrim by Alasdair Macdonald, universally popular among the Scottish Gael.

It was at Lude, hard by the future battlefield of Killiekrankie, in August 1644, that James Graham, Marquis of Montrose, in his capacity of Lieutenant-General of the royal forces in Scotland,

A cottage in Moidart

The ingle-nook of a Highland cottage. Note the heather besom and the wooden potato-masher

unfurled the standard of King Charles. Of the astonishing series of victories that followed, only one concerns us in this brief sketch of Central Highland history; but in some ways it is the most astonishing of them all. In the campaign and battle of Inverlochy, Montrose struck a shattering blow at the chief prop of the Covenanting cause in his own mountain homeland, the inaccessibility of which had prompted the Campbell vaunt: "it's a far cry to Lochow". Starting from Blair, about 11th December, 1644, with some three thousand troops, and marching in three divisions, he essayed the penetration of Argyll's fastness in mid-winter, an enterprise which no man had thought to be possible. Traversing the south shore of Loch Tay, Glen Dochart, and passing the northern elbow of Loch Awe, he poured his army down Glen Shira upon Argyll's capital at Inveraray. The Campbell Chief fled before him down Loch Fyne in a fisherman's yawl. Behind his flight the whole of Argyll's country went up in flame. Devastation on such a scale had never before been known, even in Highland warfare. Of course it was a cruel business; but there were many in Montrose's army who had experienced similar treatment at the hands of the sons of Diarmaid. When nought was left in the glens round Inverary but smoking homesteads and slaughtered kine, Montrose, his purpose achieved, turned north, traversed the Pass of Brander, crossed Loch Etive at Connel Ferry, and continuing his march by Glencoe, Loch Treig, and Inverlochy, headed up Glenmore towards the north-eastern plains. At Kilcumin (now Fort Augustus) he learned that his way was barred by the Mackenzies, under their chief, the Earl of Seaforth, one of the most powerful leaders of the Covenant. Furthermore, word was brought to the Royalist general that Argyll, thirsting for vengeance, was hot upon his track. In this dilemma Montrose took the bold decision to strike again at the Campbells. In the words of a contemporary Royalist historian, "instead of marching forward, he turned about and went to speak with Argyll". Montrose's famous flank march, by the River Tarff, Glen Turrit, and Glenroy, has rightly been saluted by John Buchan as "one of the great exploits in the history of British arms". Beneath the walls of Inverlochy Castle, on 2nd February, 1645, he fell upon and destroyed the army of Argyll. Once again the Chief of the Campbells made his escape beforehand by boat. From the stricken field Montrose wrote thus to his royal master:

Only give me leave, after I have reduced this country to your Majesty's obedience, and conquered from Dan to Beersheba, to say to your Majesty then, as David's general said to his master "Come thou thyself, lest this country be called by my name."[1]

Dis aliter visum! It was not to be Montrose's destiny to conquer Scotland for King Charles, but Cromwell's to annex it by force of arms to his English Republic. Under the Protectorate, the Central Highlands were held down by Roundhead garrisons planted at Stirling, Perth, Inverness, Inverlochy, and other places. A last Royalist effort was crushed at Dalnaspidal, below the throat of the Drumochter Pass. For Cromwell's administration it could at least be claimed that it gave the Highlands a sorely needed respite from internecine strife, and a stronger and juster government than the mountaineers had ever known. I write 'known', not 'enjoyed': for in the Highlands, no less than in the Lowlands, the Cromwellian Union was sullenly resented, because it had been enforced by England as a result of victory in war. In the Highlands, therefore, as in the Lowlands, the Restoration of Charles II in 1660 was hailed with acclamation.

Throughout the latter part of the seventeenth century, the Central Highlands may be said to have been dominated by the formidable personality of Sir Ewan Cameron of Locheil. Although the lands that gave him his distinctive designation are on the far side of the Great Glen, he also possessed a considerable holding in Lochaber. His entire active life was spent in heroic warfare on behalf of the Stewart dynasty. Macaulay, who in his History has presented his readers with a grotesque travesty of the Scottish Highlanders, was nevertheless fascinated by the colourful figure of Ewan Cameron, of whom his famous character-sketch must be quoted, even in the present brief historical outline of the Central Highlands:

> Sir Ewen Cameron of Locheil, surnamed the Black, was in personal qualities unrivalled among the Celtic princes. He was a gracious master, a trusty ally, a terrible enemy. His countenance and bearing were singularly noble. . . . Locheil was tall and strongly built. In

[1] This extraordinary campaign and battle has a unique position in historical romance because it is the subject of two famous novels, one portraying it from the Royalist and the other from the Covenanting viewpoint: Scott's *Legend of Montrose* and Neil Munro's *John Splendid.*

agility and skill at his weapons he had few equals among the inhabitants of the hills. He had repeatedly been victorious in single combat. He was a hunter of great fame. He made vigorous war on the wolves which, down to his time, preyed on the red deer of the Grampians; and by his hand perished the last of the ferocious breed which is known to have wandered at large in our island. Nor was Locheil less distinguished by intellectual than by bodily vigour. He might indeed have seemed ignorant to educated and travelled Englishmen, who had studied the classics under Busby at Westminster and under Aldrich at Oxford, who had learned something about the sciences among Fellows of the Royal Society, and something about the fine arts in the galleries of Florence and Rome. But though Locheil had very little knowledge of books, he was eminently wise in council, eloquent in debate, ready in devising expedients, and skilful in managing the minds of men. His understanding preserved him from those follies into which pride and anger frequently hurried his brother chieftains. Many, therefore, who regarded his brother chieftains as mere barbarians, mentioned him with respect. Even at the Dutch Embassy in St. James's Square, he was spoken of as a man of such capacity and courage, that it would not be easy to find his equal. As a patron of literature, he ranks with the magnificent Dorset. If Dorset, out of his own purse, allowed Dryden a pension equal to the profits of the Laureateship, Locheil is said to have bestowed on a celebrated bard, who had been plundered by marauders, and who implored alms in a pathetic Gaelic ode, three cows and the almost incredible sum of fifteen pounds sterling. In truth, the character of this great chief was depicted two thousand five hundred years before his birth, and depicted—such is the power of genius—in colours which will be fresh as many years after his death. He was the Ulysses of the Highlands.

Ewan Cameron was born in 1629. His first military service in the Royalist cause was made in the abortive rising against Cromwell's government in 1654, when he was largely instrumental in gaining a smart victory over the Roundhead forces in the Pass of Ballater—the gateway to the Deeside Highlands. To the English garrison at Inverlochy Locheil proved himself a veritable thorn in the flesh: and Macaulay's comparison is justified by his recorded exploits, which indeed have a Homeric quality. Not until the end of 1654 did he consent to lay down his arms, upon honourable conditions. In 1681, when James, Duke of York was in residence at Holyrood, Locheil visited the court in order to pay his respects to his future king; and from the Duke he received a well-earned knighthood. Resisting the offer of a higher title and a pension from William of Orange, as the price of his neutrality, despite his three-score years, he joined 'Bonnie Dundee' in Glenroy on 16th May, 1689. It is no part of our purpose to follow the track of Dundee's amazing game of march and countermarch against his able antagonist, General Mackay. The last round of this whirlwind campaign was fought out in the Central Highlands. Blair Castle was held by the Jacobites and besieged by its owner, John, Lord Murray. From Badenoch Dundee sped to its relief over the Drumochter Pass. Against him from Dunkeld marched General Mackay. Above the Pass of Killiekrankie, Mackay's troops were swept away by the headlong charge of the Jacobites. In the moment of victory Dundee was shot, and with him perished the cause for which he fought. He sleeps in the Atholl vault in the ruined church of St. Bride at Old Blair. The last words of the dying victor had been "'Tis the less matter for me, seeing the day goes well for my master!" (27th July, 1689).

In the battle Sir Ewan Cameron, despite his years, had displayed all the fire of youth. His life had been saved by his foster-brother's son, who served him as a kind of page. The over-running of Mackay's army had left many of the Government forces in the rear of the victorious Jacobites. Among them were some Highlanders who were fighting on Dutch William's side. One of these drew a bow against Locheil's back: but the page, seeing the arrow coming, threw himself in front of it, and thus saved his chief's life at the cost of his own. Killiekrankie was Locheil's last active service in the Stuart cause. He retired to Lochaber, and in 1692 made his peace with King William. He survived until 1719, when death claimed the noble old warrior in his ninetieth year.

In Scotland, the memory of William of Orange is forever clouded by the Massacre of Glencoe. The facts of this deplorable affair are so well known that no great detail is required here. At the time when the last embers of Dundee's rising were in course of being quenched, the Government, in August, 1691, issued a proclamation of indemnity, promising a full pardon to all who took an oath of allegiance not later than New Year's Day. Alexander Macdonald, otherwise known as MacIan, the Chief of the Macdonalds of Glencoe, appeared before the Governor of Fort

William in the last days of the old year, offering to take the oath—only to be told that he must go on to Inveraray to swear it before the Sheriff of Argyll. In bitter winter weather, "across eighty miles of the wildest mountain-land in Scotland", the old man made his painful way to Inveraray, where he arrived on 2nd January. But the Sheriff, the Earl of Argyll, and his deputy, Campbell of Ardkinglas, were both absent; with the result that MacIan was not able to take the oath until 6th January. The Macdonalds of Glencoe had a bad reputation, even by Highland standards, for 'cattle-lifting'. So early as September, Sir John Dalrymple, Master of Stair, the Secretary of State for Scotland, and his friend the Earl of Breadalbane, who himself had suffered at the hands of the Glencoe marauders, and moreover was a Campbell, had made up their minds that the unruly sept must be 'extirpated'. Thus the fact that MacIan had failed to take the oath before the stipulated date came as an opportunity on no account to be neglected. That MacIan had after all taken the oath, and that the delay was due to circumstances beyond his control—all this was carefully concealed from King William. Not only that, but the certificate of MacIan's having taken the oath was "deleted and obliterated" in the Privy Council Register. On 11th January the King had already signed a warrant to proceed by fire and sword against those clans whose chiefs had failed to take the oath, "to burn their houses, seize or destroy their goods or cattell, plenishing or cloaths, and to cutt off the men". Now on the 16th a second directive, likewise signed by the King (who later protested he had not read it!) contained the explicit instruction: "If MacIan of Glencoe, and that tribe, can well be separated from the rest, it will be a proper vindication of the public justice to extirpate that sect [sept] of thieves." With the first order in his hands, Stair wrote exultantly to the Commander-in-Chief in Scotland: "Just now my Lord Argile tells me that Glenco hath not taken the oathes, at which I rejoice, it's a great work of charity to be exact in rooting out that damnable sect, the worst in all the Highlands."

So far, all this was no more than just another of those "letters of fire and sword" which for centuries Scottish governments had issued against recalcitrant Highland clans or septs, and which had resulted in slaughterings and burnings on a far larger scale than the Massacre of Glencoe. What gives the latter its peculiar horror is the gross treachery and vile abuse of hospitality—that most sacred virtue among the clansmen—by which the bloody purpose of the Government was carried into effect.

The Commander-in-Chief's instructions to Lieut.-Colonel Hamilton, second in command at Fort William, were certainly explicit. "Do not trouble the Government with prisoners." For some time he had been corresponding secretly with Hamilton, by-passing the latter's chief, Colonel Hill, an elderly and humane man, who had sent MacIan on to Inveraray, with a letter entreating the Sheriff "to receive him as a lost sheep". When the royal instructions were shown to Hill, it appears that he made some protest, which drew down upon him a decisive letter from the Secretary of State, "Yours of the 14th inst. I have shown to the King"—so wrote Sir John Dalrymple. "You cannot receive further directions than what you have had under the King's hand." Thus the personal responsibility of King William seems established beyond a peradventure.

On 1st February, 1692, a detachment of Argyll's regiment, about 120 strong, marched into Glencoe, under the command of Captain Robert Campbell of Glenlyon. They told the Macdonalds that they were on their way back from the reduction of Invergarry Castle, that there was no room for them at Fort William, so could they have quarters in Glencoe? Campbells though most of them were, they were hospitably received by their predestined victims, and were put up in the three clachans of the glen. Here for all but a fortnight, says the report of the official inquiry, they "had free quarters and kind entertainment, living familiarly[1] with the people". Glenlyon, whose niece was married to a son of MacIan, "came almost every day and took his morning drink at the house". He and his two subordinate officers accepted an invitation to dine with the Chief on the 13th knowing full well that on that very morning they were due to murder him. Precisely as arranged, soon after 5 a.m. the guests rose up against their hosts. The old Chief was shot in the back as he was getting out of bed. His wife was stripped naked, and the rings torn off her fingers by the soldiery with their teeth. She died next day. Other parties of military were marching through the night, to block the exits from Glencoe by east and west. Yet, in the confusion of a dark morning and amid a heavy snowstorm, the majority of the Macdonalds succeeded in making their escape up into the bitter mountains—

[1] "Familiarly", here in the sense of en famille.

though how many, including wives and bairns, were frozen to death, was never known. In all, the soldiery butchered about thirty-five men, as well as two women and two children. All three clachans were burnt, and the cattle, horses and sheep, to the number of about one thousand, were driven away. But, as a massacre, the affair had been a flop. This was the only thing that the Master of Stair regretted. "All that can be said," so he wrote, "is that, in the execution, it was neither so full, nor so fair, as might have been."

In the two great Jacobite risings of the eighteenth century, the 'Fifteen' and the 'Forty-five', our Central Highlands were heavily involved. It was at Castleton of Braemar, on 6th September, 1715, that the Earl of Mar raised the standard of 'King James VII'. Thence he marched south over the Cairnwell Pass by the Spital of Glenshee and Kirkmichael to Dunkeld and Perth, which remained his headquarters during most of his feebly conducted campaign. Its lack of vigour is the more remarkable when we remember that, despite the need to leave substantial forces in his rear to contain the northern chiefs—Simon, Lord Lovat, Forbes of Culloden, and the Earl of Sutherland, all supporters of the Hanoverian interest—Mar was able to muster at Perth no less than ten thousand men, a much larger force than Prince Charles Edward had at his disposal at any time thirty years later. It seems indeed that Jacobite fervour reached its climax in 1715. No doubt this was in no small measure due to the discontent felt in Scotland over the way in which the Government in London had played fast and loose with the terms of the Treaty of Union. Even then, and among the followers of Highland chiefs who were 'out', as the phrase went, in the 'Fifteen', there were many who had to be coerced into supporting the Stuart cause. This is strikingly illustrated in the well-known letter which Mar addressed, on 9th September, 1715, to John Forbes of Inverernan, Baillie of his own Lordship of Kildrummy:

> Ye was in the right not to come with the hundred men ye sent up tonight, when I expected four times the number. It is a pretty thing, when all the Highlands of Scotland are now rising upon their King and country's account, as I have accounts from them since they were with me, and the gentlemen in most of our neighbouring Lowlands expecting us down to join them, that my men should be only refractory. Is not this the thing we are now about, which they have been

wishing these six and twenty years? And now, when it is come, and the King and country's cause at stake, will they for ever sit still, and see all perish?

I have used gentle means too long, and so I'll be forced to put other orders I have in execution. I have sent you enclosed an order for the Lordship of Kildrummie, which you are immediately to intimate to all my vassals. If they give ready obedience, it will make some amends; and if not, ye may tell them from me, that it will not be in my power to save them (were I willing) from being treated as enemies by those who are ready soon to join me; and they may depend on it, that I will be the first to propose and order their being so. Particularly, let my own tenants in Kildrummie know, that if they come not forth with their best arms, I will send a party immediately to burn what they shall miss taking from them. And they may believe this not, only a threat; but by all that's sacred I'll put it in execution, let my loss be what it will, that it may be an example to others. You are to tell the gentlemen that I'll expect them in their best accoutrements, on horseback, and no excuse to be accepted of. Go about this with all diligence, and come yourself and let me know your having done so. All this not only as ye will be answerable to me, but to your King and country.

That the Earl did not shrink from putting his threats in execution we learn from an inquiry held, after the collapse of the Rising, into the conduct of his tenants in Kildrummy, which shows that fifteen of these unfortunates had fled to avoid military service; that their houses and crops had been burnt; and that they themselves had been rounded up and sent as prisoners to their feudal superior in the camp at Braemar.

The failure of the Rising saw the first attempts of the Hanoverian Government to deal with the Highland problem in a civilized fashion, instead of by a mixture of bribery and brutality. In the pithy phrase of Macaulay, "experience had taught the English Government that the weapons by which the Celtic clans could be most effectually reduced were the pickaxe and the spade". Barracks to house standing garrisons were built, within or around our area, at Inversnaid on Loch Lomond, at Ruthven in Badenoch, at Fort Augustus in Glenmore, and at Inverness. These garrisons were linked up by the great system of roads and bridges with which the name of Marshal Wade will be forever associated: though only a portion of the programme was completed during his tenure of the Scottish Command (1724–33); and indeed some of his projects, such as a cross-road linking Fort William with Aberdeen, to this day await realization.

The opening round of the campaign of 1745 was fought out— or rather marched out—in the Central Highlands. It presents us with a strategic problem of no ordinary interest. When Prince Charles Edward arrived at Invergarry Castle on Loch Oich (26th August), he learned that the royal army, under Lieut.-General Sir John Cope, had already reached Badenoch, and was marching forward with all speed to seize the Corrieyarrick Pass. Two alternative courses of action were proposed to the Prince by his military advisers. One was to continue his march up the Great Glen to Inverness. With this town as his base, he would be able to rally the northern clans, and moreover would be in a position to receive the reinforcements and supplies from France upon which he counted. The other plan was to descend immediately upon the Lowlands—which involved, of course, the necessity to sweep away the army of Sir John Cope. Prince Charles decided for the bolder plan; and on the evening of the 26th his advance guard seized the Corrieyarrick.

Sir John Cope was thus presented with his antagonist's problem in reverse. He also had the two alternatives, of making a frontal attack with his small force upon the Pass, or of turning aside to Inverness, where he could await sea-borne reinforcements, under the assumption that the Jacobites would not risk a descent upon the Lowlands with the royal army, and many clans loyal to the Government, mustering in their rear. There was, of course, a third alternative open to him: to retire into the Highlands. But neither upon military nor upon moral grounds was this a thinkable proposition.

Jacobite satire, song and tradition have made 'Johnny Cope' a figure of fun. In sober truth, like Mackay before him, he was a brave and capable soldier, whose only fault was a lack of experience or understanding of Highland warfare. Moreover, his little force of less than 1,500 was of very inferior quality; for the flower of the British army was then on active service on the Continent. The evidence laid before the Board of General Officers (presided over by the veteran Marshal Wade) that investigated his conduct —it was in no sense a court-martial—affords ample proof of the vigour and rapidity of his actions when confronted with the fact of armed rebellion. No one who has diligently studied the fascinating Report of the Board can doubt the rightness of their unanimous verdict "that Sir John Cope's behaviour has been unblameable".

So far back as July, in view of repeated rumours that a Jacobite rising in the Highlands was imminent, Cope had strengthened the three garrisons in Glenmore—Fort George (Inverness), Fort Augustus and Fort William: but his requests for reinforcements and equipment, and for the recall of officers on leave, were turned down by the Government "to prevent the alarming his Majesty's subjects too much"! When the news of the Prince's landing reached Edinburgh, on 8th August, Cope acted with the utmost promptness; and his correspondence during that month fully attests the vigour, variety, and wisdom of his measures. His advance into the Highlands, instead of waiting at their gates to receive the Jacobites, as the Duke of Argyll had done in 1715, was dictated by the Government, under the vain expectation that he would immediately be joined by a great number of the "well-affected clans".

Sir John left Crieff on 22nd August. Conducting his march with all speed and every precaution against surprise, he reached Dalwhinnie on the 26th. His rapid passage through the mountains had of course been made possible by the Great North Road so recently constructed by Wade. Just beyond Dalwhinnie this road branched. The right section made for Inverness; the left climbed, by seventeen traverses, over the formidable Corrieyarrick Pass, at a height of 2,507 feet, to descend upon Fort Augustus. At Dalwhinnie Cope received the astounding news that the Jacobites, estimated at about 2,500 strong, were in possession of the Pass. To attack them there would be to invite a second Killiecrankie: all the more so as the Jacobites had in position twenty small cannon provided from the *Doutelle*, the vessel which had brought the Prince from France; whereas Cope had with him no more than eight pieces, four light guns, and four mortars—the latter better suited for siege than mountain warfare. Moreover, there were no artillerymen, and the guns had been brought, as Sir John himself quite candidly tells us, "for show only"—doubtless in view of the well-known dread felt by the Highlanders for the "musket's mother". In the Preface to the Report of the Inquiry into Cope's conduct of his campaign, a vivid picture is presented of the impregnable nature of the Pass:

The south side of the Corriarrick is of so very sharp an ascent, that the road traverses the whole breadth of the hill seventeen times before it arrives at the top. The road in descending on the north side is flanked for a considerable space by a wood, and is crossed by a large hollow, which is the bed of a torrent, and whose banks are so extremely steep that it is not passable but by a bridge, which was possessed by the rebels, and could have been broken down in a very short time, if they had found it necessary. From this description it is plain that a very small force, who were masters of this hill, were capable of stopping, or even defeating a considerable army that should attempt to dislodge them. For each traverse, in ascending, is commanded by that above it: so that even an unarmed rabble, who were posted on the higher ground, might, without exposing themselves, extremely harrass the troops in their march. Whence, the attempting to force seventeen traverses, every one of them capable of being thus defended, was an undertaking which it would have been madness to have engaged in, with a number inferior to the enemy, especially as the Highlanders, from their knowledge of the country, their natural agility, and their attachment to ambushes and skirmishes, would in this situation, have indulged their genius, and would doubtless have proved most formidable opponents. Besides, could it be supposed that by the bravery of the troops, or an uncommon share of good fortune, all these passes had been cleared, and the army had arrived on top of the Corriarrick, yet, the descent would have been still more hazardous, and, if the formentioned bridge was broken down, became absolutely impossible; for then neither a carriage nor a baggage horse could have crossed this hollow.

Although it does not appear in his printed evidence, this very cogent exposition may well have come from the pen of Sir John Cope himself, or, at all events, from that of a senior member of his staff.[1] Certainly it bears out the Commander-in-Chief's own statement that "it was utterly impracticable to force a passage to Fort Augustus over the Corriarrick".

To retreat into the Lowlands, apart from loss of face, would be

---

[1] I suspect it was written by the Quartermaster-General, Major Caulfield, who, according to Cope, had "been employed by Marshal Wade, and the succeeding Commanders-in-Chief, from the beginning, upon the roads through the same country. He has actually surveyed these roads every year since they were made, as Inspector of them, and is allowed to have a compleat knowledge both of the general and particular situation of the country, and of the disposition of the inhabitants."

equally dangerous, since the fast-moving enemy, "lightly armed and free of baggage", could with great ease slip past the royal troops and break down the bridges in their rear. Nor could the royal army blockade the Pass; for, owing to desertion of carters and pilfering in the commissariat, they had less than three days' supply of bread left. So Sir John Cope's fateful decision, unanimously supported by a council of his field officers, was taken to march north-eastward to Inverness. To quote from a paper put in at Cope's trial—if for convenience this term may be used for the inquiry—by Colonel Whiteford, his Chief of Staff: "By advancing to Inverness he secured the forts in the north, kept all the waverers from joining the rebels, and gave an opportunity for the King's friends to join him."

Thus the way was left open for Prince Charles's audacious descent upon the Lowlands and his capture, first of Perth, and then, through the poltroonery of its defenders and the treachery of its Provost, of Edinburgh, which fell on 17th September.

Meantime Sir John Cope had been acting with speed and foresight. After a two days' forced march down the Spey, he occupied Inverness on 29th August. Two days thereafter he wrote to the Lord Justice Clerk, urging prompt measures for the security of the capital: "Exert your authority—lengths must be gone; and rules and common course of business must yield to the necessity of the times, or it may be too late." Sending Colonel Whiteford in advance to arrange sea transport and supplies at Aberdeen, he himself with his whole army reached that city on 11th September, after a forced march of eight days, conducted with perfect order and discipline. Next day the transports, sent up urgently by the authorities in Edinburgh, sailed into the harbour. On the 15th the army was embarked, and on the 18th and 19th Cope's little force, with its guns and baggage, was landed at Dunbar. Stress of weather had prevented them from putting in at Leith. Had they been able to do so, Edinburgh would not have fallen to the Jacobites. His subsequent advance upon the capital, and the total destruction of his army in the whirlwind battle of Prestonpans (21st September) do not concern us here. But in justice to the memory of a capable and gallant, though most unlucky soldier, it is necessary once again to correct the old Jacobite lie that the night before the battle was spent by Sir John Cope in feather-bedded ease at Cockenzie House. The evidence presented to the Court of Inquiry makes it clear that he "lay upon his arms" among his men in the field. In the words of Rob Roy, it is high time to "let that flee stick in the wa' ".

During their final retreat to Inverness in February, 1746, the Jacobite army divided itself into two columns. One, under Lord George Murray, comprising the cavalry and the Lowland regiments, marched up by Strathmore and Aberdeenshire; while the Highlanders, led by Prince Charles, took Wade's road over the Drumochter Pass and down the Spey—in a frame of mind very different from the *élan* with which, in the preceding September, they had poured southward over the same road to descend in triumph upon the Lowlands. On 16th April, 1746, in the last battle fought upon British soil, the Jacobite cause perished for ever upon "bleak Culloden's heath"; and with that mournful event this historical sketch of the Central Highlands finds its proper end. The horrors that followed upon Cumberland's victory were no more than the first eddies upon the surface of a remorseless flood which, from that day to this, has continued to submerge the successive landmarks of a proud and ancient race. After long centuries of ding-dong struggle, the West had finally been vanquished by the East.

> A wind that awoke on the moorland came sighing,
> Like the voice of the heroes that perished in vain:
> "Not for Tearlach alone the red claymore was plying,
> But to win back the old world that comes not again."

CHAPTER V

THE HIGHLAND CASTLES

No one who travels through the Central Highlands can fail very soon to become aware of the ancient castles which—in most cases no more than weather-worn ruins, but sometimes still proudly defying the hazards of time and the slow gangrene of a hostile economic climate—add a distinctive element to the Highland scene. The picturesqueness of the buildings themselves, the romantic beauty, and often the stark grandeur of their situation, and the part which so many of them have played in the sturt and strife of olden Scotland—all these things arouse our interest and excite our imagination. And when a ruined castle is examined with some knowledge of medieval architecture, it will be found to reveal much about the life which was lived, centuries ago, within walls long bereft of their flooring and furniture—the perils against which its occupants required to defend themselves; their ideas of domestic comfort; and, not least, the brow-beating pride of feudalism or chieftainry, expressing itself in the landowner's determination, for reasons of prestige, to house himself in a dwelling that should command respect from all who approached it. The arrogance implicit in castellar construction is finely portrayed in Blind Harry's description of Ravensworth Castle in Yorkshire, said to have been besieged and captured in one of Wallace's raids. The Minstrel describes it as "a seemly place"—

> A royal stead, fast by a forest side
> With turrets fair, and garrets of great pride
> Builded about, right likely to be wight[1]
> Awful it was unto any man's sight.

Nor must we imagine that the builders of our ancient castles

[1] Wight—strong. Again I am quoting from the somewhat modernised black letter edition of 1758.

95

were wholly uninfluenced by natural beauty, as well as fencible strength, in their choice of site. For example, of Doune Castle, mentioned in the last chapter, King James VI in 1580 wrote that "at our last repairing towart our castell and place of Downe in Menteith we persavit the samin and feildis therabout to be maist pleasant for our pastyme and verray commodious for our dwelling in the symmer seasoun". And even in the purely Celtic society that preceded the Anglo-Norman infiltration, the interior splendour of a chief's house was a thing to be celebrated by the bards: for example, in the account of Fingal's palace contained in one of the poems of the Dean of Lismore's Book:

> Seven sides had the house of Cumhal's son
> Seven score shields on every side
> Fifty robes of wool around the King
> Fifty warriors filled the robes.
> Ten bright cups for drink in his hall.
> Ten blue flagons, ten horns of gold.
> A noble house was that of Finn.

The castle, in its strict definition as the private stronghold of a feudal magnate, exercising seigneurial authority over his tenants, was of course a foreign importation into the polity of the Celtic Highlands. As such it remains today as the outward and visible sign of the change-over, beginning during the Anglo-Norman penetration in the twelfth and thirteenth centuries, from chieftainry to ownership. It is now pretty well understood that our earliest Scottish castles, those of the Norman settlers, were not the ponderous stone towers, which did not become common, even in England, until the twelfth century. Although at least one Norman stone keep remains in the Highland area of the Scottish mainland, namely Castle Sween in Knapdale, the usual Norman castle, here as elsewhere in Britain, was an affair not of stone and lime but of timbered earthwork. Such a castle was called by its builders a *motte*; and pictures of them may be studied on the Bayeux Tapestry. A circular fosse or ditch was dug, and the upcast heaped up within the ditch to form a tall, conical, flat-topped mound. The word *motte* is the same as our *moat*, only we use the modern word to indicate not a mound but a ditch—just as, in Scotland a dyke means a wall of earth or stone, whereas in most parts of England it signifies a ditch. Round the summit of his *motte* the

Norman lord set a stout palisade, or it might be a rampart of gabions; and within this he built for himself a wooden tower. In the more important castles, to the *motte* was attached a *bailey*, that is to say a courtyard enclosure, likewise protected by a palisaded bank or ditch, which houses the subsidiary buildings of the lord's establishment. In these castles of timbered earthwork there was nothing in the least provisional. They were made to last, and possessed a formidable potential of defence. It was difficult for men in heavy armour, having struggled up the steep side of the *motte* amid the missiles of its defenders, to pull to pieces a stout palisade fixed on the very edge of the summit, so that the besiegers, out of breath and encumbered by their armour and weapons, had no purchase ground from which to assail it. If the wooden tower were set ablaze by fire-arrows, the castle did not thereby fall; and subsequently the tower could be quickly and cheaply replaced.

Two Norman *mottes* have been noted near Fortingall, and doubtless there are others in the Central Highlands; but no systematic search has yet been made. Our area, however, contains two Norman earthworks on a grand scale, ranking indeed among the most imposing secular monuments of the Middle Ages in the whole of Scotland. These are the Doune of Invernochty in Strathdon, and Ruthven Castle in Badenoch. They may be described as "ring castles" rather than *mottes*, since the summit area of each is so large as to accommodate the whole establishment, so that no bailey was required. In each, the mound is in substance natural, carved by the Norman engineers out of a morainic or fluvio-glacial mass. In a heavily glaciated country like Scotland, many of our *mottes* are natural in substance.

Prior to the building, in the thirteenth century, of the great stone castle of Kildrummy, ten miles down the valley of the Don, the Doune of Invernochty was the capital messuage or principal stronghold of the Earldom of Mar—one of the ancient Celtic provinces whose Mormaers had accepted the new dispensation. The fact that their fortalice at Invernochty has always been styled the Doune (Gaelic *dun*) reminds us that in the Highlands of Strathdon the old Celtic speech survived until well on into the eighteenth century. Owing to its early supersession by Kildrummy Castle, very little history attaches to the Doune. It is an oval motte, 60 feet or upwards in height, with a summit area measuring about 250 feet by 120 feet. It is enclosed by a formidable ditch; and to the north and west large-scale embankment was employed to form a broad artificial lake, with elaborate arrangements for filling and emptying the ditch at will. The whole structure presents us with a most impressive picture of Norman military engineering. Round the top of the mound run the foundations of a stone curtain wall, which may well date from the twelfth century—the more so as the remains of the first parish church of Invernochty, which stood within the curtain, and doubtless began as the castle chapel, have yielded evidence of Norman work.

The kitchen refuse found during the excavation of this great Norman castle proved that its inhabitants lived almost entirely on their domestic animals—cattle, sheep, and pigs—with only an occasional haunch of venison. It is surprising to find, in so remote a district and at such an early date, that a stock-breeding economy had so completely superseded the hunting stage of existence. Also, the midden bones clearly showed that cattle-raising rather than the herding of sheep was then the chief stock industry in upper Strathdon.

The great *motte* at Ruthven near Kingussie, now superbly crowned by the gaunt and grim ruin of the Hanoverian barracks (of which more hereafter) remains to us as the most imposing memorial of the Comyn lordship of Badenoch. Here the summit area of the mound, rising to a height of some 50 feet above a marshy plain, measures about 265 feet in length and 115 feet in greatest breadth. Its summit area must be at least in part artificial, since when the barracks were built cross-beams were discovered running through its upper portion. Here also there has been a stone curtain wall, of which a single fallen fragment still lies at the foot of the mound. In the fourteenth century Ruthven Castle was one of the chief seats of the terrific Wolf of Badenoch. In March, 1452, the castle, then recently granted to the first Earl of Huntly, was captured and 'kest doune' by the rebel Earl of Ross. It was soon rebuilt, and was visited in 1459 by James II; also in September 1506 by James IV, who there paid a gratuity in cash and provided a new wardrobe for nine Spaniards who had been shipwrecked in the Lewis. Early in the seventeenth century, after being twice burnt by negligence, the castle was rebuilt by the fifth Earl (and later first Marquis) of Huntly. Ruthven Castle played a stormy part in the Civil Wars of the seventeenth century, until in 1689 it was finally given to the flames by Claverhouse.

During the thirteenth century the typical stone castle consisted of a thick curtain or wall of *enceinte* enclosing a courtyard. The curtain was defended by flanking towers, usually round. Two of these might be placed on either side of the principal entrance, while a third, larger and stronger than the others, formed the keep or donjon. Of this type of castle the Central Highlands present us with some fine examples. One of the most interesting is the Comyn stronghold of Balvenie, near Dufftown, at the gateway of the Banffshire Highlands. It was anciently known as the Castle of Mortlach, the local centre of population long before Dufftown was thought of. Occupying in itself a strong and romantic situation where the Dullan Water joins the Fiddich, this important castle commands the approaches both up and down Glen Fiddich; blocks the outlet from Glen Rinnes, down which the Dullan Water flows; and forbids the passage eastward through the narrow slack which leads by the modern Drummuir Castle to Glen Isla and the eastern lowlands. Moreover, it sentinels the old hill road leading over by Auchindoun Castle to the Cabrach and Donside, which Edward I used on his return march from Elgin in July, 1296, and again in October, 1303, on which occasion he paused at Balvenie Castle on the 6th of that month. The primary work at Balvenie consists of a tall and massive curtain wall, constructed with the banded rubble masonry usual in Scotland at this period; the material being quarried out of the formidable rock-cut ditch by which the fortress is engirdled. At one corner was the square donjon, which was destroyed at an early date, probably during the Wars of Independence. In the fifteenth century Balvenie Castle was held by the Douglases, who built a fine stone hall, with a pointed vault. Later it passed to the Stewart Earls of Atholl, who in the mid-sixteenth century housed themselves in a handsome new mansion, with a bold round tower and provision for firearm defence. This latest addition to the castle has the distinction, unusual at that early date, of possessing a row of oriel windows, above which is displayed the arrogant motto of the Stewart Earls of Atholl: FURTH FORTUIN AND FIL THI FATRIS. *Fatris*, otherwise *ferteres*, is the plural of an old Scotch word *ferter* (Latin *freetrum*) meaning a coffer.

With its building work of three different periods, Balvenie is one of the most interesting of Highland castles. As might be expected from its strategic position, it figured prominently in the Civil Wars of the seventeenth century, and in the 'Fifteen'. Within its walls in 1582 was born Field-Marshal Sir Alexander Leslie, First Earl of Leven, the "old little crooked soldier" who commanded the Army of the Covenant, the most efficient military force that Scotland ever produced in her whole long martial history.

At the lower inlet of the Great Glen, placed so as to block any hostile effort, whether Norse or Celtic, from the Hebrides, the Comyns built themselves another powerful fortalice, more elaborately designed than Balvenie. Inverlochy Castle, famous as the scene of Montrose's masterpiece of victory described in my last chapter, is a quadrangular structure with thick curtain walls and boldly salient drum-towers at the four corners, one of which, considerably larger than the rest, formed the donjon, and to this day is known as Comyn's Tower. There are two entrances, the main gateway and a postern leading out to a small harbour on the River Lochy. The other three sides were surrounded by a deep ditch, fed from the river. Later in the thirteenth century, the fashion of providing a donjon was given up, as is illustrated in a third Comyn castle, Lochindorb, which almost completely covers its island site in one of the bleakest of Highland moorland lakes, about six miles north-west of Grantown-on-Spey. Here all four corner towers are more or less equal in size. The masonry of the original building, and in particular the broad outspreading base or apron of the curtain walls, so closely resembles the work at Balvenie as to make it practically certain that both were the work of the same masons. An outer curtain, facing the mainland, may well have been an addition made by Edward I, who stayed here from 24th September to 4th October, 1303, during which time many writs, preserved in the English public records, were issued from Lochindorb.

In 1300, 'Black' John Comyn, Earl of Buchan and Lord of Badenoch, sometime Guardian of Scotland, claimant to the throne against Balliol, and father of Bruce's murdered rival, died in Lochindorb Castle. It is recorded that when in 1295 the Earl of Buchan, in view of the proved incompetence of Balliol, assumed *de facto* power in Scotland, the titular king, whom his subjects called in mockery the 'toom tabard' was secluded in a stronghold in the Highlands. This may well have been Lochindorb. Its defence by Katherine de Beaumont in 1336, and Edward III's famous march to her relief, have been set forth in the previous chapter. Later the castle passed into the hands of the Douglas Earls of Moray, and after their rebellion and forfeiture was dismantled in 1456.

This remote Highland castle has a niche of its own in Scottish literature. As a seat of the Wolf of Badenoch, it bulks large in Sir Thomas Dick Lauder's romance, mentioned already. And, under the pseudonym of 'Loch Ruighi', the castle plays its part in a more modern work of fiction, the late Maurice Walsh's well-known yarn, *The Key above the Door*.

What has been claimed as a fourth Comyn strength in the Central Highlands is the ruin of Castle Roy, near Nethy Bridge on Speyside. Its history is a blank, but the masonry of its four-square curtain wall strongly resembles that of Balvenie and Lochindorb. A remarkable feature of this castle is the great pointed rear arches of early fashion, above the main entrance and the side gate. Probably this was the residence of Augustin, Lord of Inverallan, a local magnate of the time of the later thirteenth century; but whether he was of the Comyn kindred is unknown. It is at all events clear that this great Anglo-Norman family of wise statesmen and enlightened landowners, who deserved well of Scotland but were so ruthlessly extinguished by Bruce, were notable castle builders in their vast Central Highland possessions.

In a famous letter written to Edward II, in the early spring of 1308, Bruce's inveterate antagonist, John of Lorne, complains that "I have three castles to keep, as well as a lake twenty-four miles in length, on which I keep galleys with trusty men to each galley." The word *stagnum* means a fresh-water lake, not a sea-loch, and there can be no doubt that the lake in question is Loch Awe, which is about twenty-two miles in length. Two of John of Lorne's castles were obviously Dunollie and Dunstaffnage. The third may well have been the island stronghold of Inchconnell in Loch Awe; the more so because the 'Castle of Lochawe' was occupied by John of Lorne after Bruce deprived him of Dunstaffnage in 1308. The main feature of Inchconnell Castle, a large and picturesque ruin, is a four square enclosure which seems to fall into the thirteenth century pattern of Central Highland stronghold; but distinctive architectural features are lacking.

In Kildrummy, the chief seat of the Earls of Mar, our area possesses a thirteenth-century castle of the first rank, alike in size and in quality of architecture. This "noblest of northern castles" I have discussed at such length in other writings[1] that only the briefest notice seems called for in the present little sketch. With its mighty ring of walls and round towers, and its beautiful First Pointed chapel, all built for the most part in fine ashlar of the local red sandstone (see above pp. 21-3) it is indeed a splendid specimen of medieval castellated architecture. And on the pages of Scottish history, from the Wars of Independence to the 'Fifteen', its record is writ large, in letters of blood and fire.

Recent years have been marked by an increasing awareness, among Scottish medievalists, of the existence, in various parts of the country, of a number of stone "hall-houses". These are oblong structures, generally somewhat lightly built, of which the central feature is a hall, raised above cellarage, not always vaulted. One of the most interesting and best documented of these, the island castle of Fraoch Eilean on Loch Awe, has recently been the subject of a careful and detailed study.[2] Leaving out of account later alterations, this castle is a hall-house, unmistakably Norman in style, and therefore to be assigned to the twelfth century. The great north-western buttress of characteristic Norman aspect, rises from the spreading plinth in a manner which finds an exact parallel in the corner buttress of the twelfth-century hall at Monmouth Castle. Fraoch Eilean Castle was already in existence in 1267, when Alexander III granted it to the chief of the Clan MacNachtan, on condition that he repaired it and kept it "for the King's necessity, and that so often as he should come to it, the castle well furnished should be delivered to him to lodge and dwell there at his pleasure". Obviously these unusually explicit conditions demonstrate the importance which Alexander III ascribed to this remote island castle. His charter to MacNachtan must surely be construed as an act of state, grounded upon national policies. The danger now apprehended came from the lower end of Loch Awe—from the west, through the Pass of Brander, from whose outlet the estuary of the River Awe broadens out into the loch hard over against Fraoch Eilean. What the Scottish King feared was the continued menace

[1] See also the latest study, "Excavations at Kildrummy Castle, Aberdeenshire, 1952–62," by M. R. Apted, in *Proc. Soc. Ant. Scot.*, vol. XCVI, pp. 208–36.

[2] See Hugo Millar's important paper in *Trans. Glasg. Archaeol. Soc.*, n.s., vol. XV, pt. iii, pp. 111–28.

of Norse aggression from the Hebrides. The Treaty of Perth, following on Alexander's victory of Largs, was not sealed until 1266, the year before the grant of Fraoch Eilean; and nobody could venture to assume that the new King of Norway, Magnus Lagaböter, had in fact renounced the ambitions of his mighty father, Haakon Haakonsson. If this be the correct interpretation of the Fraoch Eilean charter, then it must be regarded as another detail of the intersecular struggle between East and West which, following O. G. S. Crawford, we are regarding as the *Leitmotiv* of Central Highland history.

Perhaps the latest, and certainly the most massive, of our Central Highland hall-houses is Kindrochit Castle, in the village of Braemar. Here the large hall, resting on unvaulted cellarage, and provided with square corner towers, appears to be the place where King Robert II kept his summer court almost annually between 1371 and 1388—after which the war with England, famous for the Scottish victory at Otterburn, brought the royal holidays in Braemar to an end; much as Balmoral, the successor of Kindrochit, was deserted by our Royal Family during the two great wars of our own time. It was in Kindrochit Castle that the poet John Barbour, the father of Scottish literature, received in 1378 a civil-list pension, in recognition of his authorship of the great national epic, *The Brus.* To Robert II's hall-house was added, under a royal licence granted in 1390, the fifth largest tower-house in Scotland.

The excavation of Kindrochit Castle yielded kitchen refuse which offered a marked contrast from that which we have already noted at the Doune of Invernochty. Here the animal bones were mainly those of red deer, with only a minor proportion of roe deer, cattle, sheep, pig and horse. It thus appears that the household at Kindrochit, unlike their opposites in Strathdon, lived mainly by the chase. It is interesting to have this medieval gloss upon the ancient rhyme:

> The river Dee for fish and tree
> The river Don for horn and corn.

Among the relics found at Kindrochit was a large, handsome, and richly wrought silver-gilt brooch, dating from the early sixteenth century. On its seven kidney-shaped bezels is the graceful inscription, in old French: "Here am I in place of a friend!"

From the fourteenth century onwards, the typical Scottish castle, in the Central Highlands as elsewhere, is some variety of a "tower-house". The tower-house is just a hall-house up-ended for security reasons: just as, for different reasons, the tower-flats in our modern cities are to be considered as streets up-ended. It is impossible to travel very far in our area, without being confronted by some grey tower looming amid trees, crowning some rocky knoll or commanding height, or occupying one of the many islands to be found in the Highland lochs. Space permits us to do no more than glance at a few outstanding examples.

The tall tower of Invermark stands at a height of about 850 feet near the head of romantic Glen Esk, on a steep bank overlooking the rocky, boulder-strewn channel of the Water of Lee, a short distance below the point where it emerges from the lonely loch of the same name. Tactically, the situation between the two streams is a strong one, while strategically the tower occupies an important position as an outpost to Edzell Castle, the headquarters of the Lindsays of Glen Esk. It sentinelled the upper reaches of the Glen and controlled the Fir Mounth, Forest of Birse Mounth, and Mounth Keen passes. The position was therefore well chosen to impede the movement of cattle thieves across the Mounth between Mar and the Braes of Angus. On closely examining the tall and narrow tower, it becomes apparent that it has been heightened. The stubs of a former corbelled parapet may still be detected, and the part above this, with its picturesque angle turret, is clearly shown by its ornate detail to be the work, *circa* 1600, of Sir David Lindsay, Lord Edzell, who at that time was making such notable additions to his ancestral seat at the foot of the Glen. As originally built, the tower dates from 1526. At ground level it is well furnished with horizontal gunloops. The only entrance is on the first floor, and was reached by a timber forestair. It still retains its iron 'yett', fashioned after a manner peculiar to Scotland, whereby the mode of penetration of the bars is reversed in opposite quarters. No better example of a Highland tower could be found anywhere than Invermark Castle. A seventeenth century topographer states very precisely the reason for its presence where it is:

In Lochlie is the great and strong castle of Innermark upon the water of Northesk. It is very well peopled and upon any incursions of the Highland Katranes (for so those highland robbers are called) the Laird can, upon very short advertisement, raise a good number of weell-armed prattie[1] men, who seldom suffer any prey to goe out of their bounds unrecovered.

Another noble example of a Highland tower is Auchindoun Castle in Glenfiddich. This massive ruined stronghold of a powerful branch of the Gordons, proudly crowning an abrupt green conical hill and overlooking from a height of 200 feet, the turbulent stream of the Fiddich, has much the aspect of a Rhineland *Räuberburg*. Round the castle are the multiple banks and ditches of a prehistoric hill fort. The great tower has a special interest for us, because a reliable seventeenth-century historian ascribes it to Robert Cochran, the master-mason, or architect as we should call him nowadays, who became a favourite of James III, and by him was made Earl of Mar. The story of how in 1482 the jealous barons, led by Archibald 'Bell-the-Cat' hanged the upstart Earl (as they deemed him) over Lauder Brig, is one of the best known episodes of Scottish history. It was James III, a great patron of fine building, who gave its great hall to Stirling Castle: and if, as has been thought, Cochran was the architect thereof, then to him is due the credit of designing the noblest of Scottish festal halls. His tower at Auchindoun is built upon the L-plan: that is to say, it is what in old Scotland was called a 'tower-house and *jam*': 'jam', nowadays spelt 'jamb', and applied to the check or side of a door or window, in former times signified a wing or 'outshot' of a building. In view of its distinguished architect, it is not surprising that the tower of Auchindoun contains a finely conceived groin-vaulted hall. It is even more interesting to find that, after the four angle corbels and the *tas-de-charge*, or level-bedded portion of the groin-ribs, had been built, it was decided to raise the vault, and a new start, with a second corbel-cap, had to be made in the corners: but the middle corbels and ribs were designed from the outset to suit the heightened vault. Round this fine and unusual tower is a 'barmkin' or courtyard, containing kitchen, bakehouse, stables, and other offices. These are enclosed within a massive wall, with a round flanking tower; and both tower and wall are well furnished with gunloops.

The Auchindoun Gordons were a turbulent brood. The best

---

[1] i.e., 'pretty', in the sense of the German *prachtig*—'splendid fellows'.

known among them was Adam Gordon, who played a leading part in the savage Civil War between the partisans of Queen Mary and those of her son, the infant James VI. The ballad of *Edom o'Gordon* has earned him a sombre though unjust fame; for he was not present at the burning of Corgarff Castle (see below p. 119). In fact, he was a chivalrous foe in all that cruel strife. In 1592 Auchindoun was plundered and burnt by the Mackintoshes, as commemorated in a well-known ballad:

> Coming owre Cairn Croom
>   And looking doun, man,
> I saw Willie Macintosh
>   Burn Auchindoun, man.
>
> Light was the mirk hour
>   At the day dawing;
> For Auchindoun was in flames
>   Ere the cock crawing.

Every Scottish tower-house had attached to it a 'barmkin'. This was a courtyard defended by a curtain wall, so as to afford protection for outbuildings, and, if need be, for the owner's livestock. Should the castle be a large one, and its owners rich, the barmkin might in course of time be occupied by domestic buildings enclosing a small courtyard. The result could be a castle of considerable size providing a large amount of domestic accommodation. Of this development, by far the finest example in the Central Highlands is Kilchurn Castle on Loch Awe, the ancient seat of the Breadalbane Campbells. This imposing and well-preserved ruin, so finely situated on a low, rocky platform thrust forth into the marshy northern apex of Loch Awe, and surrounded by a superb mountain panorama, culminating in Cruachan Ben, has long enjoyed the attention of artists, whether with brush, pen, etching tool, or camera. It also inspired a well-known sonnet by Wordsworth, beginning

> Child of loud-throated war! the mountain stream
> Roars in thy hearing; but thy hour of rest
> Is come, and thou art silent in thy age.

To the architectural antiquary, Kilchurn Castle is of special value because, thanks mainly to the *Black Book of Taymouth*, the chronology of its various parts is fully known. The great tower that forms the nucleus of the structure was built in the mid-fifteenth century by Sir Colin Campbell of Glenorchy, the 'Black Knight of Rhodes', uncle and 'tutor', that is to say guardian, of the first Earl of Argyll. He was a man of international renown, who thrice visited Rome, and (as his *soubriquet* indicates) had served with distinction against the Moslems under the banner of the Knights of St. John. His career is therefore yet another instance of the point made in a preceding chapter, that the Highland magnates were not barbaric chiefs cut off from the wide world amid their mountains. The tower which he "biggit to him self" on "Ilankeilquhirn in Glenurquhay" is a lofty and massive rectangular structure, and with the four oversailing corner turrets added by the sixth Lord of Glenorchy (also Sir Colin) who ruled from 1550 until 1583, still dominates the castle. The second laird, Sir Duncan (1480–1513, who fell at Flodden) built the "laich hall", that is to say a festal hall within the courtyard, as distinct from the old family hall in the tower. The sixth laird, above referred to as having built the "four kirnellis" on the keep, likewise added the "north chalmeris" of the castle. The seventh laird, the famous 'Black Duncan' (1583–1631, see above p. 80) repaired the whole castle "inwardlie and outwardlie". In 1614 he rebuilt the "laich hall" and its kitchen, both being raised to a height of two storeys "with ane chymnay on the syde wall thairof". The cost of this work, it is interesting to be told, was 3,000 marks—the mark being 13s. 4d., and the Scotch pound being then 1s. 8d. sterling! Two years later still further improvements were made:

Item, upone the south syd of the clos betwix the great toure and kitchin of Glenurquhay the twa laich sellaris with ane loft abone (above) thame and ane capell abone the loft wer compleit in Mairche in anno 1616 zeiris, the expenss quhairof debursit be Sir Duncane Campbell of Glenurquhay Knicht is fywe hundreth pundis money, at quhilk tyme the stair going frome the clos to the said tour wes biggit.

Finally, the castle was once more remodelled in 1693, which date, with the arms and initials of the first Earl of Breadalbane and his Countess, appear on a new lintel inserted over the door of the keep. As a result of all these additions and re-handlings, the courtyard buildings form a spacious, well-articulated mansion, in part embodying the ancient barmkin wall with its three round towers.

It is noteworthy that the only entrance to the inner court is through the basement of the keep.

Kilchurn Castle played a notable part in Central Highland history. Here, in February 1629, was born Sir Ewan Cameron of Locheil, 'the Ulysses of the North', of whom we heard in the last chapter. In 1654 the castle was burnt by General Middleton, during the Royalist rising against Cromwell's Government. In 1740 the Earls of Breadalbane finally deserted Kilchurn for their seat at Balloch, now Taymouth Castle. Yet the ancestral stronghold was still capable of housing a Hanoverian garrison in 1746; after which it rapidly fell into decay. Some time prior to 1769 the keep was damaged by lightning. In the great gale that destroyed the Tay Bridge, on 28th December, 1879, a segment of one of the corner towers was blown down, and the fallen mass now lies overturned on the ground. The castle is now under the guardianship of the Ministry of Public Building and Works, and awaits happier times for the necessary measures of conservation.

In our last chapter we heard about Montrose's devastating invasion of the fastnesses of Clan Campbell in December–January 1644-5. From the carefully detailed *Black Book of Taymouth* we learn just what this signified on the Breadalbane estates:

> In the zeiris of God 1644 and 1645 the laird of Glenurquhay his whole landis and esteatt betwixt the foord of Lyon and point of Lesmoir weir brunt and destroyit be James Grahame soumetymes Earl of Montrois, and Alexander McDonald sone to Coll McDonald in Colosna, with their associattis. The tennants ther quholl cattell weir takine away be these enimies, and ther cornes, houses, plenisching, and whole insight[1] weir brunt. And the said Sir Robert [ninth of Glenorchy], pressing to gett the inhabitants repairit, warrit[2] XIs Scottis upon the bigging of every cuple in his landis within the shirrefdoomes of Perth and Argyll, and als warrit seed cornes upon his awine chairgis to the most of his inhabitants in Perthshire. Yett by the providence of God his garisone housis, to wit, Balloch, Ile of Lochtay, Finlarg, Aucallader, Castelkylchorne, and Barchaltan, weir keipit from these enimies.

The loveliest of all these composite castles in the Central Highlands is Lochaneilean near Aviemore. This is indeed a beryl of

---

[1] 'Inside plenishing' form a single idea, namely the whole interior contents of a house.

[2] i.e., 'laid out'.

mountain scenery, and in that context we shall look at it again later. The loch, so haunting in its lonely beauty, is encradled in the heart of the ancient Forest of Rothiemurchus, of which something was said in Chapter II. Many able writers have extolled the beauties of Lochaneilean Castle; but none better than the unknown author of a sonnet written in 1903:

> The mountain tops rise into spectral mist,
> The wind is moaning in the forest fir;
> The steel-blue waters scarcely are astir
> That darkly mirror those gaunt hills, cloud-kissed,
> And gently lap that islet's mantling green
> Where stand the castle ruins, old and grey,
> Silent and grim that rang with old-time fray—
> The terror of a wild, long-dead Has-been!
> Formless and dark the shadowed waters sleep,
> While on the mountain tops the wind shrieks shrill
> And, rioting in passes scarred and deep,
> Strikes the black Larig with a death-like chill.
> But here the silent waters darkly keep
> Lost untold stories, safely hidden still.

The ruins of the castle are of small extent. Yet they are of interest because they show work of five building periods; and because these seem to be the result less of haphazard addition and alteration, than of a consequential development of the whole insular site up to the limit of its restricted possibilities. In order of date, the structures are: (1) the tower-house; (2) a hall-house; (3) the fore-curtain with its entrance; (4) a guard house adjoining the entrance; and (5) a long narrow lodging. Part of the castle is said to be built upon piles; and as there has been serious settlement, it is likely that the building occupies the site of a crannog or lake-dwelling.

Lochaneilean is said to have been a stronghold of the Wolf of Badenoch. Later it was occupied by the Mackintoshes, who held it from the Bishops of Moray for the yearly rent of a fir-cone, payable on demand at the castle. From the Mackintoshes in the sixteenth century Lochaneilean passed to the Gordons. A writer of about 1680 reports that the castle "is usefull to the countrey in times of trouble or wars: for the people put in their goods and children here, and it is easily defended, being environed with steep hills and craigs on each side, except towards the east". It is stated to have been attacked by the Jacobites in 1690, after the battle of Cromdale (see below p. 192) but was successfully defended by the laird's wife, Grizel Mor. The active history of the castle ends in 1715, when it was used as a prison to prevent Mackintosh of Balnespick and some others from joining the Hanoverian forces.

As is well known, up till 1902 Lochaneilean Castle was the last breeding place in Britain of the osprey, until that beautiful and interesting bird was introduced again to Rothiemurchus in 1959. The remarkable triple echo obtained from the shore opposite the castle is familiar to every visitor. In Sir Thomas Dick Lauder's stirring romance, *Lochandhu*, which gives us a vivid picture of the disturbed state of the Speyside Highlands for years after Culloden, Lochaneilean Castle figures as the scene of Eliza Malcolm's captivity and her daring rescue by Amherst Oakenwold, aided by the *Dwarfie Carline o' the Cove*.

Perhaps I may be pardoned for concluding these few particulars about a famous castle upon a personal note. While the ospreys bred on the ruin all access to it was strictly forbidden. The castle was therefore not surveyed by MacGibbon and Ross for their standard work; and no proper plans of it had been made before my own expedition in 1935, nor did any architectural description or analysis exist of the ruined structure. Thus I went there not knowing what I should find, and with a pleasurable sense of the pioneer or explorer which is seldom enjoyed by the investigator of medieval monuments in Britain—a feeling not altogether dissimilar to the sensation of Keats on a similar experience in the realm of letters:

> Then felt I like some watcher of the skies
>   When a new planet swims into his ken;
> Or like stout Cortez when with eagle eyes
>   He stared at the Pacific—and all his men
> Looked at each other with a wild surmise—
>   Silent, upon a peak in Darien.

In the sixteenth century the general use of arquebuses or handguns led to important changes in the design of our Scottish castles. The central structure, be it tower-house or hall-house, now comes, in many cases, to be built with angle towers designed to provide

flanking defence at ground level by means of gunloops. Charac-
teristically, two towers are often made to do the work of four, in
covering all four sides of the central building, by disposing them
en échelon—i.e., one at each of two diagonally opposite corners.
Another advantage of this canny scheme is that the angle towers,
holding on to the main building as it were by their finger-tips,
interfered as little as possible with the lighting. Such buildings are
known, descriptively, as 'three-stepped' or Z-castles. A fine example in the Central Highlands, dated 1577, is Castle Menzies,
near Aberfeldy, the chief seat of that most famous clan. Here the
flanking towers are square: and the castle, proudly displaying its
steep roofs, crow-stepped gables, corbelled turrets with their conical helmets, and enriched dormer windows, makes a massive and
imposing appearance. In 1840 a large addition, not to its advantage, was made to the castle. At Edinample Castle, near Lochearnhead, the flanking towers are round. This was another seat of the
Breadalbane Campbells. The Water of Ample here makes a fine
multiple water-fall, first in two separate cascades and then, after
uniting, in a single fall; the entire descent is about sixty feet.

One of the finest among the still inhabited castles on the three-
stepped plan is Grandtully, also near Aberfeldy. It has been claimed
as the original of Tullyveolan, the Baron of Bradwardine's mansion in Waverley; but from a note by Sir Walter in the later
editions of that splendid novel, it is clear that when he wrote it he
had not seen Grandtully. Here the wings are square, but a round
staircase tower caps the heel of one of them. In 1626 this tower was
heightened and finished with an ogee helmet, so as to form a
commanding and most satisfying feature of the building. There
are the usual crow-stepped gables and corbelled turrets with
"candle-extinguisher" roofs. Grandtully is the ancestral seat of the
Stewarts of Innermeath. In the last century a chapel was added to
the castle; this was remodelled in 1893.

Our old Scottish architects loved to ring the changes on their
plans. So we have examples of three-stepped castles where one
tower is square and the other round—as in the modest but pleasing
mansion of Newton near Blairgowrie, where the round tower is
developed above into the square by boldly salient corbelling, in a
highly effective manner.

Of all the Z-castles in the Central Highlands none exceeds in
historic fame the picturesque ruin of Glenbuchat in Strathdon. At

this castle, which occupies a commanding situation in the angle where the Water of Buchat meets the Don, and backed by the great 'nose' of Ben Newe—the Holy Mountain of Strathdon— the flanking towers are square. Between each of them and the main building is a stair turret. These are not carried, as usually in Scotland, upon corbel courses, but upon squinch arches or *trompes*. This is a French mannerism, much favoured by the great architect Philibert de l'Orme, who built so many beautiful palaces for François I and Henri II—the designer of the Tuileries and the gallery at Chenonceaux. Now John Gordon, the builder of Glen- buchat Castle, married a daughter of Sir Robert Carnegie of Kinnaird in Angus, who had been Ambassador-extraordinary to the court of Henri II, the patron of Philibert de l'Orme. Sir Robert can hardly have failed to meet the great French architect; and, himself a notable builder, may well have become interested in his ideas about *trompes* as a form of construction preferable, in de l'Orme's opinion, to the usual Scottish corbelling. It is note- worthy that the whole character of Glenbuchat Castle differs from its Aberdeenshire contemporaries, and suggests that the master mason came over the Mounth from Angus.

Above the castle doorway is the inscription (now, alas! weath- ered out):

IOHN GORDONE HELEN CARNEGE 1590
NOTHING ON EARTH REMAINS BOT FAIME

This motto has about it an intriguing air of enigma: for is not fame the most perishable of mortal attributes? The engima is solved when we realize that 'faime' has here its former meaning of 'good repute'[1] and that 'bot' is the old Scotch word for 'with- out'—as in the motto of Clan Macpherson "Touch not the cat but a glove". So the meaning of our motto is "nothing earthly can endure without good repute". This is a common theme in the literature of antiquity, and became again a favourite in the Re- naissance.

Glenbuchat Castle is forever associated with 'Old Glenbucket'[2] of the 'Forty-five', whose unswerving devotion to the Jacobite

---

[1] Thus in the records of old-time Scottish trials 'famous witnesses' does not imply celebrity, but simply that they were respectable.

[2] This is really the better form of the name, which was changed in 1902 to pedantic antiquarianism of 'Glenbuchat'.

Glencoe
Loch Lomond and Ben Lomond

cause earned him, even during his lifetime, a legendary fame. As a teenager he had been present at the battle of Killiecrankie: he was a prominent figure in the 'Fifteen'; and in 1737 and 1739 he paid secret visits to Paris and Rome, in order to concert measures for a second rising. The late Dr. Walter Blaikie, a distinguished authority on the Jacobite period, considered him a principal architect of the 'Forty-five'. In that heroic campaign he served with distinction as a Major-General, albeit by this time "an old man, much crouched", who had to be lifted on to his horse. After Culloden he was hunted like a partridge on the braes, with £1,000 on his head, until finally he escaped to France, to die there in sickness and poverty.

It is characteristic of the inveterate ignorance among writers about Highland affairs, that a former Historiographer Royal for Scotland could say about this Jacobite leader that "it would depend entirely on the turn taken by intrigues in London, about which the Laird of Glenbucket knew no more than he did of the politics of the court of Cathay, whether he should be called out to fight for King George or King James!"

Among those few ancient castles in our area which are still inhabited by the descendants of their builders, pride of place must surely be given to two: Blair and Ballindalloch.

Standing as it does in the gate of the Highlands, Blair Castle, north-west of Blair Atholl, the ancestral seat of the Duke of Atholl, inevitably has had a stormy history. A fortalice is known to have been built here in 1269 by John Comyn, Lord of Badenoch; and part of this early castle is thought to be incorporated in the north-eastern tower of the present large white-washed mansion. In 1653 the Castle was blown up by the Roundheads, but had been restored before 1689, in which year it was occupied by Claverhouse before the battle of Killiecrankie. For about a week it was unsuccessfully besieged, on behalf of the Williamite Government by John, Lord Murray, brother of its owner, the Marquis of Atholl, who himself held aloof from the civil strife. It was to relieve the Castle that General Mackay undertook the famous march that brought him to disaster at Killiecrankie. From Blair Castle, the day before the battle, Dundee wrote his last letter—a personal appeal to Cluny Macpherson to join the Jacobites: "If you have a mynd to preserve yourself and save the King, be in armes

Kilchurn Castle and Loch Awe

to morou, then when the letter comes you may be here in a day. All the world will be with us, blissed be God." After the battle, Blair Castle was dismantled, in order to prevent it again falling into Jacobite hands. In his Latin poem, the *Grameid*, chronicling Dundee's heroic campaign, James Philip of Almericlose described Blair Castle with its "lofty battlements":

> *Per densas coryli silvas, et curva Timellae*[1]
> *Flumina ad alta Blari tendit munimina castri.*

Once again the Castle was restored, and gave lodging to Prince Charles Edward, both on his daring southward march in 1745, and on his mournful retreat to the north next year. Before Culloden it admitted a Hanoverian garrison, and was successfully defended against Lord George Murray, the Jacobite commander —a brother of the Duke of Atholl, who supported the Hanoverian interest. So in 1746 the history of 1689 repeated itself at Blair. In this, the last of its sieges (and the last siege on British soil), the Castle was bombarded with red-hot shot. After the 'Forty-five' the damaged building was remodelled, in such fashion as to divest it of much of its baronial character: Queen Victoria, who visited it with the Prince Consort in 1844, describes it as "a large plain white building". In 1872, however, it was restored, and further alterations were made in 1903. It is now an imposing pile, and contains many features of architectural interest; notably the fine eighteenth-century panelling, and the ornate stucco ceilings made by Thomas Clayton, Adam's plasterer.

The contents of this famous castle are such as would be expected in the ancestral seat of a distinguished Highland family. Naturally, they include armour and weapons, and many relics of the Jacobite period. The family portraits are of special interest, and so also is the fine library, including many books belonging to Lord George Murray. Most valuable of all, perhaps, is the vast collection of muniments, illustrating every aspect of the life of a long series of Highland chiefs, whether in war, in politics, or in estate management. These papers are now being systematically investigated and catalogued by Aberdeen University Library. When the task is completed, we shall know a great deal more about Highland history and economy. The Castle stands amid extensive ornamental

---

[1] *Timella* is the River Tummel. It is interesting to learn that in 1689 the glen was clad in dense hazel woods.

grounds, and is approached from the village along an avenue of patriarchal limes.

His Grace the Duke of Atholl is the only subject of the British Crown who is entitled to keep a private army. The Atholl High-landers are a corps of some thirty men: needless to add, they are now used for purely ceremonial purposes!

In 1529 the third Earl of Atholl of the Stewart line built a second castle somewhere upon his estates. The circumstances of its build-ing were so extraordinary that the matter deserves, even in this little book, to be recorded with the fulness of picturesque detail in which it has been preserved to us in the narrative of Lindsay of Pitscottie:

> Wpoun the nixt sommer thairefter, the King, togidder with his mother, and ane ambassadour of the Paipis wha was in Scotland for the tyme, went all togidder to Atholl to the huntis. The earle of Atholl heiring of his coming, maid great and gorgeous provisioun for him in all thingis pertaining to ane prince, that he was als weill eased in all thingis as if he had beine in ane of his awin pallaces. For this noble earle of Atholl caused mak ane curious pallace to the King, his mother, and the ambassadour, quhairby they were als weill eased as if they had beine in ony pallace aither of Scotland or Ingland, and equivalent for the tyme of thair hunting; quhilk was biggit in the midle of ane greine medow, and the wallis thairof was of greine timber, wovin with birkis, and biggit in four quarteris, as if it had been ane pallace, and in everie quarter ane round lyk ane blokhous, quhilkis war loftit and jeasted thrie hous hicht; the floore was laid with grein earthe, and strowed with sick floures as grew in the medow, that no man knew quhair on he yead,[1] bot as he had beine in ane greine gardeine. Fardder, thair was tuo great roundis on everie syd of the yett and ane great portcullies of trie falling doun as it had beine ane barrace yett with ane gritt draw bridge, and ane foussie of sixteine fute deip, and thrittie fute broad of watter. This pallace was hung with fyne tapistrie within, and weill lighted in all necessar pairtis with glassin windowis.
>
> The King was verrie weill intertained in this wildernes the space of thrie dayes, with all sick delicious and sumptuous meattis as was to be hade in Scotland, for fleschis, fischis and all kindis of fine wyne, and spyces, requisit for ane prince. Fardder, thair was no fisches that could leive in fresch watteris, but was thair swimming in the foussie about the pallace. That is to say, all kind of drink, as aill, beer, wyne, both whyte and claret, malvasie, muskadaill, eligant hippocras, and

[1] went, trod.

aquavitae: farder, thair was of meattis, wheat bread, maine bread,[1] and ginge bread, with fleshis beiff and mutton, lamb, veill, and vennison, goose, gryse,[2] capon, cunning,[3] cran, swan, pairtrick, plever, duik, drake, brissel,[4] cock, and paunies,[5] black cock, and muirfoull, capercailles. And also the stankis that were round about the palace were full of all delicat fishes, as salmond, trouttis, pearshis, pykes, eiles, and all other kind of delicat fishes that could be gott in fresch water, and were all readie for the banket. Syne were ther proper stuarts, cunning baxters, excellent cooks, and potingaris, with confections, and drugs for ther disserts. It is said, by the space of thir thrie dayis that his grace was thair, the earle of Atholl was everie day ane thousand pundis of expenss. This Pope's ambassadour sieing so great ane triumph in ane wildernes, quhair thair was no toun neir be twentie myllis, he thought it ane great marvell that sick ane thing sould be in Scotland: that is, so court lyk and delicious intertainment in the Highlandis of Scotland, quhair he saw nothing bot woodis and wildernes. Bot most of all, this ambassadour, when the King was cuming back from the huntis, marvelled to see the Highlanderis sett all this pallace on fire, that the King and the ambassadour might sie it. Then the ambassadour said to the King, "I marvell, Sir, yea latt burne yon pallace quhair in yea war so weill eased." The King answerit, "It is the vse of our Highland men, that be they nevir so weill lodged all the night, they will burne the same on the morne!"

Where was this wondrous timber palace of three days that the Earl of Atholl created for his royal master? Since we are told that the King rode back to Dunkeld on the evening when it was burned, it cannot have been so far away. Probably indeed it was in the neighbourhood of Blair Castle. A 'foussie' 30 feet wide and 16 feet deep ought to leave some trace; and perhaps the site could be identified by an air survey. Pitscottie tells us that the 'bag' of three days hunting included "threttie scoir of hart and hynd, with other small beastis, sick as roe and roe-buck, woulff, fox, and wyld cattis".

Ballindalloch Castle, the ancestral seat of Sir George Macpherson Grant, Bt., is finely situated opposite the point where the Water of Avon pays its tribute to the Spey, a dozen miles southwest of Craigellachie. It provides us with the perfect picture of a Highland castle, where a noble river, spacious and finely wooded grounds, and a background of forest rising into a crest of wine-dark hills, all combine to set forth a coronet of turrets, steep roofs

---

[1] manchet bread.   [2] grouse.   [3] rabbits.   [4] turkeys.   [5] peacocks.

with crow-stepped gables, and picturesque dormer windows. A fireplace in the old portion bears the date 1546; the cap-house, oversailing upon corbels from the round entrance tower with its spiral stair, was added in 1602; two long wings were built early in the eighteenth century; and the entire structure was skilfully remodelled in 1845–50.

Ballindalloch Castle is one of several ancient Scottish mansions the site of which was dictated by supernatural agency. Work was started on the brow above; but every night, precisely when the clock struck twelve, a sudden tempest, sweeping down from Ben Rinnes, carried all the building materials headlong into the River Spey. The storm ceased as suddenly as it began; and the resultant silence, all the eerier by contrast, was broken only by an unearthly laugh in the middle air. At last the laird determined to watch for himself, accompanied only by his faithful henchman. Shortly before midnight they took up position upon the rising walls of the castle:

As the 'witching hour' of night approached, the wail of the rising tempest was heard—it was speedily upon them, and in an instant master and man were both whirled through the air, and jammed into the branches of a holly-bush, while they heard the stones of the building plunging into the river below, and the awful laugh of the preceding nights was followed by an eldritch voice, which thrice repeated, "Build in the cow-haugh".

Finally some account must be given of those castles in the Central Highlands which were rebuilt or adapted to serve as Hanoverian garrison posts during the eighteenth century. Of these by the far most important is Ruthven Castle, in Badenoch, which we have already noted as an early stronghold of the Comyns. Having been burned by Claverhouse in 1689, its ruins were finally cleared away in 1719, when the present barracks were built. These form a massive and lofty rectangular structure, comprising two barrack ranges facing each other across a narrow courtyard, with curtain walls on the other two sides. At each of two diagonally opposite corners are square towers, quite in the style of the old Scottish Z-plan; but originally four towers were planned, the full design being curtailed upon grounds of economy. The curtain walls have broad ramparts carried on vaulted undercrofts; and the whole building is fully loopholed for musketry. West of the main structure is a large stables block, added in 1734 by General Wade.

In August, 1745, Ruthven Barrack was attacked in strength by the Jacobites. Its garrison consisted of Sergeant Terence Molloy and fourteen privates. The stout-hearted Irish sergeant's report to Lieut.-General Sir John Cope deserves a niche among the great documents in the history of the British Army:

Ruthven Redoubt, August 30th, 1745.

Honourable General,

This goes to acquaint you, that yesterday there appeared in the little town of Ruthven above 300 men of the enemy, and sent proposals to me to surrender this redoubt, upon condition that I should have liberty to carry off bag and baggage. My answer was, that I was too old a soldier to surrender a garrison of such strength without bloody noses. They threatened hanging me and my men for refusal. I told them I would take my chance. This morning they attacked me about twelve o'clock, by my information with about 150 men. They attacked Fore-gate and Sally-port, and attempted to set the Sally-port on fire with some old barrels and other combustibles, which took blaze immediately; but the attempter lost his life by it. They drew off about half an hour after three. About two hours after they sent to me, that two of their chiefs wanted to talk with me. I admitted, and spoke to them from the parapet. They offered conditions; I refused. They desired liberty to carry off their dead men; I granted. There are two men since dead of their wounds in the town, and three more they took with them, wounded as I am informed. They went off westward about eight o'clock this morning. They did the like march yesterday in the afternoon, but came back at night-fall. They took all the provisions the poor inhabitants had in the town; and Mrs. McPherson the Barrack-wife, and a merchant of the town, who advised me to write to your Honour; and told me there were above 3000 men lodged in the cornfields west of the town last night, and their grand camp is at Dalwhinny. They have Cluny McPherson with them prisoner, as I have it by the same information. I lost one man shot through the head, by foolishly holding his head too high over the parapet, contrary to orders. I prevented the Sally-port taking fire by pouring water over the parapet. I expect another visit this night, I am informed, with their pateraroes,[1] but I shall give them the warmest reception my weak party can afford. I shall hold out as long as possible. I conclude, Honourable General, with great respect,

Your most obedient and humble servant,

MOLLOY, Sergeant.

[1] Small cannon.

This splendid performance, and no less splendid letter, earned the gallant sergeant an immediate commission. It was therefore as Lieutenant Molloy that the defender of Ruthven Barracks, on 10th February, 1746, faced a second Jacobite onslaught, now under the command of the redoubtable Gordon of Glenbucket. This time the attackers had cannon, so that Molloy was constrained to surrender on terms. Thereafter the barracks and stable were burnt. Ever since then they have remained an imposing ruin on their lofty stance. They are now under the guardianship of the Ministry of Public Building and Works, and are in process of thorough conservation.

In Aberdeenshire, after the 'Forty-five', two ancient castles of the Earldom of Mar, Braemar and Corgarff, were remodelled and furnished with Hanoverian garrisons. Braemar was a ruin, having been burned in 1690 to prevent it falling into the hands of General Mackay: but Corgarff, burned at the same time, had been repaired, and had served as a Jacobite post during the last Rising. Both were now refurbished, and enclosed by a rectangular wall, with salients on all four faces, the whole being well loopholed for musketry defences. More will be said about these castles when we come to deal with the Highlands of Braemar and Strathdon.

In 1717-19 a barrack building was erected by the Government at Inversnaid, on a most picturesque site near the eastern shore of Loch Lomond. Its purpose was to control the pass between Loch Lomond and Loch Katrine, and thus to bridle the depredations of the redoubtable Rob Roy. It followed the standard pattern exemplified at Ruthven; and, as at Ruthven, four flanking towers were originally planned. Now a total wreck, the ruins are partly embodied in a farm steading. The future General Wolfe was at one time commandant of Inversnaid.

CHAPTER VI

LOCH LOMOND,
THE TROSSACHS, AND BALQUHIDDER

In the last chapter, we finished our brief sketch of the military architecture of the Central Highlands at Inversnaid Barracks, on the eastern margin of Loch Lomond. With Loch Lomond we now begin the topographical survey of our area—under the reservation that its southern end, between Alexandria and Balmaha, does not belong to the Highlands.

Loch Lomond is the largest fresh-water lake in Britain. It is twenty-two miles in length and five in greatest breadth at its southern end, with an area of twenty-seven square miles. Almost to its northern tip the eastern shore is in Stirlingshire; while the whole western flank, and the eastern side of the northern tip, pertain to the county of Dunbarton. The surface of the loch is 23 feet above sea-level. It is drained by the River Leven, which, emerging from the Loch at Balloch, flows into the Clyde at Dumbarton. The deepest part (105 fathoms) is in Stirlingshire, off Cailness, south of Inversnaid. The lake contains abundant salmon, sea trout, lake trout, pike, and perch, and is celebrated for the Loch Lomond 'powan', a fresh water herring of great delicacy. On the Stirling side, near the southern end, the scenery of Loch Lomond is soft and verdant, embosomed in the rich plain of Drymen and Killearn, and studded with romantic wooded islands; while across the water in Dunbartonshire the stern hills behind Luss, culminating in Doune Hill (2,409 feet) lend a Highland character to the scene. Further north along both sides succeed the rugged mountains, but these never reach the savageness of some parts of the Scottish Highlands. Their outlines, though imposing through their mass, are rounded, and their flanks are richly wooded. The lake is a true rock basin, having been hollowed out by the action of ice. The diversity and contrast of its scenery is due to the fact that it occupies a 'transverse' valley, cutting across the 'strike' or general trend of the outcropping beds of rock. The rocks out of which the basin has been gouged belong to the Dalradian schists. A notable feature in the geology of Loch Lomond is a basalt dyke, no less than 30 feet thick, which, first traceable at the head of Loch Long, traverses Ben Vorlich in Dunbartonshire at a height of 2,950 feet, then descends into Loch Lomond, on the other side of which it rises again to a height of over 2,000 feet, until it finally disappears at the head of Loch Katrine. Now the difference between the highest point of the dyke, far up Ben Vorlich, and the bottom of Loch Lomond, has been computed to be no less than 3,130 feet. Since the dyke belongs to the period of Eocene vulcanicity, which I have described in my previous volume in this series, it is obvious that in the time which has elapsed since that epoch—a mere forty millions of years, or thereby, in the stupendous time-scale of the geological record—the obdurate schists have been denuded to a depth now unmeasurable, but at least of 3,000 feet.

Loch Lomond has been truly termed the Queen of Scottish lakes. Many writers have extolled its beauties, and I do not propose to add to their number. Something, however, must be said about its thirty islands, the majority of which, like emeralds in a silver setting, are clustered in its broad southern end. In general they are low, rocky, and clad in coppice or heath. Some of them are of historical interest: notably Inchcailleach near the south-eastern corner of the loch. Here we find the overgrown foundations of a small Romanesque church, with nave and chancel, enclosed in a forlorn graveyard which contains one or two tombstones of the typical West Highland fashion.[1] At Inchcailleach the silent witness of archaeology is confirmed by historical record; for here, on 7th January, 733, as a recluse on this remote islet, died St. Kentigerna, sister of St. Comgan, Abbot of Turriff in Aberdeenshire, and mother of St. Fillan. The name Inchcailleach means the island of the nuns: so we may presume that Kentigerna, like other holy women of the Celtic Church, had gathered around her a community of dedicated virgins. If, as seems probable, the Fillan or Faolan whose mother was Kentigerna is the same early missionary whose name is commemorated, along with those of his mother and his uncle Comgan, in far-off Kintail, and again by himself at Kilallan or Kil'illan in Renfrewshire, then there is perhaps some

[1] See my *Ancient Stones of Scotland*, chap. XVII.

warrant for the imaginative fancy of a modern historian of those ancient and obscure times, who, contemplating this family partnership in far-flung missionary enterprise, pictures the Lady of Inchcailleach in her declining years as follows:

From the high ground beside her island retreat, in the intervals of work, she could often look across the intervening Clyde to the plains of Renfrew, and assure herself that at Kil'illan the one soul she held dearest was responding to her tenderest thoughts.[1]

Beneath an uninscribed white sandstone slab in front of the high altar of the island church were found the bones of a skeleton, which has been conjectured to be that of the Lady Kentigerna.

The graveyard on Inchcailleach was the burial place of Clan Gregor. The yew trees which once enclosed the consecrated ground provided the "Fiery Cross" that figures in Scott's *Lady of the Lake*:

> The grisly priest, with murmuring prayer,
> A slender crosslet formed with care.
> A cubit's length in measure due;
> The shaft and limbs were rods of yew,
> Whose parents in Inch-Cailliach wave
> Their shadows o'er Clan-Alpine's grave.
> And, answering Lomond's breezes deep,
> Soothe many a chieftain's endless sleep.

The largest of the Loch Lomond islands, Inchmurrin, enjoys interests both ecclesiastical and secular. It measures about a mile and a half in length by less than half a mile in greatest breadth, and rises at its northern end to a height of 291 feet. With its low rocky shores and shadowy woodlands, Inchmurrin is a haunt of sheer delight. The name is said to mean St. Mirren's island. St. Mirren was the founder of the Celtic monastery at Paisley, which in the twelfth century was superseded by the famous Cluniac Abbey, a daughter house of Wenlock. The new foundation, planted by Walter, son of the High Steward of Scotland, was dedicated to St. Milburga of Wenlock, St. James (the patron of the Stewarts), and St. Mirren—thus, as Bishop Forbes rightly pointed out "indicating a previous local veneration" of the Celtic missionary, who came in the later sixth century from that great

----

[1] A. B. Scott, *The Pictish Nation*, p. 359.

hive of evangelistic enterprise, the monastery of Comgall the Great at Bangor in the Ards of Ulster. Since Paisley Abbey had a considerable interest in the lands around the base of Loch Lomond, we cannot be sure that the ancient chapel on Inchmurrin was not a medieval foundation from Paisley, rather than a church planted by St. Mirren in person: though the island position is such as was much favoured by the Celtic missionaries. Hard by the chapel site are the foundations of a fourteenth-century castle of the Earls of Lennox, in which the Duchess of Albany found refuge after the execution of her husband, Duke Murdoch, her two sons, Walter and Alexander, and her father, the aged Earl of Lennox, by James I in 1425. Later monarchs of the Stewart line, James IV and James VI, visited the island castle. In the eighteenth century, Inchmurrin, like other islands on Loch Lomond, was used as a place of confinement for lunatics and confirmed drunkards.

Five of the Loch Lomond islands, including Inchcailleach, along with part of the mainland shore, are now included in the Loch Lomond Nature Reserve.

Along its western shore, Loch Lomond is traversed throughout its length by the trunk road from Dumbarton to Crianlarich—a route which, for scenic qualities, is unsurpassed even in the Central Highlands. The villages of Luss, on the broader part of the Loch, and Tarbert, in its narrow northern portion, deserve every whit of their renown as holiday resorts. Both have piers, at which the summer steamers once called on their voyage to Inversnaid near the northern apex of the lake. From Tarbert—the name means isthmus—strikes off a road traversing the narrow neck between Loch Lomond and the salt-water Loch Long, branching at Arrochar, on the left down Loch Long to Garelochhead, and on the right through Glen Croe and Glen Kinglas to the head of Loch Fyne.

On the eastern shore of Loch Lomond a good road exists only as far as Rowardennan. Inversnaid and the northern end of this side of the Loch are reached either from Callander, *via* the Trossachs, or from Aberfoyle by Loch Ard and Loch Chon, and the head of Loch Arklet, down the north bank of which the road descends to Inversnaid (see p. 134). At Inversnaid Wordsworth in 1803 met the 'Highland Girl' whose charms he has sung in two of his poems. The tourist with antiquarian interests approaching Rowardennan up Loch Lomond will not fail to turn aside at Cashel; where, upon a promontory jutting forth into the lake, he will find the very distinct foundations of a Celtic *cashel* or small fortified religious establishment.

Ben Lomond (3,192 feet) though by no means among the highest, is one of the grandest of Central Highland mountains. Since it forms the westmost bastion of the watershed betwixt Forth and Clyde, it may properly be regarded as the southern end of Drumalban, the *dorsum Britanniae* or backbone of the Scottish Highlands (see p. 31). Its splendid cone is visible from many points far and near—for example, from Arthur's Seat and Edinburgh Castle; from Stirling Castle; from the Forth Bridges, both road and rail; from the Rock of Dumbarton; from many other points around the Firth of Clyde; from far-off Tinto Hill in Lanarkshire and Goatfell on the Island of Arran; and needless to say, from scores of summits in the Central Highlands, ranging from Cruachan Ben in the west to Ben Lawers in the east. The most gentle slope is from the south, up which the summit is usually approached by a grassy track from Rowardennan, passing the Half-way Well and breasting the toilsome ridge of Sron Aonaich (the 'moorland nose'). To the west the mountain almost plunges into Loch Lomond, so that its aspect, seen from the further shore, is grandly picturesque. On the north and north-east the summit overhangs a fine corrie (Coire-a-bhathaich, the Sanctuary Corrie, so called as a shelter for deer). On a fine day the view from the top is breath-taking. To the north extends, in a vast panorama, the dissected plateau of the Highlands, a veritable sea of mountains, from the twin summits of Cruachan Ben on the left to Ben Lawers on the right; immediately below on the west is Loch Lomond, bespangled with islands, and cradled in its 'transverse valley'; while south and east is spread out before us the rich and diverse scenery of the Central Lowlands, bounded by the far off screens of the Pentlands and the Ochils, with the basin of the Forth between them. To the south-west, beyond the Firth of Clyde, is seen the mountain mass of Arran; and, on a fine day, across the open waters, it is even said that a glimpse may be obtained of the Ulster coast. No wonder that James Alexander Haldane and Charles Simeon, those stalwart leaders of the evangelical movement at the close of the eighteenth century, having gained the mountain top on a glorious day in 1796, fell on their knees in presence of this view, and "solemnly consecrated their future lives to the service of Almighty God".

The geology of the Loch Lomond basin presents us with much interest. The northern end of the Loch, including Ben Lomond, is eroded out of the Ben Ledi Schists, a group of stubborn metamorphic rocks to whose resistance to aeons of denudation some of the wildest scenery of our Central Highlands is due. Further south, a composite assemblage of rock-types, coarse grits and slates, margins the track of the great Highland Boundary Fault, which traverses the Loch through Inchcailleach and Inchmurrin. In the former island, Lower Old Red Conglomerate is seen up-ended owing to the intense downthrow of the Fault—just as it may be seen at Stonehaven, on the opposite side of Scotland. The summit of Ben Lomond itself, where the surfaces are exposed, reveals evidence of intense glaciation. Of Loch Lomond it is recorded, as of Loch Ness (see p. 27) that its waters were violently agitated during the Lisbon earthquake of 1775. Without doubt this is due to the fact that the Loch lies athwart the Highland Boundary Fault. Some of the islands have beds of clay containing arctic marine shells, showing that at some time during the Ice Age the lake was a salt-water fiord, communicating with the Firth of Clyde.

Westward from Loch Lomond, between it and two famous sea-lochs, Loch Long and the Gareloch, lies a large triangular tract of tangled and almost roadless mountainland, traversed from west to east by four valleys, Glen Fruin, Glen Finlas, Glen Luss and Glen Douglas. Owing to its lack of communications, this area is not so well known as it deserves to be, for it offers some magnificent scenery. The highest summit is Doune Hill with its twin peaks, 2,409 feet and 2,298 feet. Of the valleys, the best known is Glen Fruin, which is served by a reasonable road coming out on the Gareloch at Belmore. Glen Fruin is famous for the extraordinary battle fought on 7th February, 1603, at Strone, between the MacGregors of Glenstrae (in Glenorchy) and the Colquhouns of Luss. A vivid account of this sanguinary event is given by Sir Walter Scott in his Introduction to Rob Roy. The Colquhouns, though more than twice as numerous as their adversaries, were completely defeated, with heavy losses. What rendered the memory of this conflict peculiarly horrible was its bloody sequel, which must be told in the language of Sir Walter. A party of schoolboys from Dumbarton, together with their clerical teacher, chanced to be near the scene of battle. The Chief of Clan Gregor committed the

lads to the charge of his foster-brother, Dugald, known as the
Ciar Mhor, or 'Great Mouse-coloured Man',

with directions to keep them safely till the affray was over. Whether
fearful of their escape, or incensed by some sarcasms which they
threw on his tribe, or whether out of mere thirst of blood, this
savage, while the other MacGregors were engaged in the pursuit,
poniarded his helpless and defenceless prisoners. When the chieftain,
on his return, demanded where the youths were, the *Ciar Mhor* drew
out his bloody dirk, saying in Gaelic "Ask that, and God save me!"
The latter words allude to the exclamation which the victims used
when he was murdering them.

Doubt has been cast upon this blood-curdling story by the fact
that it is nowhere mentioned in the proceedings which followed
against Clan Gregor before the Privy Council; or in an account
of the battle compiled within thirty years of the event. It was the
battle of Glenfruin that caused the celebrated edict of the Privy
Council, which followed (3rd April, 1603) within a month of the
event, proscribing the name of MacGregor. On pain of death, all
who had hitherto borne it were ordered to change their surnames;
while all who had taken part in the battle against the Colquhouns
were prohibited from carrying weapons, other than a pointless
knife to carve their meat. It is easy to understand that such dracon-
ian legislation was easier enacted than enforced. Again to quote
Sir Walter Scott, the anger of the King was particularly excited
by the manner in which the losses sustained by the Colquhouns
was brought to his royal attention:

That James might fully understand the extent of the slaughter, the
widows of the slain, to the number of eleven score, in deep mourning, riding upon white palfreys, and each bearing her husband's
bloody shirt on a spear, appeared at Stirling, in presence of a monarch peculiarly accessible to such sights of fear and sorrow, to demand vengeance for the death of their husbands, upon those by
whom they had been made desolate.

The upper part of Glen Finlas has been converted into a reservoir in connexion with the Dunbarton County Council water
supply. The little Water of Finlas emerges quite dramatically from
its highland glen into an embayment of rich lowland country,
where it divides into two amid the spacious policies of Rossdhu,
the ancestral seat of Colquhoun of Luss. Part of the old tower still

remains, but the present mansion dates from about 1774. The situation is a striking one, on a horn-shaped promontory jutting northward into Loch Lomond.

Glen Luss is associated with St. Kessog, or Mokessog,[1] a sixth-century missionary who came over from Munster, and is said to be buried in the old churchyard of Luss. Primarily he is credited with the evangelization of Lennox; but ancient church sites bear his name also in Perthshire (at Auchterarder, Callander and Comrie), and even in distant Carrick. Indeed Kessock Ferry, Ross-shire, in Gaelic Port Cheiseig, has been associated with this early evangelist. He is said to have founded a monastery upon Inchtavannach, 'Monks Island', in Loch Lomond southward from Luss. Tradition has it that he was martyred, and a prehistoric burial cairn, Carn-macheasaig at Bandry, south of Luss, has been alleged to mark the site. At Luss in 1315 King Robert Bruce granted to the parish church a girth or sanctuary of three miles, which sufficiently indicates the ecclesiastical importance of the site. St. Kessock's bell, no doubt a hand-bell of the well-known Celtic type, was reverenced as late as the seventeenth century.

My readers will not have failed to remark the intensely ecclesiastical character of the early sites on the islands and shores of Loch Lomond. Island monasteries, for the safety and quiet that they offered, were much favoured by the Celtic Church. Naturally these were places where treasures would be accumulated—the most famous instance being St. Ninian's Isle in Shetland—and whither in an emergency the inhabitants of the surrounding country made haste to transport their stock and valuables. This, therefore, may be the reason for the plundering raid on Loch Lomond made by troops of King Haakon during his celebrated attack on Scotland in 1263. Sixty ships came up Loch Long; they were drawn over land, evidently between Arrochar and Tarbet, and launched again upon Loch Lomond. The sequel is told, with terse vigour, in Haakon Haakonsson's Saga:

Round the lake lay an earl's realm which is called Lennox. There were also very many islands on that lake and well tilled. These islands the Norsemen wasted with fire and sword. They burned too the whole district round the lake, and wrought there the greatest mischief. As Sturla sang:

---

[1] i.e., the personal name with the honorific prefix, *mo*.

> "These soldiers so flight-shy
> Of dart-storms bold wielder,
> Drew boats over dry land
> For many a length;
> Those warriors undaunted,
> They wasted with war-gales
> The islands thick-peopled
> On Lomond's broad loch."

The fourth valley that opens from the Dunbartonshire side of Loch Lomond is Glen Douglas. This is a typical Highland glen, now almost uninhabited. An inferior road ascends it, and, after crossing the West Highland Railway, at a height of some 500 feet traverses the *col* to descend at Gorten upon Loch Long. This railway, linking Glasgow with Mallaig, passes over to Loch Lomond at Tarbert, and from the head of the Loch makes for Crianlarich and Tyndrum, whence its course lies over the Moor of Rannoch to Glen Spean and so down to Fort William on the Great Glen.

North of Tarbet the western shore of Loch Lomond is fronted by a noble group of mountains, including such famous summits as Ben Arthur (otherwise known as the Cobbler, 2,891 feet); Ben Ime (3,318 feet); Ben Vane (3,004 feet); and Ben Vorlich (3,092 feet). Of these the first two are in Argyll; the others in the long northward tongue of Dunbartonshire. 'The Cobbler', a name which invites explanation, is said to be merely a corruption of *Gaelic An Gobaileach*, the twin peak. Its fantastically serrated crests afford good rock climbing—not to be attempted, however, by the inexperienced. Ben Arthur overlooks wild Glen Croe, at the head of which is the famous stone seat inscribed "Rest and be thankful". This marks, at 860 feet, the summit of the road from Arrochar to Glenkinglas, and so down to the head of Loch Fyne. The former military road here, completed in 1748, ascended in successive traverses, like the Corryarrick road mentioned in a former chapter. Wordsworth, who with his sister Dorothy, came over the Glen Croe pass in 1803, describes the old road in words that show how much he had appreciated the injunction carved by the soldiery on the stone bench:

> Doubling and doubling with laborious walk,
> Who that at length has gained the wished-for height,

Ruthven Barracks

> This brief, this simple wayside call can slight,
> And rest not thankful?

Ben Vane and Ben Vorlich overlook between them Loch Sloy and its effluent stream, the Inveruglas Water, which enters Loch Lomond at the place of that name. North of Inveruglas is the power station for the Loch Sloy hydro-electric scheme. The size of the Loch has been doubled by a dam, from which the water is conveyed in a tunnel underneath the skirts of Ben Vorlich to the Inveruglas power-station. Opened in 1950 by H.M. Queen Elizabeth The Queen Mother, this was the first scheme to be completed by the North of Scotland Hydro-electric Board.

Strictly speaking, the term 'The Trossachs' (Gaelic *na Troisea-chan*, the cross places) is applicable only to the region between Loch Katrine and Loch Achray, rendered so famous by Scott in his *Lady of the Lake*. Owing, however, to the current vogue of what is called 'The Trossachs Tour', the term has now come to be associated in many minds with the whole tract of country, unsurpassed alike for natural beauty and for historical and literary interests, contained in the elongated triangle, whose base rests on Aberfoyle and Callander, and whose apex touches Loch Lomond at Inversnaid. It is this tract which we have now to consider. We follow first the northern side of our triangle, starting from Callander and passing along four famous lakes, Loch Vennachar, Loch Achray, Loch Katrine, and Loch Arklet. A large portion of this area, extending from the Trossachs and Ben Venue round by Aberfoyle, Loch Ard, and Loch Chon to include Ben Lomond and the adjoining shores of the Loch, is now designated the Queen Elizabeth National Forest Park, containing 25,000 acres of forest and 20,000 acres of mountain and moorland.

Callander, the starting point of our exploration, is also one of the gateways of the Central Highlands; for through it run the road and the railway (the latter, alas! closed in 1964) which traverse the Pass of Leny and conduct the traveller along Loch Lubnaig to Lochearnhead, and so by Killin and Crianlarich to the western coast. This is the main route from Edinburgh to Oban, and as such we shall deal with it later (see p. 153). Callander is a pleasant little town, deservedly popular as a holiday resort. It is beautifully situated at the junction of the Teith with the Leny,

The Broch of Dun Troddan, Glen Beag

and on three sides, west, north, and east, is engirdled by a fine panorama of mountain scenery. Prominent in the north-westward view is the imposing profile of Ben Ledi (2,873 feet). This is by no means an easy hill to climb, but is best tackled, perhaps, from Callander by way of Coilantogle. On a clear day the view is claimed to extend from the Bass Rock to the Paps of Jura, while to the north the Central Highland *massif* is seen to great advantage. The summit of Ben Ledi is said to have been a scene of the observance of *Beltane*, the May Day festival, which seems to have been specially popular in Perthshire. It is thus described by Pennant, writing in 1769:

On the 1st of May, the herdsmen of every village hold their *Beltein*, a rural sacrifice: they cut a square trench on the ground, leaving the turf in the middle; on that they make a fire of wood, on which they dress a large caudle of eggs, butter, oatmeal and milk; and bring, besides the ingredients of the caudle, plenty of beer and whisky; for each of the company must contribute something. The rites begin with spilling some of the caudle on the ground, by way of libation: on that, every one takes a cake of oatmeal, upon which are raised nine square knobs, each dedicated to some particular being, the supposed preserver of their flocks and herds, or to some particular animal, the real destroyer of them: each person then turns his face to the fire, breaks off a knob, and flinging it over his shoulders, says, *This I give to thee, preserve thou my horses; this to thee, preserve thou my sheep;* and so on. After that, they use the same ceremony to the noxious animals: *This I give to thee, O Fox! Spare thou my lambs; this to thee, O hooded Crow! this to thee, O Eagle!* When the ceremony is over, they dine on the caudle; and after the feast is finished, what is left is hid by two persons deputed for that purpose; but on the next Sunday they re-assemble, and finish the relics of the first entertainment.

On the flank of Ben Ledi is a small tarn, Lochan-nan-corp, 'the lake of the dead bodies'—so called because a party of mourners, returning from a funeral in Glenfinglas, sought to cross the frozen lake, but the ice gave way and all were drowned.

North-east of Callander a hill track ascends to Kelty Water, and crosses over to Glen Artney, which opens upon the River Earn opposite Comrie. Glen Artney claims attention now, because here begins the action of *The Lady of the Lake*, a poem about which we shall hear much in the rest of this chapter:

> The stag at eve had drunk his fill,
> Where danced the moon on Monan's rill,
> And deep his midnight lair had made
> In lone Glenartney's hazel shade.

We now return to Callander, and commence our approach to the Trossachs by the northern route—with (of course) a copy of *The Lady of the Lake* in our pockets. Our first stop is at Coilantogle Ford on the River Teith, the scene of the Homeric single combat between Fitz-James and Roderick Dhu. Sad to say, the ford no longer exists, having been obliterated by the sluices of the Glasgow water-works. Beyond Coilantogle our route takes us along the north bank of Loch Vennachar, following the course of the famous stag-hunt until we approach its upper end at Brig o' Turk—by which time, as readers will recollect, "the headmost horseman rode alone". Here we come into contact with another facet of Sir Walter's genius: for on our right the Turk water hurries down from rocky Glenfinglas, the scene of his first ballad—a weird composition on the 'Gothick' manner, written so early as 1799. It has its own niche in literature, for its warm reception by the public encouraged the author to publish, in 1802, *The Minstrelsy of the Scottish Border*. 'Glenfinlas' is an eerie tale of gramarye, ending in a frightful demonic catastrophe. It is impossible here to give even a summary of the ballad; more important is it to note how it reveals, even at this early date, Scott's intimate knowledge of the tract of country which, eleven years later, he was to make immortal in English literature.

The Water of Turk, which drains Glenfinglas, has now been impounded, so as to form a reservoir about twelve miles long.

Loch Vennachar, some four miles long, terminates at its upper end in Lanrick Mead, where Clan Alpine, summoned by the Fiery Cross, gathered for their battle with the royal forces. Here our road diverges from the head of the Loch, and passes Duncraggan, where "Angus, heir of Duncan's line" is summoned to leave his father's death-bed and carry the Cross of Fire on the next stage of its fatal circuit.

From Duncraggan we pass on to lovely little Loch Achray, cradled in coppice of indigenous birch, hazel and oak. The popularity of the district is attested by the presence at this 'gentle place', so Dorothy Wordsworth calls it, of two hotels. In front of us the scenery is dominated by Ben Venue (2,393 feet). We now enter the actual gorge of the Trossachs, formed between Ben Venue on the south, and on the north a much lower summit, Ben A'an (1,750 feet). This amazing piece of scenery can be described only in the language of Scott—the whole famous passage affording a remarkable example of the poet's singular ability to give us, in noble verse, what is really an accurate inventory of the scenery and natural history of a high complex landscape. Scott's description is too long to be reproduced *in extenso*, and it would be unthinkable to mutilate it; my readers will find it in stanzas XI–XIII of the first canto of *The Lady of the Lake*. Anybody who has read the passage on the spot will surely agree with Sir Walter's verdict that the prospect is

> So wondrous wild, the whole might seem
> The scenery of a fairy dream.

Although Loch Katrine has fared ill at the hands of the Glasgow Corporation water-works, it remains a scene of haunting beauty, and still deserves every whit of the descriptive eulogy of Sir Walter, who introduces the disguised King James V to its charms on a summer evening:

> Gleaming with the setting sun,
> One burnished sheet of living gold,
> Loch Katrine lay beneath him rolled,
> In all her length far winding lay
> With promontory, creek, and bay,
> And islands that, empurpled bright,
> Floated amid the livelier light,
> And mountains that like giants stand,
> To sentinel enchanted land.
> High on the south, huge Ben Venue
> Down on the lake in masses threw
> Crags, knolls and mounds, confusedly hurled,
> The fragments of an earlier world;
> A wildering forest feathered o'er
> His ruined side and summit hoar,
> While on the north, through middle air,
> Ben-an heaved high his forehead bare.

Loch Katrine is about nine miles long, and somewhat under a mile in greatest breadth. Owing to the steepness of its banks, its outline has not been greatly altered, but the depth has been increased by 17 feet, so that the lake is now about 495 feet in greatest depth. The use made of the loch for Glasgow's water needs will be apparent to all who visit it. The mercy is that the damage to this gem of Highland scenery has not been greater. Sir Walter Scott's poem has stamped itself indelibly upon the loch's topography. The 'silver strand' where the daughter of the proscribed Earl Douglas came over to ferry the disguised monarch to the island stronghold of Roderick Dhu has, alas! been drowned. But Ellen's isle survives; as also, high above the lake, the Goblin's Cave, with its wierd supernatural legends, whither Ellen Douglas and the minstrel Allan sought refuge, and where they received an unexpected and perilous visit from 'James Fitz-James'. Beal an Duine, where Fitz-James lost his 'gallant grey', and where the battle between Clan Alpine and the royal troops was fought, is at the eastern end of the Trossach defile. More authentic is Bealach-nam Bo, the pass along the northern flank of Ben Venue, in which the MacGregors were wont to hide their stolen cattle.

There is no access for vehicles along either side of Loch Katrine, for the road along the north bank of Loch Achray turns south towards Aberfoyle. The Trossachs, however, are traversed by a road ending at the pier on Loch Katrine, whence a steamboat service is available as far as Stronachlachar, at the opening of the "slack" through to Loch Arklet (see p. 134). On the north side of the Loch there is a pedestrian road to the head of the Loch at Glengyle, and thence round to Stronachlachar. Glengyle was the birthplace of the redoubtable Rob Roy.

If the northern route of our Trossachs tour is consecrated to *The Lady of the Lake*, the southern side of the triangle has been made almost equally famous by *Rob Roy*—surely one of the greatest of the Waverley Novels. We begin our pilgrimage at Aberfoyle, now a smart little village, but in Rob Roy's time a rude Highland clachan of thatched cabins, including the inn in which Baillie Nicol Jarvie performed his redoubtable exploit of singeing Iverach's plaid with a red-hot poker. Our road thence leads us through the Pass of Aberfoyle, along the steep northern bank of Loch Ard, a typical Highland lake, most truly described by Scott as "an enchanting sheet of water". This was the scene of the successful ambush laid by Helen MacGregor, Rob Roy's wife, for Captain Thornton's detachment on their way to Inversnaid with Frank Osbaldistone and the Baillie as their prisoners. Here during the brief conflict the worthy Baillie hung, suspended from a tree, like the Golden Fleece, by the skirts of his riding coat; and into Loch Ard the wretched Morris was pitched to his doom by order of the pitiless virago. Near the eastern end of the lake, on the southern margin, are the scanty remains of a castle belonging to the Duchess of Albany. On the opposite side the road passes below the Falls of Ledard, which Sir Walter tells us supplied the prototype of the cascade where Edward Waverley listened to the impassioned minstrelsy of the beautiful Jacobite enthusiast, Flora MacIvor. Two further lakes, Loch Chon and Loch Arklet, are passed before the road descends by a steep traverse upon Loch Lomond at Inversnaid (p. 123). Loch Chon is a wild and lonely lake, embosomed in birch and ash trees, and dominated from the west by the huge yet graceful outline of Ben Lomond. Though the loch itself has not yet been harnessed, the aqueduct of the Glasgow water supply, heading south from Loch Katrine, passes along its western margin. Loch Arklet, on the other hand, is now a reservoir, and has been doubled in size. Between Loch Chon and Loch Arklet we cross the watershed of Drumalban: for the former is the cradle of the Forth, whereas the latter, before its impounding by a dam at its western end, delivered its tribute undiminished into Loch Lomond, and thence to the Clyde.

At Corriearklet, midway along the north side of the Loch, was the birthplace of Helen MacGregor. All this is very much Rob Roy's country. He had purchased the wadset of Craigroyston, described by Sir Walter Scott as "a domain of rock and forest, lying on the east side of Loch Lomond, where that beautiful lake stretches into the dusky mountains of Glenfalloch". Overlooking the Loch, north of Inversnaid, 'Rob Roy's Cave', where the freebooter lurked when pursuit was hot, is still pointed out. Furthermore he had acquired some right to Glengyle. Finding the English garrison at Inversnaid too close for his liking, he transferred himself to Balquhidder, where he died in 1734 (see p. 138).

In *The Lady of the Lake* the Fiery Cross is carried from Duncraggan over the shoulder of Ben Ledi to St. Bride's Chapel at the foot of Loch Lubnaig, thence to the "swampy course" of Balvaig and so up Strathyre and westward athwart the "heathery braes" of Balquhidder and along "the sullen margin of Loch Voil" and "still Loch Doine",

> Then southward turned its rapid road
> Adown Strath Gartney's valley broad.

—thus fetching a compass round the lands of Clan Alpin, that is to say the MacGregors. Let us therefore follow the course of the Fiery Cross, and so complete our survey of the country which is forever associated with the name of Rob Roy.

St. Bride's Chapel, mentioned above, is the place where young Angus of Duncraggan hands the fatal symbol over to "Norman, heir of Armandave", thus tearing the new messenger of war away from his bridal, as he himself had been snatched from his father's bier. Little now is left of the building; but the situation is fine, on a small rough knoll, at the upper end of the Pass of Leny, overlooking the long curving vista of Loch Lubnaig. The Pass of Leny, running for about a couple of miles along the steep eastern flank of Ben Ledi, contains within its narrow, wooded and rocky gorge the tumultuous Water of Leny (a head stream of the Teith); the road to the north; and the disused railway from Callander to Oban. Loch Lubnaig, about four miles in length and in outline like a sickle, is grand but gloomy, since it is overshadowed on the west by the beetling brow and craggy skirts of Ben Ledi. The road follows the east side of the lake, while the railway, as a later interpolation, had to cling to the western declivities. It was about half way along Loch Lubnaig that, in Scott's *Legend of Montrose*, the disguised Royalist commander, along with the Earl of Menteith, met the immortal Rittmaster Dugald Dalgetty of Drumthwacket—surely one of those characters who, as Sir Walter Scott himself acknowledged, "seats himself on the feather of my pen when I begin to write, and leads it astray from the purpose". Beyond doubt he is the real hero of the tale; but what is not so well understood is the vast amount of learning which enabled Scott to realize so completely the type of hard-boiled Scottish mercenary, trained in the Thirty Years' War, who hurried back to sell their swords to whichever side offered them most in the struggle of King against Covenant.[1]

We are now in a country rich in literary and historic associations. At the head of Loch Lubnaig is Kingshouse, whence a road ascends the meandering course of the River Balvaig for a couple of miles to Balquhidder, the burial place of Rob Roy. He lies in the churchyard surrounding the former and now ruined parish kirk, which dates from 1631. But the grave of the famous outlaw is unknown. Three monuments, allegedly covering his own resting place and those of Helen MacGregor and two of their sons, Coll and Robin, are typical Highland grave slabs of late medieval date—though the third stone certainly covers a MacGregor, since it displays the arms of the clan: a sword in bend applied saltierwise to a pine tree 'eradicated', or torn up by the roots: with, on the point of the sword, a crown, in assertion of Clan Alpine's ancient claim to be descended from the sire of Kenneth MacAlpin, who in 843 united the realms of Scots and Picts, and thus took the first effective step towards the emergence of a Scottish nation. The rooted-up pine tree of course portrays the tragic fortunes of the 'Nameless Clan':

> Through the depths of Loch Katrine the steed shall career,
> O'er the peak of Ben Lomond the galley shall steer,
> And the rocks of Craig Royston like icicles melt,
> Ere our wrongs be forgot, or our vengeance unfelt!

It is easy to dismiss Clan Alpine as incorrigible thieves, harriers and slaughterers. Yet of Rob Roy himself it is proper to remember, as Scott himself points out, with characteristic fairness, that

No charge of cruelty or bloodshed, unless in battle, is brought against his memory. In like manner, the formidable outlaw was the friend of the poor, and, to the utmost of his ability, the support of the widow and the orphan—kept his word when pledged—and died lamented in his own wild country, where there were hearts grateful for his beneficence, though their minds were not sufficiently instructed to appreciate his errors.

[1] Perhaps filial pride may earn me indulgence for pointing out that the extent of sheer hard study which went into the creation of Dugald Dalgetty, which seems so spontaneous in the story, was first pointed out by my father in his Cambridge edition of *A Legend of Montrose*.

Nor was Rob Roy an illiterate barbarian. His letter to Marshal Wade, exculpating himself after the 'Fifteen', is a model of business-like English; and, if it be imagined that it may have been written for him, no one surely will deny the patent authenticity of his flamboyant challenge to the Duke of Montrose, offering His Grace single combat "that at once you may extirpate your inveterate enemy, or put a period to your puny life in falling gloriously by his hands!" As to the clan, in remembering their savage deeds let us not forget the wrongs that they had suffered. In the days when the greater Highland chiefs were transforming themselves into feudal magnates by seeking Crown charters of the lands of which, by fair means or foul, they had secured possession, the Campbell Earls of Argyll and Breadalbane, and the Stewart or Murray Earls of Atholl, had hit upon, and urged to the uttermost limit, the ingenious practice of getting written into their charters grants of lands which in fact did not belong to them, and thereafter subjugating, or if they resisted, dispossessing, those who had occupied the glens in question, perhaps from time immemorial. Of such an unscrupulous policy the MacGregors had been prime sufferers; and their passionate resistance made it only too easy for their powerful neighbours, having access to the ears of the Privy Council in far-off Edinburgh, to obtain "letters of fire and sword" against them as "the wicked Clan Gregor, so long continuing in blood, slaughter, theft, and robbery".

Treatment such as this, prolonged through generations, may explain, though it cannot excuse, such a deed of horror as is connected with this ruined church of Balquhidder, in which we are now standing. A part of the clan had surprised and slain their inveterate enemy John Drummond of Drummond-Ernoch, the King's Forester of Glenartney. They cut off his head, and carried it, wrapt in a plaid, to his house, where his sister, with true Highland hospitality, set immediate light refreshment before her unexpected guests. While she was in her kitchen preparing a meal for them the MacGregors placed her dead brother's severed head upon the table, "filling the mouth with bread and cheese, and bidding him eat, for many a merry meal he had eaten in that house". Thereafter they carried the bloody trophy to the Church of Balquhidder, where the Chief of the Clan, having gathered together all his available followers, made them swear upon the severed head to defend the perpetrators of the ghastly crime. This atrocious deed, which is said to have been done in 1589, is, as Scott lovers will not have forgotten, worked, *mutatis mutandis*, into the *Legend of Montrose*.

Loch Voil and Loch Doine are fine Highland lakes, remarkable for their emerald grassy margins. In times of spate, the two are sometimes merged into one. The rough road along the north bank ceases about a mile above the head of Loch Doine, at Inverlochlarig, the site of Rob Roy's house. Here, on 28th December, 1734, he died, peacefully in his own box-bed, after such a career of sturt and strife. It is said that on his death-bed he was urged by his wife to banish from his mind any thoughts of regret for all his deeds of violence. "You have put strife" gravely replied the dying outlaw, "betwixt me and the best men of the country; and now you would place enmity between me and God."

It was in a cottage, somewhere on the Braes of Balquhidder, that Alan Breck Stewart had his celebrated piping contest with Robin Oig, a son of Rob Roy, as described in R. L. Stevenson's *Kidnapped*. "Robin Oig", said Alan, in conceding victory to his rival, "ye are a great piper. I am not fit to blow in the same kingdom with ye. Body o' me! ye have mair music in your sporran than I have in my head!"

CHAPTER VII

DUNKELD AND THE GREAT NORTH ROAD

Dunkeld, *Dun Chaillean, Calèdodunum* as the Romans may have called it, is the *dun* or fort of the Caledonians. It is also, as noted by Pennant, who had formed a most accurate knowledge of Scottish topography during his first tour in 1769, one of the four principal gates into the Central Highlands. Here is what he wrote down in his journal, under date 7th September:

> Before I take my last leave of the Highlands, it would be proper to observe that every entrance into them is strongly marked by nature.
> On the south, the narrow and wooded glen near Dunkeld instantly shows the change of country.
> On the east, the craggy pass of Bollitir [Ballater] gives a contracted admission into the Grampian hills.
> On the north, the mountains near Lough Moy appear very near, and form what is properly styled the threshold of the country; and on the
> West, the narrow road impending over Lough Lomond forms a most characteristic entrance to this mountainous tract.

To these four he might have added the Pass of Leny (p. 135)—which, however, he had not visited. The entry above Dunkeld seems particularly to have impressed him:

> The pass into the Highlands is awefully magnificent; high, craggy, and often naked mountains present themselves to view, approach very near each other, and in many parts are fringed with wood, overhanging and darkening the Tay, that rolls with great rapidity beneath. After some advance in this hollow, a most beautiful knoll, covered with pines, appears full in view; and soon after, the town of Dunkeld, seated under and environed by crags, partly naked, partly wooded, with summits of a vast height.

Although now no more than a charming townlet of under 900

inhabitants, Dunkeld retains much of the dignity of a cathedral city, and is fully conscious of its ancient renown as the former capital of the vast medieval diocese of the Central Highlands. It is certainly one of the loveliest, as it is perhaps the tiniest of cathedral cities in Britain. The little town lies on the left or north bank of the Tay, here a broad, ample, clear and swift-flowing river, across which it is approached by a fine stone bridge of seven arches, erected by Telford in 1805–9. Some years ago the antique character of Dunkeld was in grave danger of being ruined for ever by the desire of insensitive 'developers' to pull down the 'little houses', ancient dwellings in the cathedral precinct, which, following a sadly familiar pattern in such cases, had been allowed to fall into such decrepitude that the 'powers that be' could pronounce them with assurance to be fit only for demolition. Fortunately the National Trust for Scotland intervened, and, with the active co-operation of the Perthshire County Council, restored the majority of the group, and replaced those which had disappeared or were incapable of preservation. About the same time, six acres of ground to the north, including the wooded Stanley Hill—an artificial mound raised about 1730 by the Duke of Atholl in memory of his grandmother, Lady Amelia Stanley —were presented to the Trust; so that, as far as anything is certain in these uncertain times, the romantic setting of town and cathedral seems to be secured. The restoration of the 'Little Houses' earned public recognition both from the Saltire Society and from the Civic Trust. In their original state, most of them dated from the rebuilding of Dunkeld after its destruction in 1689.

Something has been said in Chapter IV about the remote history and vast extent of the Diocese of the Central Highlands. Its cathedral occupies an enchanting site on the north bank of the Tay. The choir, restored in 1815 and again in 1908, dates from the turn of the thirteenth century; it is now used as the parish church. North of it, and forming a structural unit with the choir, is the rectangular vaulted chapter house, dating from the time of Bishop Lauder, by whom the completed church was consecrated in 1464. The chapter house now forms the mausoleum of the Ducal House of Atholl, and contains some fine monuments of the seventeenth and eighteenth centuries. The nave, now in ruins, was built by Bishop Cardeny in the early fifteenth century, and with its great cylindrical piers and high, simply moulded pointed arches, forcibly recalls the contemporary naves of St. Machar's Cathedral, Aberdeen, and the great burghal church of the Holy Rude at Stirling. Only the aisles were vaulted; the north vault, indeed, was never completed. A remarkable peculiarity of the lofty western window, which was much altered by Bishop Lauder, is that it is not set centrally in its gable. The great north-western tower, as shown by coats of arms which it bears, was begun by the same bishop and completed by his successor, Bishop Levingston. It retains some precious remnants of early sixteenth-century wall-painting, including the Judgment of Solomon and the Woman taken in Adultery. The Cathedral contains a number of medieval effigies, of which the most notable, now in the choir, is the altar-tomb of the Wolf of Badenoch (see p. 75). He is shown in full armour of plate, surrounded by mourning figures also in armour; and round his effigy is an inscription proudly proclaiming his royal birth and titles. The ruined parts of the Cathedral are carefully preserved as a national monument by the Ministry of Public Building and Works; and the enclosing grounds, lapped by the rapid Tay, are laid out with the utmost taste.

The most famous Bishop of Dunkeld was Gavin Douglas (1516–1522)—statesman, scholar, and poet, whose translation of the *Aeneid* into the Scottish vernacular was "the first version of a great classic poet in any English dialect". In our time, unquestionably the most distinguished native of Dunkeld was Professor J. J. R. Macleod, whose name will forever be associated with the discovery of insulin.

To the north of the town lies Dunkeld House, formerly a seat of the Dukes of Atholl, but now a hotel. Both the House (or rather its predecessor, demolished about 1828) and the cathedral played a prominent part in the heroic defence of Dunkeld by the Cameronian Regiment under Colonel Cleland against the victorious Highlanders led by General Cannon at the end of August, 1689, after Killiecrankie. This epic story aroused in the Whig historian Macaulay the same enthusiasm of narrative which he displays, on a much ampler scale, in his immortal description of the defence of Londonderry. Let us therefore hear in full his account of the siege of Dunkeld:

That night the regiment passed under arms. On the morning of the following day, the twenty-first of August, all the hills round

Dunkeld were alive with bonnets and plaids. Cannon's army was much larger than that which Dundee had commanded, and was accompanied by more than a thousand horses laden with baggage. Both the horses and baggage were probably part of the booty of Killiecrankie. The whole number of Highlanders was estimated by those who saw them at from four to five thousand men.[1] They came furiously on. The outposts of the Cameronians were speedily driven in. The assailants came pouring on every side into the streets. The church, however, held out obstinately. But the greater part of the regiment made its stand behind a wall which surrounded a house belonging to the Marquess of Athol. This wall, which had two or three days before been hastily repaired with timber and loose stones, the soldiers defended desperately with musket, pike and halbert. Their bullets were soon spent; but some of the men were employed in cutting lead from the roof of the Marquess's house and shaping it into slugs. Meantime all the neighbouring houses were crowded from top to bottom with Highlanders, who kept up a galling fire from the windows. Cleland, while encouraging his men, was shot dead. The command devolved on Major Henderson. In another minute Henderson fell pierced with three mortal wounds. His place was supplied by Captain Munro, and the contest went on with undiminished fury. A party of the Cameronians sallied forth, set fire to the houses from which the fatal shots had come, and turned the keys in the doors. In one single dwelling sixteen of the enemy were burnt alive. Those who were in the fight described it as a terrible initiation for recruits. Half the town was blazing; and with the incessant roar of the guns were mingled the shrieks of wretches perishing in the flames. The struggle lasted four hours. By that time the Cameronians were reduced nearly to their last flask of powder: but their spirit never flagged. "The enemy will soon carry the wall. Be it so. We will retreat into the house: we will defend it to the last; and, if they force their way into it, we will burn it over their heads and our own." But, while they were revolving these desperate projects, they observed that the fury of the assault slackened. Some of the Highlanders began to fall back: disorder visibly spread among them; and whole bands began to march off to the hills. It was in vain that their general ordered them to return to the attack. Perseverance was not one of their military virtues. The Cameronians meanwhile, with shouts of defiance, invited Amalek and Moab to come back and to try another chance with the chosen people. But these exhortations had as little effect as those of Cannon. In a short time the whole Gaelic army was in full retreat towards Blair. Then the drums

[1] The Cameronian Regiment was 1,200 strong (W.D.S.).

struck up: the victorious Puritans threw their caps into the air, raised, with one voice, a psalm of triumph and thanksgiving, and waved their colours, colours which were on that day unfurled for the first time in the face of an enemy, but which have since been proudly borne in every quarter of the world, and which are now embellished with the Sphinx and the Dragon, emblems of brave actions achieved in Egypt and in China.

Such, in a sequestered glen at the gateway of the Central Highlands, was the baptism of fire of a famous British regiment, the disbandment of which in 1966 must be accounted as a deadly sin on the part of the War Office. Today, the little town of Dunkeld —at least out of the tourist season—seems to dream in peace beneath the venerable walls of its ancient cathedral. It is not easy, on this quiet spot, to realize the stour and fury of that terrible day, two hundred and seventy-nine years ago. But not a few visitors to the ruined nave of the cathedral pause over the modest gravestone of the heroic Colonel Cleland, or beneath the tablet that recalls his fame within the choir.

Over against Dunkeld, on the right bank of the Tay, a low hill is covered with Birnam Wood—which, remarks Pennant, "seems never to have recovered the march its ancestors made to Dunsinane". Dunsinane, more properly Dunsinnan, a prehistoric hill-fort crowning a conspicuous peak on the other side of Strathmore, can in fact be seen from Birnam Hill.

North of Dunkeld the road and railway carry on up the Tay for about eight miles to Logierait. Here they part company with the Tay, which comes down on the left hand from Loch Tay, while rail and road continue north up the Tummel towards Pitlochry and Blair Atholl. Pitlochry, a fashionable tourist centre, has suffered somewhat in its environs by hydro-electric installations, connected with the Tummel-Garry scheme. It is a well-built town of some 2,500 inhabitants, situated in superb scenery, overlooked from the north by Ben Vrackie (2,757 feet), "the dappled mountain". The well known Pitlochry Festival attracts many visitors during the summer months. Curiously enough, Pitlochry was originally planned as a commercial centre, and once had woollen textile mills. By contrast, Blair Atholl remains a typically feudal village, which has grown up under the protection and patronage of the successive owners of Blair Castle (see

p. 113). Between Pitlochry and Blair Atholl road and railway, closely elbowing each other, find their way through a quartzite ridge by the Pass of Killiecrankie, scene of Claverhouse's victory and death (27th July, 1689: see p. 85). Through the Pass the River Garry hurries southward to join the Tummel, thus further reducing the space available for the traveller by train or car. Many writers have described the beauties of the Pass of Killiecrankie—none with more eloquence than Macaulay. The eastern side of the Pass now belongs to the National Trust. In the Pass the traveller is offered an interesting study in communications. General Wade's road, still traceable in places, as a rule lies higher than the turnpike, which modern drainage enabled to be sited lower down in the Pass. Next came the railway, which had to be interpolated between the turnpike and the river. This involved some notable feats of engineering, in particular a tunnel and a curving viaduct, 40 feet above the river, which affords the traveller some wonderful views of this grand and historic Pass. Finally, at more than one point along this Great North Road, we are accompanied by the pylons, striding along the skyline—in their fitness for their purpose asserting a just claim for recognition, here as elsewhere, as no unseemly contributions to the ever-changing Highland landscape. How proudly do they pursue their way across hill and brae and howe and glen, proclaiming their beneficent mission of bringing the comforts of modern life to remote clachan and lonely cottage, and thereby playing their part in arresting the canker of depopulation in the Highlands!

At Blair Atholl the River Garry is joined on our right by the brawling Tilt. Glen Tilt formed one of the ancient routes from Atholl across the Mounth into Mar, by a bridle path joining the Geldie Burn, one of the sources of the Dee, at Bynack Sheiling, and so eastward down to Braemar, a distance from Blair of some thirty miles. On the east side of Glen Tilt is Ben-y-Gloe (3,671 feet), with its three peaks, commanding a fine panorama of mountains, including the Cairngorms and Lochnagar towards the north, Ben Lawers on the south-west, and on the west Ben Nevis. Pennant, who rode over by Glen Tilt to Braemar in 1769, describes the road as "the most dangerous and the most horrible I ever travelled".

The country round Blair Atholl is celebrated in the annals of Scottish forestry. From three seedlings planted in 1737 at Dunkeld have arisen the larch woods that are the scenic glory of the Atholl estate. The intention of the large-scale plantings, carried out in particular by the 'planting Duke' between 1774 and 1830, was not so much aesthetic as commercial. Oak was becoming scarce for ship building, and it was thought that larch might provide a substitute. This was in a manner proved by the fact that the frigate *Atholl* (28-guns) launched at Woolwich in 1820, remained in service for forty-five years. The introduction of iron vessels put a stop to this hopeful venture: but the coming of the railway provided an alternative in a huge demand for sleepers. By 1830 more than 140 millions of larches had been planted; and their sale has proved a boon to the Atholl estates in these unfriendly times. Since the European larch is liable to disease, the Japanese larch was introduced to the estate in 1883: and now a cross-breed, immune, or at least resistant to infection, is the only larch planted in Atholl. So precipitous were some of the hill-slopes afforested by the 'planting Duke', that, in at least one case near Dunkeld, the seed was fired against them in canisters from a cannon!

Three miles above Blair Atholl the road and rail, still keeping close company, cross, on the right, Glen Bruar, with its famous falls, which in 1787 inspired Burns to address to the 'planting Duke' his "Humble Petition of Bruar Water":

> Here, foaming down the shelvy rocks
>   In twisting strength I rin
> There, high my boiling torrent smokes
>   Wild-roaring o'er a linn:
> Enjoying large each spring and well
>   As nature gave them me,
> I am, altho' I say't mysel,
>   Worth gaun a mile to see.
>
> Would then my noble master please
>   To grant my highest wishes,
> He'll shade my banks wi' towering trees
>   And bonnie spreading bushes;
> Delighted doubly then, my Lord,
>   You'll wander on my banks,
> And listen mony a grateful bird
>   Return you tuneful thanks.

To which appeal His Grace promptly responded by planting

the Glen with pine, larch and beech, improving .the walks, and providing seats and shelters.

Above Glen Bruar our route now enters a long tract of wild and almost uninhabited country, skirting on the right along the immense Forest of Atholl. In Scotland, it is perhaps needful to point out, a 'forest' means simply a tract of country reserved for deer, and therefore typically treeless. Road and railway, arm in arm, climb steadily until they reach the summit of the Drumochter Pass (1,484 feet)—the highest point on any British railroad. Hence the Mounth meets Drumalban, and here we pass from Perth into Inverness. An inscribed stone on the road, below the summit, marks the point where the two parties of Wade's road-making troops, one working from Inverness and the other from Dunkeld, met on Drumochter, their great task completed. Snow-screens and snow ploughs left by the roadside, testify to the stress of winter upon this desolate moorland. Two summits on the left hand side, the Sow of Atholl and the Boar of Badenoch, define the two great ancient territorial divisions which meet on this famous Pass.

At Dalwhinnie, below Loch Ericht, we enter Glen Truim, and begin our descent towards the Spey. Here, on 26th August, 1745, Sir John Cope made his fateful decision to turn aside from the Corrieyarrick Pass and march north-eastward to Inverness. We shall follow him as far as Loch Moy, Pennant's northern entrance to the Central Highlands.

Glen Truim presents few features of interest or beauty, until we reach the Falls, below which the valley widens and becomes softer and more fertile of aspect, with plantations of fir, larch and birch on its flanks. At Invernahavon, where the River Truim joins the Spey, is a field of battle, famous in Highland history, fought in 1386 between Clan Chattan and Clan Cameron, to the discomfiture of the latter.

We now enter upper Strathspey. This splendid valley is enclosed between two mountain ranges. On the east are the Cairngorms, more properly, and anciently, known as the Monadh Ruadh, the Red Mountains, from the prevailing tint of their granite. On the west is the Monadh Liath, the Grey Mountains, formed of Moine schist and quartzite, with some granitic intrusions. The Spey Valley will come up for fuller consideration in

Chapter XI: here we are concerned only with that portion of it which is followed by our Great North Road—that is to say, from Kingussie to Aviemore.

Kingussie, the capital of Badenoch, is a well-built and well-equipped little town of just over 1,000 inhabitants. Beautifully situated on the north bank of the river, and commanding fine views of the noble strath with its flanking mountains, blessed also with a fine dry climate, it is furthermore a place of high historic interest. On the opposite side of the river it is dominated by the great *motte* of Ruthven Castle, formerly a stronghold of the Comyns, later of the Gordons, and today crowned by the vast ruins of the Hanoverian barracks (pp. 98, 117). In the now extinct clachan of Ruthven, crouching at the foot of the barracks, the remnants of the beaten Jacobite army disbanded on 20th April, 1746, after receiving a message from the fugitive Prince, to whom they had sent an aide-de-camp, asking what to do: "Let every man seek his safety in the best way he can"—"an inconsiderate answer", bitterly comments one who was there, "heartbreaking to the brave men who had sacrificed themselves for him."

Kingussie was the site of one of the latest monastic foundations of the Middle Ages in Scotland—a Carmelite Friary established before 1501 by George Gordon, second Earl of Huntly. It was dedicated to St. Columba; and, as there appears to be no other indication of any special devotion of the Gordon family to the Apostle of the Scots, it is more than likely that here there had been a clachan chapel or preaching station founded by Columba in person. Our Great North Road was a major line of communication through the Central Highlands long centuries before Wade's road: and quite possibly Columba may have come this way on one of his visits to the Pictish King, Brude MacMaelchon, at his capital in Inverness. Perhaps it is not without significance that at Invermoriston on Loch Ness in the Great Glen—another ancient line of communication between Dalriada and Pictland—there is likewise a church site bearing the name of St. Columba. In the little old ill-kept graveyard at Kingussie a tablet bears the inscription, in Gaelic and English: "Here is the hallowed site of the old church of Kingussie, dedicated to St. Columba and according to tradition planted by himself."

When the Jacobite army dispersed at Ruthven in 1746, it is possible that the melancholy scene may have been watched by a bare-footed laddie, not yet ten, who afterwards became famous throughout Europe as the 'translator' of Ossian. His father was a crofter in the clachan of Ruthven. From Sergeant Molloy's celebrated despatch (p. 118) we learnt that the 'barrack wife' at Ruthven in 1745 was a Mrs. Macpherson: and I often wonder if she might have been the mother of the young man who set the literary world ablaze within twenty years of the 'Forty-five', and who now rests in the 'Poets' Corner' of Westminster Abbey. In his later days of wealth and fame, 'Ossian' Macpherson did not forget his homeland. He bought an estate and built himself a fine house (designed by Robert Adam) at Belleville, now Balavil, near Kingussie, where also there is an obelisk of grey and white marble, erected in his memory in terms of his will. Several stories have been preserved about his generosity to the humble companions of his boyhood. When building his mansion he employed none but local craftsmen, and paid them half as much again as the current rates. The tenant of his parental croft had now become his 'vassal', as the legal term still is in Scotland: and to him Macpherson gave a freehold life-rent, along with a generous extent of pasture land.

Am Fasgadh (the Shelter), the Highland Folk Museum, is one of the principal attractions of Kingussie. The nucleus of this remarkable collection was brought together by a gifted Highland lady, Dr. Isabel F. Grant, author of the standard history of the great Clan MacLeod. It was bought by the Pilgrim Trust and presented to the four Scottish Universities. Further expansion has been facilitated by the Douneside Trust. The museum, open from May till September, may rightly be described as a priceless collection, since it consists to a large extent of what used to be clumsily termed 'neo-archaic' items, but now, more simply 'byegones', that is to say, those obsolete relics of old-time Highland life, arts and crafts, and building fashions, which, not yet having acquired the prestige of 'antiquities', are all too liable to be unthinkingly destroyed or cast aside.

In the angle where the Feshie joins the Spey, about six miles below Kingussie, we find the ancient church of Insh, beside the pretty little loch of the same name. Under the common local form of Eunan, this church bears the name of St. Adamnan, ninth Abbot of Iona, who ruled over the island monastery from 679 until 704, and is famous because of his Life of Columba—"the most complete piece of such biography that all Europe can boast of, not only at so early a period, but throughout the whole Middle Ages". The knoll on which the little church stands is still known as Tom Eunan, Adamnan's Mount; and in the church is preserved a very precious relic, St. Eunan's Bell, a bronze hand-bell of the type carried by Celtic missionary monks. We have already noted that the neighbouring church of Kingussie is under the invocation of St. Columba. Long ago, Bishop Reeves pointed out that, alike in Ireland and in Scotland, dedications to St. Columba and St. Adamnan tend to occur side by side. Reeves knew nothing about Insh Church; but, having regard to all the facts, we can hardly doubt that this church is in origin a foundation by Adamnan in person, or by a mission sent forth from Iona during his abbacy—following the ancient route taken by Columba before him. These two Celtic church sites, Kingussie and Insh, stand today as a monument to the early influence of the Scotic Church in the heart of the Pictish homeland.

Some one and a half miles below Kingussie is Aviemore. Here the now disused railway down Speyside to Forres diverges to the right from the trunk line to Inverness, which follows the route of our Great North Road. Within the last decade the little village of Aviemore has been transformed in the process of creating here a centre for summer pleasures and winter sports in the Cairngorms. Since these mountains nowhere reach to the level of what is called 'eternal snow', and having regard to the variable character of our Scottish climate, the future of ski-ing in the Cairngorms is a matter which the investors of capital in Aviemore and its eastern neighbour, Coylum Bridge, have no doubt fully pondered; but certainly their plans for developing both as holiday centres, all the year round, do not err on the side of timidity. At Aviemore we have now two large and very modern luxury hotels, incorporating in and around them, such attractions as a cinema; a dance hall; an ice rink for skating and curling; a swimming pool; a bowling alley, and a display of stuffed wild animals found in the Highlands, expounded by a record-player. For those with less money to spare there are mountain châlets of the Swiss type; while the Scottish Youth Hostels Association have provided one of their most up-to-date establishments. The Aviemore Centre was the brain child of a great Scotsman gifted with vision, the late Lord Fraser of Allander—surely one of those "rich men furnished with ability, living peaceably in their habitations" whom we are enjoined to praise. All lovers of the Highlands must wish every success for this bold and imaginative venture, and everyone will concede that buildings intended to cater for modern pleasure must be designed in a modern manner. Yet there are not a few who regret that the new scene at Aviemore is dominated by a structure externally so brash as the towering Strathspey Hotel. *De gustibus non est disputandum* is a wise old maxim; and the building has found its defenders, on the ground that "architecture is a personal matter". This, however, is hardly the case; notably in rural areas, where every new building, if it is to occupy a conspicuous site, should be devised with due regard to the *mise-en-scène*. An exalted personage, whose comments on matters of public interest always merit respect, once remarked upon the peculiar responsibility that rests on the profession of architecture. If you do not like a picture, you can sell it, turn it to the wall, or relegate it to the lumber room; if the picture is in a public gallery, you don't need to look at it. So also with sculpture. But nobody can avoid looking at architecture!

Overlooking Aviemore from the west is the bold rocky front of Craigellachie (1,500 feet) amid whose frost-riven clefts the graceful but hardy birch finds a precarious footing. It is this, not the lower Craigellachie, which gives Clan Grant their rallying cry: "Stand fast, Craigellachie!" The name means 'stony crag'. Craigellachie is worth the exertion of climbing because of the superb view that it affords of the Cairngorms, sundered by the Larig Ghru and fronted by the sombre pine forests of Rothiemurchus and Glenmore.

At Aviemore railway and high road diverge to the left, forsaking Speyside and climbing over the Monadhliath to Strathdearn, and thence to Loch Moy, Pennant's northern threshold of the Highlands. At Carr Bridge the road crosses the River Dulnan, a major tributary of the Spey, which it enters about three miles above Grantown. Carr Bridge is a beauty spot, fragrant with the scent of birch and pine. The arch of an older bridge, dating from 1719, still stands above the modern one, and is a favourite subject with artists. Hereabouts turnpike and railway leave Wade's road far to the left: the latter crossed the Dulnan at Sluggan, a good two miles above Carr Bridge. From here the military road passes round the south side of Inverlaidnan Hill, and so joins the turnpike and railway again in the narrow gorge of *Slochd Mor*, 'the Big Pass', alternatively *Slochd Muick*, 'the Pigs' Pass'. In his famous forced march from Dalwhinnie to Inverness, General Cope on 28th August covered the distance of some nineteen miles from Ruthven to Dalrachny, fearing lest the Highlanders might attack him "in the strong pass of Slockmuick". Apparently his scouts found the gorge unoccupied, and next day he completed another forced march to Inverness. From the summit of the Slochd (1,333 feet) the road and rail have a long steep ascent into Strathdearn. The River Findhorn is crossed above Tomatin. Wade's road has diverted to the right since we left the Slochd, and made the river passage at Raigbeg; but the present bridge is modern.

From Tomatin another half dozen miles, or thereby, bring us to Loch Moy, where we quit the Central Highlands. The Loch is a pretty sheet of water, snugly set amid plantations and containing an island with the ruins of a castle, the ancient seat of Clan Mackintosh. Moy Hall, its modern successor, is at the north end of the loch, which is closely elbowed in by wooded heights. Along its western margin pass the road and railway. Since the level of the loch was reduced in 1884 by about five feet, the pass was even narrower in former times, and well deserves Pennant's claim for it as the northern threshold of the Central Highlands. From Loch Moy Wade's road diverges to the west on its way to Inverness, crossing the River Nairn above Fairlie Bridge.

Moy Hall was frequently visited by King George V, who enjoyed the sport provided for him by The Mackintosh. It has now been superseded by a more modest edifice.

Thus we have reached the end of our pilgrimage along Wade's Great North Road. Surely the Marshal's wraith has accompanied us—marvelling, it may be, at the new roads that have superseded his own, at the streams of cars speeding smoothly over the tarmacadam surfaces and at the diesel-electric locomotives thundering along their iron track, making light of the steep passes which his red coats mastered only with sweat and toil. Most of all assuredly, he will marvel at Aviemore.

CHAPTER VIII

THE WESTERN PASSES

From the Great North Road three major lines of communication, following the river systems, lead through Drumalban towards the Atlantic seaboard. These are:

1. From Perth by Methven and Crieff, entering the Highlands at Comrie, thence by St. Fillans along the north shore of Loch Earn, and so northward through Glen Ogle to Killin, and westward along Glen Dochart to Crianlarich and Tyndrum on the West Highland Railway.

2. From Ballinluig, between Dunkeld and Pitlochry, up the Tay valley, passing through Aberfeldy and along Loch Tay to Killin at its head, thence joining the first route at Killin.

3. From the throat of Killiecrankie Pass due westward along Loch Tummel and Loch Rannoch to Rannoch Station on the West Highland line, beyond which there is no further road.

It is no purpose of the present *Portrait of the Highlands* to give a detailed description of these transverse roads. That is the function of a guide book, and of these there are plenty. Let us therefore consider them briefly, so as to portray their general character and to indicate the points in which each differs from the others.

The most important route is that which enters the Highlands at Comrie. The entry is not only physical but geological, for here we cross the Highland Boundary Fault. Comrie is therefore one of the principal centres in Scotland for earthquakes—or rather, earth tremors, since they are seldom serious enough even to crack a window or dislodge a chimney (see p. 27). The little town is pleasantly placed on the north bank of the River Earn, at the point where Glen Lednock opens from the north and Glen Artney from the south. It is thus a capital centre for hill walkers. As it approaches its junction with the Earn, the River Lednock flows turbulently through a rocky and wooded channel, in which is the Devil's Cauldron, a spectacular example of a 'breached pot-hole'. The upper part of the Lednock has been harnessed for the Dalchonzie power station, and an artificial lake has been formed. Of 'lone Glenartney' mention has been made in Chapter VI.

From Comrie to St. Fillans we follow the north bank of the Earn. On the opposite side is the great Dark Age multiple hilltown of Dundurn, the capital of Fortriu (see p. 48). At the pretty village of St. Fillans we strike the lower end of Loch Earn. There are routes along both sides of it: but the main road is on the north. It commands notable views of Ben Vorlich (3,224 feet), which is easily ascended from the southern road. The beauty of the lake and its surroundings, and its ready accessibility, have ensured the popularity of Loch Earn. In summer it is bright with the sails of yachts, for which, and for boat-hiring and water ski-ing, special provision is made. Towards the upper end of the south side of the loch is Edinample Castle (p. 111).

Beyond Lochearnhead our road plunges northward into wild Glen Ogle, and a short run of five or six miles brings us through to the scenic glories of Glen Dochart. The River Dochart, rising as the Fillan Water on the very spine of Drumalban, flows southeastward into Loch Dochart and Loch Iubhair, from which it emerges as the River Dochart, and pursues its way eastward till at Killin it pays its tribute to Loch Tay. Glen Dochart may not be the grandest of Highland valleys, but it is certainly among the most historical. Towards its lower outlet, before it debouches upon Loch Tay, the glen is narrow, and the course of the river is rocky: but above the point where the road through Glen Ogle comes down upon it, the glen is wider than usual, and the bottom flat, alternating between meadowland and marsh. There is not a great amount of wood. At the Luib Hotel, a noted resort of salmon and trout fishers, Wordsworth and his sister Dorothy spent the night of 4th September, 1803. They did not order wine, and in consequence, reports Dorothy, "the servant was uncivil". Just before we reach Loch Iubhair, the southern bank of the glen becomes extremely steep, rising continuously up to the conical summit of one of the grandest and most shapely mountains in the Central Highlands, Ben More (3,843 feet). Directly to the south and separated from Ben More by a deep defile, *Beal-eadar-bheinn*, "the pass between the Bens", rises another summit of almost equal height and majesty, Stobinean (3,827 feet), the southern skirts of which overlook the Braes of Balquhidder.

Loch Iubhair and Loch Dochart are virtually one, and become actually so in time of spate. On an islet in Loch Dochart, picturesquely embosomed in coppice, stands a small ruined castle or hall-house, built by Black Duncan Campbell of Glenorchy (see p. 80). It is well seen from the road, a conspicuous feature being its enormous 'lum'. The castle was surrendered to Montrose during his famous march through Glendochart to Argyll in December, 1644, and subsequently burnt. Ample proof of the conflagration was forthcoming when the ruins were excavated. An earlier, but much more melancholy march, or rather flight, through this glen, was that of Bruce, after his defeat at Methven (19th June, 1306). At Dalry, near Tyndrum, he was waylaid by John of Lorne, and sustained his second defeat. This was the action, so vividly described by Barbour, in which Bruce is averred by later (though still ancient) tradition to have lost the famous Brooch of Lorne. Lovers of Scott will remember how dramatically the incident is worked into the second canto of *The Lord of the Isles*:

> When the gem was won and lost,
> Widely was the war-cry tossed!
> Rung about Ben Dourich fell,
> Answered Douchart's sounding dell.
> Fled the deer from wild Teyndrum,
> When the homicide, o'ercome,
> Hardly 'scaped with scathe and scorn,
> Left the pledge with conquering Lorn!

Glendochart and Strathfillan formed part of the ancient Celtic ecclesiastical domain associated with the name of St. Fillan. We have discussed this in Chapter IV, in which its particular connexion with King Robert was set forth. There seems little doubt that the King's deep veneration for this saint was connected with the memory of his delivery from extreme peril in Strathfillan; and it cannot be without significance that long afterwards, the victor King granted the lordship of Glendochart to Alexander Menzies of Weem in Strathtay, one of the forlorn band who had stood by him in that desperate clash at Dalry. In this way, Sir Alexander became the founder of the Clan Menzies. Originally his family, like other progenitors of Highland clans, seem to have been of

Lowland origin; and indeed it has been claimed that they derived from the Norman house of Manners, now represented by the Duke of Rutland.

At Crianlarich the railway up the west side of Strathfillan, on its way to Dalmally and Oban, leaves the West Highland line, heading on the opposite side for the Moor of Rannoch and so to Glen Spean and Fort William. The scanty ruins of St. Fillan's Priory lie on the left side of the river, halfway between Crianlarich and Tyndrum; and in the river is St. Fillan's Pool, immersion wherein was thought to be a cure for lunatics. Crianlarich is a little railway village, dominated by the spectacular viaduct of six spans, over 300 feet in length, which conveys the West Highland Railway, first over the Oban road and line, and then across the River Fillan. The railway system here is absurd, due to the fact that the two lines were once owned by competitive companies. Just beyond Tyndrum we cross over from Perthshire into Argyll; and also, at a height of 872 feet in a landscape heavily glaciated, over Drumalban.

The great names of Barbour, Scott and the Wordsworths do not exhaust the literary associations of Strathfillan: for it is also the scene of the "Ettrick Shepherd's" weird ballad, "The Spirit of the Glen":

> O dearest Marjory, stay at home
>   For dark's the gate you have to go:
> And there's a maike[1] adown the glen,
>   Hath frightened me and mony moe.
>
> His legs are like to pillars tall,
>   And still and stalwart is his stride
> His face is rounder nor the moon,
>   And och, his mouth is awesome wide!
>
> I saw him stand the other night,
>   Yclothéd in his grizly shroud;
> With one foot on a shadow placed,
>   The other on a misty cloud.
>
> As far asunder were his limbs
>   On the first storey of the air.
> A ship could have sailed through between,
>   With all her colours flying fair.

[1] 'a shape'.

eroded out of the crown of the corresponding 'anticline' or arch. So an uninstructed observer of Loch Tay and Ben Lawers, seeking to interpret the scenery before him in terms of upheaval and depression, would arrive at an exact inversion of the truth!

The interest of Ben Lawers is so manifold as to deserve more attention than the limits of the present work would normally justify in the case of a single mountain. The Ben Lawers complex forms a triangle defined on the west by its base, the defile through which runs a mountain road from Edramucky on Loch Tay northwards to Bridge of Balgie in Glen Lyon; and the two sides formed respectively by that glen and by Loch Tay. The blunted apex, towards the east, is defined by another and shorter cross-country road, between Fearnan and Fortingall. Within this area, in addition to Ben Lawers itself, other four summits exceed 3,000 feet. The road through the western defile, after passing lonely Lochan-na-lairighe—'the lochan of the pass'—now harnessed by the North of Scotland Hydro-Electric Board—climbs to a height of no less than 1,805 feet. Within the triangle, some eight thousand acres now belong to the National Trust. Ben Lawers itself has justly been described as "the most famous mountain in Britain from the botanist's point of view". Here, since the last Ice Age have survived in their special habitats a remarkable assemblage of Arctic and Alpine plants, including such specialities as the mossy cyphel with its tiny green flowerets and the Alpine forget-me-not, besides many others such as the Alpine mouse-ear chickweed, Alpine lady's mantle, the small gentian, the rock speedwell, the saxifrages (including the rare species, *Saxifragia nivalis*, almost unknown elsewhere in Britain), and the reindeer moss. Generally, the Ben Lawers group present a green aspect which contrasts strongly with the sombre hue of the mountains further west. In June, parts of their middle slopes are bright with lowly flowers. Great care is taken by the National Trust to preserve this precious flora from attacks by sheep and human beings. Every climber, be he botanist or not, should regard the uprooting of any of them as a sin against the Holy Ghost.

No less interesting is the animal life of Ben Lawers. The layman will be surprised to learn that molluscs are found to a height of 3,800 feet. The golden eagle is scarce, but the buzzard, that much persecuted bird, seems to be common. The peregrine falcon is occasionally seen. Nests of the ring-ouzel, a bird which appears

Loch Katrine and Ben Venue

to be on the decline in Scotland, have been found near the summit. For the rest, the game birds and animals are such as are to be expected on a Highland mountain. That large and handsome bird, the capercailzie—"the old man of the woods"—which had become extinct in Scotland before the end of the eighteenth century, was reintroduced from Sweden at Taymouth Castle in 1837. My readers will remember that this bird was among the delicacies served up to James V in the wooden palace near Blair in 1529. But few modern palates like the resinous taste of its flesh, which derives from the pine woods upon which the capercailzie depends for shelter and food.

All in all, the Ben Lawers area is without doubt the best terrain in which to explore the natural history of the Central Highlands. It is easily accessible; good accommodation is available near at hand; and an admirable handbook is provided by the National Trust. Since the last war, the potentialities of ski-ing on Ben Lawers have been vigorously exploited. The Trust has provided a car park in the *larig*, and the Scottish Ski Club has a well-equipped hut at a height of 2,400 feet.

Glen Lyon, which forms the northern limb of the Lawers triangle, is served by a fair road along the northern bank of the river: but there is no through access across Drumalban. Fortingall, near the foot of the Glen, is famous for its hoary churchyard yew tree, about whose age some extravagant ideas have been current. It is now sorely wasted since Pennant visited it in 1769, when he records that "its ruins measured 56½ feet in circumference". He gives a vignette of it, showing that even then it was divided into two, the central portion having completely decayed. What remains is still alive, and carefully protected.

Glen Lyon, at least thirty miles in length, claims to be the longest glen in Scotland. It is certainly one of the most beautiful in the Central Highlands. The rocky river scenery is particularly fine, and as the glen is deep, narrow and sinuous, the visitor who penetrates its sombre recesses is gratified by a surprising variety of views. The road, which runs along the north side of the clear and rapid river, terminates at the foot of Loch Lyon, surrounded by green and pleasant hills. It is now a reservoir in connexion with the Breadalbane Hydro-Electric scheme.

Our third route towards Drumalban ascends Loch Tummel,

Dunkeld Cathedral

Wade's Bridge and the Black Watch Memorial, Aberfeldy

and after it Loch Rannoch. Scenically the roads which follow both banks of these two lakes offer us as fine a feast as any in the Central Highlands. But the multiplication of pen-pictures of mountain landscapes is hardly the purpose of the present work; and it must suffice here to say that these beautiful lochs, and the river which drains them, have been harnessed for the Rannoch and Tummel-Garry hydro-electric schemes—yet in such a way as to damage as little as possible their splendid natural setting. Perhaps the worst sufferer has been the 'Queen's View' on the north bank of the lower of lengthened portion of Loch Tummel. The place was given its name because of the impression it made upon Queen Victoria when she visited it in 1866. In spite of the inevitable disturbance caused by the beneficent triumphs of modern engineering, the Queen's View remains indeed a regal one—if only for the prospect which it offers towards the south-west of the noble quartzite cone of Schiehallion (3,547 feet).

General Wade's road from Crieff to Dalnacardoch crosses the saddle northward from Coshieville at the foot of Glenlyon to descend upon Tummel Bridge at the head of the loch. This remains unaltered as a fine example of a Wade bridge, with its single lofty arch carrying the hump-backed road. Close by is a power station. Above Tummel Bridge is the Dunalastair reservoir, an artificial lake over two miles long; and then we come to Kinloch Rannoch—wrongly so named, for it stands at the foot not the head of the loch. Loch Rannoch itself is now entirely a huge reservoir, ten miles long and a mile in breadth. From the head of Loch Rannoch the road continues westward to end at Rannoch station on the West Highland Line. We are now within a mile or two of the county boundary between Perth and Argyll, which here follows the course of Drumalban—striding from summit to summit at heights between 2,000 and over 3,000 feet.

No one who has penetrated as far as Rannoch should fail to visit the Black Wood—one of the surviving portions of the ancient native Caledonian pine forest (see p. 40). This lies on the south side of Loch Rannoch, and is partly maintained by the Forestry Commission and partly well cared for in private hands. In 1918 the whole wood was scheduled for felling, but fortunately the outbreak of peace in that year saved it; with the renewal of war in 1939–45 much was sacrificed.

CHAPTER IX

THE BRAES OF ANGUS
AND THE MOUNTH GLENS

In the second chapter of this book I pointed out that the line of uplands bordering the north-western side of Strathmore, along which the name 'Grampian Mountains' is sometimes printed upon our maps, is not really a mountain chain, but merely the delusive appearance of one, caused by the lateral spurs running out from the two real systems, Drumalban and the Mounth, and terminating upon the Highland Boundary Fault, to the down-folding attendant whereupon is due the syncline or basin of Strathmore. These lateral spurs are divided from south-west to north-east, by six typically Highland glens—Strathardle, Glen Shee, Glen Isla, Glen Prosen, Glen Clova and Glen Esk. All share one feature in common: they begin among the Dalradian Schists, pass over the Fault, and terminate in the Old Red Sandstone. All therefore offer much of special attention to the geologist. Between the two major formations, along the line of the Fault, occur a very interesting series, the Highland Border Rocks. These are disconnected wedges of rocks, more ancient by far than the Old Red Sandstone, which have been caught, as it were, in the downslip of the Fault, and thereby preserved from denudation. They include igneous rocks, both plutonic and volcanic, and sediments, the oldest of which by their fossils may be referred to the Cambrian period (p. 19).

These Highland Border Rocks have been found at various points along the line of the Fault: for example, on Loch Lomond, Aberfoyle, and at Callander. They are exposed in Glen Prosen; but perhaps the best place to study them is in the valley of the North Esk some three or four miles above Edzell.

All our six glens offer in their upper portions fine stretches of mountain scenery. The Highland portion of Strathardle is entered at Blairgowrie, an attractive town of some 5,400 people, the centre of raspberry growing. From here a useful cross-road connects with Dunkeld. About six miles above Blairgowrie the River Ericht divides into two, the River Ardle coming down its Strath from the left, while on the right opens Glen Shee. At the junction is Bridge of Cally, between which and Blairgowrie the "ireful Ericht" runs through a deep rocky gorge between Old Red Conglomerate cliffs, forming one of the most striking pieces of scenery in the Eastern Highlands. Sir Archibald Geikie describes it as "a true canyon eroded in the conglomerate": it "averages about 150 yards in width by 150 to 180 feet in depth" and is due to erosion by the river along parallel lines of joint which "enable the ravine to maintain the verticality and parallelism of its walls". Elsewhere he has this more to tell us about the geological interest of our Eastern Highland glens:

I have already alluded to the remarkable series of deep gorges which the streams descending from the Highlands have cut in the Old Red Sandstone of Perthshire and Forfarshire. They are true canyons, which, for picturesqueness of river scenery, are almost unrivalled in any other part of this country. They display with singular clearness the influence of variation in rock structure upon the process of erosion. The gorge of the Ericht, for example, though excavated mostly in a coarse conglomerate, reveals some of the volcanic rocks of the Lower Red Sandstone, and allows their contrasted forms to stand out conspicuously against the walls of conglomerate. In the ravine of the Isla, an intrusive boss of porphyry makes itself prominent at the picturesque Reekie Linn. The bed of the North Esk, above Gannochy Bridge, is a mere chasm through which the stream foams in its headlong course from the Highland glens above. The Old Red Sandstone, as already remarked, yields the most striking river scenery in Scotland.

When we come to deal with the Northern Straths, we shall have occasion to recur to this theme.

It lies outwith the scope and character of the present work to provide detailed descriptions of our six eastern glens, beautiful and varied though they are. The River Ericht, with the two streams out of which it is formed, lies wholly in Perthshire. Along its left hand affluent, the River Ardle, an excellent road is available up the Strath to Kirkmichael, thence across the western hills to descend upon Pitlochry. The summit of this cross road, at a height of 1,260 feet, provides us with a superb view of the Perthshire Highlands with Schiehallion in front and Ben Lawers away towards the left.

Much more important is the right-hand tributary of the Ericht: for although the Black Water is itself a stream of no great consequence, Glen Shee, down which it flows, affords one of the main lines of communication between Atholl and Mar. The present highroad follows pretty closely to the track of the military road built in 1749-50, after the suppression of the last Jacobite Rising led to the resumption, as a matter of emergency, of Wade's policy of road-building in the Central Highlands. But this passage from Atholl to the Braes of Mar is older, far older, than the days of the Hanoverian engineers. Along it, in the eighth century, journeyed St. Rule and his companions, to present themselves, with the relics of St. Andrew, at Kindrochit in Mar, before Angus I Mac-Fergus (729-61), the most powerful of Pictish kings. Hither, more than six centuries later, came Robert II and his royal court, almost annually between 1371 and 1388, to enjoy at Kindrochit Castle their summer hunting in the Braes of Mar. On this almost prehistoric road, therefore, we are accompanied by the shades, not only of the patient anonymous road builders of the eighteenth century, but of saints and monarchs and men of affairs famous in Scottish history.

It is not surprising that the green and pleasant Glen Shee is full of antiquarian and historical interest. The huts of a village community who dwelt here about the end of the Bronze Age have been excavated north of Blairgowrie; and in early Celtic legend the Glen is the scene of the famous hunt of the Fingalian hero, Diarmad Mac O'duine, after the boar on Ben Gulbain or Gulabin, a high green mountain (2,641 feet) on the left side of the road, near the head of the Glen: below it, near the Spital of Glenshee, a tumulus marks the hero's tomb. The story is told at length in the Book of the Dean of Lismore. It opens with our earliest word picture of Glen Shee:

> Glen Shee, the vale that close beside me lies,
> Where sweetest sounds are heard of deer and elk,
> And where the Feinn did oft pursue the chase,
> Following their hounds along the lengthening vale.
> Below the great Ben Gulbin's grassy height

> Of fairest knolls that lie beneath the sun
> The valley winds. Its streams did oft run red,
> After a hunt by Finn and by the Feinn.

The tale is told of a fierce and furious boar, whom arms had never subdued:

> The great old boar, him so well known in Shee
> The greatest in the wild boar's haunt e'er seen.

Diarmad slew the monster, and was asked by Fingal to measure it. In doing so, he passed the sole of his foot backwards against the bristles, one of which pierced him, so that he died of the wound. The hero who then perished in Glen Shee is said to have been the eponymus of Clan Campbell, 'the children of Diarmad'. In this tale of Diarmad Mac O'Duine the reader will not fail to have noted parallels with the old Greek legends of Adonis and Achilles: and as at Fraoch Eilean, we are again struck by the links between Celtic and classical mythology.

At the Spital of Glen Shee, as its name betokens, the medieval church maintained a hospice for the benefit of travellers across the Mounth. Here Robert II on his way to Kindrochit, paused on 27th June, 1376. In modern times this glen of ancient memories has acquired a new celebrity as a centre of Scottish ski-ing and pony-trekking. Our road crosses over from Angus to Aberdeenshire by the Cairnwell Pass (2,199 feet), the highest mountain pass on a main road in Britain. Before reaching it, the motorist has to cope, at 1,950 feet, with the Devil's Elbow, a double hairpin bend with a gradiant of 1 in 5. The summit itself lies between two mighty bens, the Cairnwell (3,059 feet) on the left and, on the right, Glas Maol (3,502 feet). On top of the latter meet the three counties of Perth, Angus, and Aberdeen. From the Cairnwell Pass the road descends bare and desolate Glen Clunie towards Braemar. Near the head of Glen Clunie, Shean Spittal (the old hospital) was another hospice maintained by the ancient church. The road keeps on the right side of the Water of Clunie: but at Fraser's Bridge, three miles short of Braemar, the old military road crosses the river, and descends by its left bank to Braemar. Fraser's Bridge, with its two low arches, is kept in repair, and the old road is still in use as a pleasant walk by Braemar golf course.

The military road whose course we have thus followed from Blairgowrie to Braemar—a distance of thirty-four miles—was completed in 1750 by a detachment of one hundred men belonging to Viscount Bury's regiment: the engineer was G. Morrison. Of these and other road builders in whose tracks we have been pilgrimaging, it may be said with truth that "they rest from their labours, and their works do follow them".

We return now to the sunward side of the Mounth. Our next three glens—Glen Isla, Glen Prosen, and Glen Clova—introduce us to the homeland of the Ogilvies. In them this historic old Scottish family once possessed four castles, three of which remain in their hands. Airlie Castle, at the junction of the Melgam Water with the Isla, is the seat of the Earl of Airlie. A portcullised gateway and a long curtain wall, incorporated in the eighteenth century mansion, remain of the 'Bonnie House o' Airly' destroyed by the Marquis of Argyll on 7th July, 1640—as described, somewhat fictitiously, in the well-known ballad. The walled garden adjoining the castle is one of the beauty spots of Angus. In Glen Isla, about seventeen miles above Airlie, is Forter Castle, a lonely ruined tower-house likewise burned by Argyll in 1640, and never since repaired. It was here, and not at Airlie, as the ballad says, that the Countess of Airlie, her husband being in England in attendance on Charles I, was in residence on that occasion; nor did she die of grief, as the ballad avers. Cortachy Castle, the seat of Lord Ogilvy, the eldest son of the Earl of Airlie, stands within fine grounds where the Water of Prosen, coming down its wooded glen, joins the River South Esk, emerging from Glen Clova. Part of the castle is ancient. Lord Airlie's herd of polled Angus cattle have achieved international renown. Inverquharity, the fourth castle of the Ogilvies, has long passed out of their hands. It stands near the junction of the Carity Water and the South Esk, a little south of Cortachy. This is one of the finest remaining fifteenth-century tower houses in Scotland. Built on the L-plan, pursuant to a royal licence granted in 1444, the castle survives, intact and roofed, except only for the wing, which was taken down long ago, to provide stone for the nearby farm-steading. Unfortunately it is now fast falling into decay. By these four Ogilvy castles cattle reivers from the upper parts of Glen Isla, Glen Prosen, and Glen Clova were hindered from 'down-falling' upon Strathmore

All three glens present many features of natural beauty and varied interest. Their bold scenery has been explained by Geikie in the passage quoted above; but something should be added about the Reekie Linn—so called from the cloud of spray in which it is always invested. The Linn is a narrow gorge, 120 feet in depth, hemming in the turbulent river, which emerges by a cataract of two separate stages, with a total descent of some 80 feet. In time of spate these become a single splendid fall. So abrupt is the descent of the river that at such times it is liable to do widespread damage in the 'laich country'. The Isla rises in the corrie of Canlochan, on the east side of Glas Maol, mentioned above. Almost immediately it is joined on the left bank by the Canness Burn, which rises a mere matter of yards from the Aberdeenshire boundary. Certain localities near the head of the Canness Burn, which had better not be more narrowly specified, afford a refuge for rare Alpine plants. Above Forter Castle the road deteriorates progressively, but a footpath traverses the Monega Pass, crosses the eastern shoulder of Glas Maol at a height of 3,318 feet, and conducts the hardy pedestrian through to the Cairnwell Road, which it joins amid the headstreams of the Clunie, at Shean Spittal, the medieval hostelry already mentioned, whose position, where the mountain passes meet, is thus explained. The Monega Pass, an ancient right-of-way, is claimed to be the highest public path in Britain.

Glen Prosen, a finely wooded glen, has its niche in history because here, in a charming bungalow near its mouth, Captain Scott and Dr. Wilson made their plans for the expedition to the South Pole which, though successful, cost the whole party their lives. A memorial fountain by the roadside, recently repaired, commemorates their achievement and sacrifice. There is no track across the Mounth from the head of Glen Prosen. Glen Clova, on the other hand, conducts us up to the Tolmounth Pass (2,863 feet)—one of the major crossings of the Mounth, leading down to Glen Callater and thus to Braemar. Before reaching the summit, the Tolmounth road forms a 'ladder' or zig-zag which, for some unexplained reason, is known as 'Jock's Road'. Also from the head of Glen Clova, the Capel Mounth Pass leads across to Glenmuick, and so down to Deeside above Ballater.

Glen Clova, which affords a passage for the River South Esk from its source on Cairn Bannoch (3,314 feet), a Mounth summit north-east of the Tolmounth, is a Highland glen as far as Cortachy. Milton of Clova, far up the Glen, has its niche in history as the scene of a little known episode in the Civil War, nicknamed 'The Start'. Charles II, having signed the Treaty of Breda on 1st May, 1650, had landed at Speymouth as a Covenanted King, with the hope of at least recovering his ancestral realm. Although the people at large received him well, he soon found himself the virtual prisoner of the violent fanatics who now had collared the Covenanting movement. Claiming the direct inspiration of Almighty God, these 'Presbyterian Popes' assailed their wretched King with interminable thundering sermons, sometimes six in a day: he was required to forswear his father and to denounce his mother's 'idolatry'; he was forbidden to walk abroad on the Sabbath; and, if on a week day he ventured a game of cards, the ministers scolded him before his royal face. Small wonder that the persecuted King in after days declared his conviction that Presbyterianism was "not the religion of a gentleman". Small wonder also that he sought to regain his freedom in the Highlands, where there were many who had served under Montrose, and who could not away with the Covenant and all its works. So, on 4th October, 1650, with a mere handful of companions and no baggage, he gave his tormentors the slip at Perth, and headed for the north. At Cortachy Castle he was provided with a guard of sixty Ogilvies, and word came in that a large force of loyal clansmen was assembling at the head of the Glen. But Argyll, by now the dictator of Scotland, was quick to act. A cavalry detachment was sent after the royal fugitive; and on Sunday the 6th, sheltering in a poor hut at Milton, "in a nasty room, on an old bolster, above a mat of seggs and rushes, over wearied and very fearful", they found their miserable sovereign and carried him back in shame to an even more rigorous captivity.

The upper parts of Glen Isla, Glen Prosen and Glen Clova are now in the beneficent hands of the Forestry Commission. In Glen Isla, Scotch pine, Norway and Sitka spruces, and Japanese larch have been planted; in Glen Prosen, pines, spruces, and some European larch: and in Glen Clova, Norwegian spruce, Japanese and European larch, and Scotch and Lodgepole pines. Most of the Glen Clova plantations in fact encircle Glen Doll, down which flows one of the headstreams of the South Esk, and are therefore officially styled the Glen Doll Forest. Here "the forester has to wage a constant struggle with hill torrents that can wash away trees, and avalanches of snow that break his fences and let in the hungry red deer of the peaks". Glen Doll is now being developed as a ski-ing centre.

Perhaps the most popular among the six Mounth Glens is Glen Esk. Its accessibility from large centres of population like Perth, Dundee, Arbroath, Montrose, and Aberdeen; the fact that it is served to the head by an excellent road; the variety and charm of its scenery (though there are few plantations), culminating in rugged grandeur about desolate Loch Lee; its historical and literary associations; and the Glen Esk Folk Museum at The Retreat, so beautifully housed amid the fragrant birch trees of Ardoch—all these attractions combine to lure visitors in their thousands into this favoured glen throughout the summer season.

The River North Esk, which descends the Glen, is formed by the junction of two head-streams, the Lee and the Unich. After flowing through Loch Lee, the river receives from the north successively the Water of Mark, the Branny Burn, the Water of Tarff, and the Turret Burn. About Auchmull it emerges from its Highland surroundings, and thereafter pursues a meandering course past Edzell and across Strathmore until it enters the North Sea about three miles above Montrose. At Edzell it receives its one considerable tributary on the right bank, the West Water which in its upper part, known as the Water of Saughs, flows down a fine though little known Highland glen. From the handsome eighteenth-century mansion known as The Burn—which, with its beautiful grounds overlooking the rocky gorge of the river, is now a students' hostel and conference centre, administered jointly by the four older Scottish Universities—the River North Esk forms the county boundary between Angus and the Mearns.

Like Am Fasgadh at Kingussie, the Glen Esk Folk Museum is the creation of a woman, a retired teacher in Glen Esk, Miss Greta Michie. It is both wider and narrower in its scope than Am Fasgadh, since on the one hand it is confined to Glen Esk, while on the other it includes natural history collections illustrating the geology, flora and fauna of the Glen. Of special interest are the examples of lead, silver, and iron ore from the head of the Glen, where German mining engineers were employed by Lord Edzell as far back as the first decade of the seventeenth century. As far as my knowledge goes, no other Scottish glen is so completely illustrated, in all its aspects, as is Glen Esk by the rich collection of exhibits which has been brought together and beautifully arranged in The Retreat. The finely illustrated catalogue is, in itself, a valuable contribution to the study of the Central Highlands.

Just below Loch Lee is the tall, ruined tower of Invermark (p. 104). Loch Lee, with the ruined old parish church at its lower end, has been harnessed, and its level raised, in connexion with the county water supply. Though the place is now utterly desolate, here there was once a clachan, of which the 'dominie' for many years was Alexander Ross, who died there in 1784, and has an enduring if modest niche in the gallery of Scottish vernacular poets. Some of the tombstone inscriptions in the forlorn little kirkyard are of Ross's composition, including that of his wife; but his own grave is unknown. One of his funerary compositions, on the stone of a young man who perished in an accidental fire, is perhaps worth quoting for its 'auld-farran' quaintness:

> From what befalls us here below,
> Let none from thence conclude,
> Our lot shall afterwards be so—
> The young man's life was good.
> Yet, heavenly wisdom thought it fit,
> In its all-sovereign way,
> The flames to kill him to permit
> And so to close his day.

Incidentally, the visitor will be struck by the fine quality of the design, carving and lettering of some of the eighteenth-century monuments in this sequestered kirkyard, as also in the old parish graveyard of Edzell, at the foot of the Glen. No doubt this excellence is attributable to the presence of a school of mason-craftsmen working in the seventeenth century at the great and ornate Castle of Edzell.

From the head of Glen Esk access is obtained to Deeside by the Fir Mount, Forest of Birse Mount, and Mounth Keen passes (p. 104), all of which, however, are now mere hill tracks.

We have yet to consider the last, and most important, of all the Mounth Passes—the Cairnamounth, which traverses the eastern margin of our area from Fettercairn in the Howe o' the Mearns to Kincardine O'Neil on Deeside. Like most of the Mounth Passes, it is less a pass in the accepted sense than a passage across the hills. From the old royal Castle of Kincardine, near Fetter-cairn, the road, now an excellent motorway, holds northward by Clattering Bridge, whence it 'takes the hill' to reach its summit (1,475 feet) amid bare moorland at the Cairnamounth, from which a fine view may be enjoyed to the west of the dusky High-lands and southward of smiling Strathmore. The road then des-cends towards Deeside through the splendid woodlands of Glen Dye, crossing the Water of Dye by an ancient bridge of a single ribbed arch. As early as before the year 1233, the road was carried across the River Dee by a bridge at Kincardine O'Neil.

In ancient times the Cairnamounth Pass was the principal cross-ing from Strathmore into Mar, except for those who had business in Aberdeen. There is a long chain of recorded evidence for its military use from the eleventh century onwards. By this road Macbeth fled northward to make his last stand at Lumphanan (15th August, 1057):

> Oure the Mounth thai chast him then
> Rycht to the wod of Lumfanan.
> Thus Makbeth slew thai than
> Into the wode of Lunfannan.

By the same route, in the reverse direction, the 'Men of Moray', heirs of Macbeth's quarrel, *invaded Scotland*—so it could still be said in the year 1130—and were met and turned back at Stracathro: their leader, Angus, *King of Moray*, being left behind on the stricken field. At Stracathro, also, at the foot of the mountain pass that offered him the last refuge which he despaired to take, John Balliol the luckless 'Toom Tabard', gave in his abject sub-mission (7th July, 1296) to Edward I's representative, Anthony Bek, the warrior Bishop of Durham. Over the Cairnamounth King Edward himself returned in triumph, after his victorious march to Elgin; by the same route, also, he marched back in 1303, from his second great invasion of the North. In the Civil Wars of the seventeenth century, the Cairnamounth Pass was used by both sides—by Montrose, first in 1639 as a Covenanter, and again as a Royalist in 1645, and by 'Bonnie Dundee' and his antagonist General Mackay in their whirlwind campaign of 1689. The old military road, precursor of the modern motorway, was made in

1779; in the days of the great cattle 'trysts' it was a favourite route for the drovers.

What a road of ancient memories is this Cairnamounth! For a thousand years or more it has echoed to the march and counter-march of embattled hosts; the swift passage of the royal messenger; the patient plodding progress of the merchant's caravan; the dust and sweat of the drovers and their cattle. In a motley throng they move along the moorland track before our fancy's eye: Macbeth, so ill-used by bogus history and world-famous drama; his con-queror, big-headed Malcolm; the great Plantagenet, with his long shanks and his drooping left eyelid, proudly astride his gallant charger, Bayard; at his side the warrior-bishop—surely a strange by-product of the faith whose Founder had foretold that they that take the sword shall perish with the sword; the grave Montrose; the fiery Dundee—'Dark John of the Battles' so the clansmen loved to call him—the captains and the kings, and all the unre-membered throng of lesser folk.

CHAPTER X

THE HIGHLANDS OF MAR

The Aberdeenshire Dee and Don are generally spoken of as sister streams. Doubtless this is because they both rise, within a few miles of each other, in the Cairngorm Mountains; flow in roughly parallel courses eastward; and discharge themselves into the North Sea, within a mile of each other, on either side of the City of Aberdeen. Yet in fact the two rivers differ widely in character, as sisters are apt to do. To begin with, the Dee has a much straighter course than that of the Don. This appears to be largely due to the fact that in its central portion the channel has been incised by the stream into a more or less straight band of Dalradian limestone, running from west to east. Then again, the Dee has a light sandy soil, which is easily dried up if the rainfall should fail. Hence the Deeside farmer is credited with requiring a shower a day to ensure a good crop. On the other hand, the Don valley is largely composed of fat, deep loam, so that agriculturally it is far richer than the basin of the sister stream. Hence the ancient couplet:

> Ae mile o' Don's worth twa o' Dee
> Except for salmon, stone and tree.[1]

Thus the Don valley was more important alike in prehistoric and in medieval times: so that, while Deeside bears the palm for picturesqueness, the Don valley offers superior historical and antiquarian attractions.

Not only is the valley of the Dee straighter than that of the Don, but it is less varied in character. From the part where it emerges from the Highlands at Ballater, it presents the general picture of a more or less uniform strath, widening gradually as it approaches the sea. In marked contrast, the Don valley, right down to the mouth, offers a succession of "close gorge and open

[1] Compare the variant rhyme quoted on p. 103.

reach". It consists of a series of alluvial basins, separated by narrow glens, or even gorges, so that the traveller ascending Donside is confronted with a succession of unexpected and pleasant changes of landscape. Thus though the valley of the Don cannot compare for scenery with its southern neighbour, it is distinctly less monotonous—using the term *sensu stricto*, and not implying dullness. The reason, or reasons, for this peculiarity of Donside are not fully understood: but it seems likely that the present course of the river is largely a succession of what may perhaps be termed 'fossil meanders'—the original channel having been incised, in a wandering course, upon an eastward sloping plain of Old Red Sandstone, long since removed by denudation.

Another important respect in which Deeside differs from Donside is in respect of their tributaries. In the Highland portions of both valleys, the tributaries are of course Highland in character, descending to the main valley in typically Highland glens. In lower Donside, the principal tributary is the Urie, which, draining the fertile basin of the Garioch, is wholly a Lowland stream. On Deeside, owing to the nearness of the Mounth, some of the affluents which enter the main stream on its right bank, well east of the Highland 'gate', and are quite Lowland in their lower reaches, debouch from truly Highland glens. This is notably the case in the valley of the longest tributary of the Dee, the Feugh (already discussed, see p. 33) and its own affluent, the Dye (p. 172). Likewise Glentanner, though it debouches on Deeside opposite Aboyne, and therefore well within the Lowlands, is in its whole course a splendid Highland glen.

Where do we enter the Deeside Highlands? It is unfortunate that in modern times it has become habitual to fix the point on the insignificant Burn of Dinnet, which plays no part either in topography or in history. It is true that the Moor of Dinnet (p. 38) thanks to the fact that it has grown upon a platform of boulder clay and morainic detritus—the apron of the Deeside glacier during a long pause in its gradual shrinking—partakes somewhat of a Highland character; but it is not itself in the Highlands, for it lies in the Howe of Cromar, which forms part of what the geomorphologists call the 'Grampian Lower Surface', as contrasted with the 'Grampian Highlands'. The identification of the Dinnet Burn with the Highland line, which has recently been asserted by a monument, has no justification. It seems to have originated in a whimsical remark, made anonymously, and with his tongue in his cheek, by a well-known writer of the early nineteenth century.

The true 'Highland Gate' of Deeside is unquestionably the Pass of Ballater. This was clearly understood by Pennant, who in 1765 describes it as "the eastern entrance into the Highlands" and includes it among his four principal entrances (p. 139). So also William MacGillivray, who wrote a classic on the Deeside Highlands, speaks of the "Pass of Tullich" as the "entrance to the Highlands of Aberdeenshire". And it was through the Pass of Ballater, on 10th February, 1654, that the Roundhead Colonel Morgan forced his entry into the Braemar Highlands, in teeth of severe opposition from that redoubtable Royalist of whom we have already heard, Sir Ewan Cameron of Locheil.

We enter the Deeside Highlands, then, through the Pass of Ballater, following the track of the old Deeside Road. Ballater itself, the capital of the Deeside Highlands, is quite a modern village, dating from the later eighteenth century, and owing its rapid growth to the extension of the Deeside Railway hither in 1866. Alas! the railway is now no more. With more imagination and less control from London, there are many who believe that it might have continued as a going concern. The abrupt and shaggy hill of Craigendarroch (1,300 feet) which forms one side of the Pass, is still clad with oak trees, the product of natural regeneration which doubtless has gone on for centuries, since the Gaelic name signifies 'the Craig of the oaks' (p. 40). The Pass itself is a typical Highland gorge, with bold granitic crags overhanging scree slopes, between which there is barely room for the road.

The beauties of upper Deeside have been extolled by so many able writers that there seems to be no point in attempting to add to their number. From Ballater westward to Braemar the valley presents some of the finest mountain scenery in Scotland. It is narrow and winding, affording a succession of unexpected and picturesque views. The surrounding hills, always bold, are often precipitous, and despite the ravages of two world wars, their under-slopes are still richly clothed in stalwart pine and graceful birch. On all the great estates—Balmoral, Invercauld, and Mar—a vigorous policy of re-afforestation is now in full progress. Abergeldie

Modern architecture at Aviemore. Behind are the
Cairngorms with Larig Garu

Castle, six miles above Ballater, is an ancient turreted stronghold of the Gordons, still belonging to the family, but now leased by H.M. the Queen. Two miles above Abergeldie is Balmoral Castle, the beautiful Highland home of the Royal Family; and opposite to it, Crathie Church, where they attend divine service when the Court is in residence. Built in 1893-5, of the local white granite, the church is deservedly admired as a fine modern building in the traditional late medieval Scotch manner. It contains many memorials of the Royal Family.

Few buildings in Scotland are probably more familiar to the world at large than Balmoral Castle. As the Highland summer residence of the British Royal Family, it has been visited by a long succession of princes and statesmen, and by distinguished figures in every walk of life and from all the five continents; while the thousands of ordinary folk who year after year throng to taste the scenic glories and breathe the pure air of Braemar, have admired the Castle as seen from across the river, or have enjoyed a closer inspection of the building when its spacious lawns, umbrageous woods and glowing gardens are thrown open to the public. The Castle lies low and sheltered, so that it is difficult to remember that it stands at a height of 926 feet above sea-level. The gardens yield an ample return in flowers and fruit, and the plantations include noble specimens alike of conifers and hardwood. Of especial beauty are the natural birches. The castle, erected in 1853-6, is built of the local white granite, which today looks so fresh that it is hard to believe that it has endured over a century of Highland weather. Extravagantly praised in its early days, the building has suffered since from the unthinking depreciation of everything 'Victorian' that was the fashion until quite recent times. A more discerning taste will recognize in it an outstanding pioneer essay in Scottish baronial architecture as the mid-nineteenth century conceived it. As a testament of finished masonry it can have few rivals; and despite inevitable modern alterations, its Victorian interiors retain their very worthy place in the history of British homes.

On the south side of the Dee, the whole scene from Ballater to Braemar is dominated by the vast bulk and graceful profile of Lochnagar—probably the most famous, as it is certainly among the noblest, of Scottish mountains. Though quoted in almost

The roof of Britain: on top of Ben Nevis
The parallel roads of Glen Roy

every book dealing with the Deeside Highlands, it seems impossible not to repeat, once again, the famous lines of Byron:

> England! thy beauties are tame and domestic
> To one who has roved o'er the mountains afar:
> Oh for the crags that are wild and majestic!
> The steep frowning glories of dark Lochnagar!

The name Lochnagar properly refers to the tarn which lies at the foot of the eastern corrie, justly regarded as the grandest of British rock basins, and described already (p. 36) in the present work. The meaning of the name is uncertain; but the ancient Gaelic term for the mountain was Mon' Gheill, the White Mounth, and this is still applied to the summit plateau, from which rises the highest point, Cac Carn Beg (3,786 feet). This name again is a distortion of the Ordnance Survey: properly it should be Ca Carn or Ca Chuirn—but here again the meaning is unknown. From the top, under favourable conditions, can be seen, on the south the Cheviot Hills, and on the north Morven of Caithness—in other words, the entire length of mainland Scotland! Lochnagar has an extensive literature, and indeed a whole book has been written upon it. Suffice it, therefore, here to quote once more Lord Byron's verdict, this time in prose: he considered it "the most sublime and picturesque of the Caledonian Alps". While it is easily ascended by the ordinary hill walks, its great corries, east and west, afford gruelling and dangerous challenges to the rock climber; and indeed some of the gullies in the eastern corrie have never yet been scaled. The Lochnagar massif, eroded out of a coarse pink granite, forms a well-defined area, bounded on the east and west by two glens very different in character: Glen Muick on the east and Glen Callater on the west. These two glens, curving inwards towards themselves, almost meet on the south; while on the north the boundary is, of course, the Dee. Probably the most popular ascent is by Glen Muick, which opens upon the Dee Valley about a mile west of Ballater. The public road is on the east side. Near the foot of the glen are the picturesque ruined tower of Knock, and the mansion of Birkhall, originally built in 1715, but much reconstructed and enlarged as the Deeside residence of H.M. Queen Elizabeth The Queen Mother. The lower part of the glen is finely wooded, the upper part bare and desolate. The area between the Muick and the Dee, on the left bank of the former, is dominated by the Coyles of Muick, three striking conical summits which, with Lochnagar as a majestic background, are conspicuous in the westward views from Ballater. The Coyles owe their distinctive outline, and the bright green grass which clothes them, to the fact that they are formed of serpentine.

Passing the Falls or Linn of Muick, some ten miles up the glen we come to Loch Muick, so closely hemmed in by steep, bare, and rocky braes that, except on the brightest summer day, it presents a daunting aspect. This is a true glacial lake. Its greatest depth is 256 feet. It is about two and a quarter miles long and half a mile in greatest breadth; the surface of the water is at 1,310 feet. At the foot of the loch is Spittal of Glenmuick, the site of a hostel maintained of old for the benefit of travellers coming over from Angus by the Capel Mounth Pass. It is pleasant so often to meet, in these desolate Highlands, such evidences of the care of the medieval Church for the lonely wayfarers. Here also is Allt-na-Guibhsaich Lodge, a royal shooting box where the Muick is spanned by a wooden bridge, giving access to the path which conducts up to the summit of Lochnagar. At the head of Loch Muick is the Glasallt Shiel, built by Queen Victoria in 1868, but now leased to Aberdeen University as a winter sports centre.

Still further up the glen at 2,091 feet is Dubh Loch, where the path ends. As its name indicates, this is indeed a dark lake; and we are not surprised to learn that it is haunted by a 'spectral stag'.

The western approach to Lochnagar, from Braemar by Glen Clunie and Glen Callater, is much less picturesque. This is the ancient route over the Tolmounth Pass to the head of Glen Clova (p. 168). Glen Callater is bare and desolate; its loch, at a height of 1,627 feet, and just under a mile in length, is set amid the broad peat moss through which its head streams flow. In keeping with its melancholy aspect, the Glen is associated with some weird and tragic legends of love and jealousy.

The village of Braemar consists of two portions, one on each side of the Water of Clunie, which hurries northward through a rocky gorge to join the Dee. The eastern and older portion of the village is known as Castleton, from the Castle of Kindrochit, of which mention was made in our account of the Cairnwell Pass (p. 165). The ruins, which have been excavated (p. 103), though picturesquely perched above the Clunie gorge, do not bulk large in the landscape. The western portion of the village is called Auchendryne, 'the field of thorns'. In the main, the folk on the west side of the Clunie are Roman Catholics: this is said not to be an uninterrupted survival from pre-Reformation times, but due to the fact that the Farquharsons of Inverey turned back to the ancient faith at some period in the seventeenth century; and, as a matter of course, the clansmen followed their chief.

At the east end of Castleton, on a site now occupied by the Invercauld Arms Hotel, the Jacobite flag was raised on 6th September, 1715:

> The Standard on the Braes o' Mar
> Is up and streaming rarely;
> The gathering pipe on Lochnagar
> Is sounding lang an' sairly.

The historic event is commemorated by a brass plate in the hotel, and by a monument erected by the Deeside Field Club on the opposite side of the road. It is said that the unfurling ceremony took place after the insurgent chiefs had fortified themselves by partaking of a banquet at the Castle of Invercauld, the ancient seat of the Chief of Clan Farquhar. Most of the mansion is modern, but it still retains the vaulted basement of a tower built by Findla Mhor Macfarquhar, who was killed at Pinkie in 1547. The view from the terrace in front of the Castle, terminated upstream by the mighty corries of Beinn a' Bhuird, and downstream by the beautiful cone of Lochnagar, is unsurpassed on Deeside. In winter, the red deer wander freely round the Castle. On the outskirts of Braemar is the tall embattled keep of Braemar Castle, which was burned by the Jacobites in 1690, and after the 'Forty-five' was rebuilt and garrisoned by the Government (see p. 119). A celebrated beauty spot, beloved of artists, is the four-arched Invercauld Bridge, erected in 1753 to carry the military road from Blairgowrie over the Dee on its way by Glen Gairn to Corgarff at the head of the Don.

Pennant, who visited Invercauld in August, 1769, was much struck by the magnificent scenery around Braemar, of which he has left us a description at once vivid and careful. About the inhabitants he was less complimentary:

> The houses of the common people in these parts are shocking to humanity, formed of loose stones, and covered with clods, which

they call *devish* [divots] or with heath, broom, or branches of fir: they look, at a distance, like so many black mole-hills. The inhabitants live very poorly, on oatmeal, barley-cakes, and potatoes; their drink whisky sweetened with honey. The men are thin, but strong; idle and lazy, except employed in the chace, or anything that looks like amusement; they are content with their hard fare, and will not exert themselves farther than to get what they deem necessaries. The women are more industrious, spin their own husbands' clothes, and get money by knitting stockings, the great trade of the county. The common women are in general most remarkably plain, and soon acquire an old look, and by being much exposed to the weather without hats, such a grin, and contraction of the muscles, as heightens greatly their natural hardness of features.

Six miles west of Braemar, at the picturesque clachan of Inverey, are the poor remnants of an old castle of the Farquharsons, which also was burned in 1690, in retaliation for the destruction of Braemar Castle. The then laird, Colonel John Farquharson of Inverey, still remembered as 'Black Jock', fled up Glen Ey and hid himself in the 'Colonel's Bed', a narrow ledge of rock a few feet above the black boiling torrent, which here flows between precipices covered with ferns, flowers and shrubs.

In and above Inverey dwelt the last native Gaelic speakers in Aberdeenshire. I remember them well: Lamonts, Gruers, and others. But between the two wars, alas! they died out or left Inverey; and the ancient tongue is now extinct in the county. Any who now speak it have come in from elsewhere.

Opposite Inverey is Mar Lodge, the former seat of the Dukes of Fife. It is reached from Braemar by crossing the Dee over the stone bridge built in 1857 over the Linn of Dee, a chasm in some places no more than 4 feet across, through which, for a distance of perhaps 400 yards, the river descends in a series of foaming cascades, having in the process eroded a fantastic series of 'potholes'. It is an unforgettable experience to see the salmon 'louping' the Linn. This is the last stone bridge across the Dee: and here the motor-way ends. Mar Lodge is now a hotel in connexion with the ski-ing centre on the Cairngorms. To this famous mountain group we now must turn.

The Cairngorms form the highest large area (about twenty miles by fifteen miles) of mountain land within the British Islands. They include four of the five highest summits in Britain: Ben

Macdhui (4,296 feet); Braeriach (4,248 feet); Cairn Toul (4,241 feet); and Cairngorm (4,084 feet): besides three others that very nearly approach the four-thousanders: Cairn Lochan (3,983 feet); Beinn a' Bhuird (3,924 feet); and Ben Avon (3,843 feet). Among this tremendous mountain group, as elsewhere in the Central Highlands, the true ancient nomenclature has been bedevilled by modern innovation. The name Cairngorm—'the Blue Cairn', properly applied to the mountain still so called, has now been appropriated to the whole group, the ancient name of which is Monadh Ruadh (pronounced Monarua), the Red Mountains, so called to distinguish them from the Monadh Liath (Monalea, Grey Mountains) on the other side of Strathspey (see p. 146). It is probably now too late to restore the authentic terminology.

As a whole, the Cairngorms are best seen from Speyside, since that valley is both further away and lower. Braemar is too near them, and since the Dee valley here is over 1,100 feet above sea level, the great mountains, seen from this side, are abated somewhat in grandeur. In common with granitic mountains, they present, when viewed from a distance, broad lumpish and heavy masses with rounded slopes and tabular summits—although one, Cairn Toul (pronounced like 'towel') rises into a singularly graceful peak. It is only on a near approach, or from the actual summits, that the real grandeur of this mountain scenery becomes apparent: the giant tors rising abruptly from the broad saddle-backs of shattered granite; the deep ravines with their dangerous screes; the frowning corries, encradling lonely black tarns; the sudden foaming cascades, dwindling almost to nothing during the short summer season; the silence of the great snow-fields, persisting sometimes almost the whole year round; the treacherous over-hanging cornices of frozen snow, which have cost many a life; the unexpected swirling mists; the roar of the sudden avalanche; and the awesome reverberation, in ravine and corrie, of the mountain thunderstorm.

The corries and the tors provide all that the rock climber can wish to test his skill and nerve: but everywhere the Cairngorms can be easily climbed by the ordinary hill-walker, if he possesses the necessary physical stamina and has brought the right kit and clothing. All six major summits—Ben Avon, Cairn Gorm, Ben Macdhui, Cairn Toul, and Braeriach—were climbed, in that order, by a party of five on 21st June, 1909. The time taken was nineteen hours, and the distance covered was twenty-eight miles, with 9,000 feet of climbing. Needless to say, this amazing *tour-de-force* has never been repeated. No hill walker should ever set out on his own. The minimum party should be three: one to have an accident, one to stay beside him, and the third to go for help.

Four of the major summits group themselves in pairs on either side of the gorge of the infant Dee and the famous pass, the Larig Ghru, leading northward from its source through to the Forest of Rothiemurchus and Speyside. On the west of this pass are Cairn Toul and Braeriach; on the east, Ben Macdhui and Cairngorm. To the east of the main group are Beinn a' Bhuird and Ben Avon; while to the south-west across Glen Guisachan is Ben Bhrotain (3,795 feet). Cairn Lochan, though in its own right a major summit, is really a western spur of Cairn Gorm, to which it is united by two immense corriès, veritable curtains of rock. Far below Cairn Gorm, on the south, between it and Ben Macdhui, lies the largest of the Cairngorm lakes, Loch Avon, at a height of 2,377 feet. It is one and a half miles in length and a quarter of a mile in breadth; and since there is no path of approach to it, it has been saluted as the loneliest and grandest loch in the Scottish Highlands. At its head is the famous Shelter Stone, a perched block of granite 43 feet in length, 20 feet in breadth, and 22 feet in height: the computed weight is 1,361 tons. Under this enormous boulder eight or ten men can huddle, and many a mountaineer has owed to it a night's uneasy sleep. Readers of Sir Thomas Dick Lauder's fine yarn, *The Wolfe of Badenoch*, will remember the dramatic part played in it by the Shelter Stone of Loch Avon. From Loch Avon the water of Avon emerges on its long descent by Inchrory to Strathspey.

The shores of Loch Avon are haunted by a kelpie, white, beautiful, and fierce. If any hardy Celt managed to bestride him, the water-horse promptly galloped off and plunged with his rider into the loch. At last he was captured, with the aid of a silver bridle; whereupon the kelpie at once became perfectly tame, and was led in triumph to Tomintoul.

The Larig Ghru, a boulder-strewn pass between Braemar and Braeriach, affords the most direct and shortest route between Braemar and Aviemore on Speyside. The total distance is about twenty-seven miles, of which fifteen miles, between Derry Lodge and Coylum Bridge, can be negotiated best on foot, since the ground is rough for bicycle or pony.

Ben Macdhui, as everybody has read, is haunted by a giant spectre, like the Brocken of the Alps. On one occasion, its un-expected manifestation so scared a distinguished F.R.S. that he fled from the mountain top! Even the most obdurate sceptic, if he is alone among these wild and awesome hills, must be prepared for unexpected sights and sounds.

At the height of 3,058 feet, Loch Etchachan on Ben Macdhui is said to be the highest lake (as distinct from mere tarns) in Britain. On its bank, in March 1963, was picked up the point of a leaf-shaped arrow-head, carefully worked in Buchan flint. Alike in height above sea-level and in sheer remoteness, this seems to be the most outlying vestige of prehistoric man in Mar. One must assume that the arrow-point was lost by a Neolithic or Bronze Age hunter in pursuit of the red deer among the Monadh Ruadh.

This great group of mountains is perhaps best known today, among thousands who have never beheld them, because of the coloured quartz crystals found in them, to which the name 'Cairn-gorm stones' has long been given. They are found in what are termed 'drusy cavities' among the veins or bands of white quartz by which the mountain is seamed. These seams used to be regularly 'worked' for them; and they may also be picked out of the gravel in the mountain streams. Typically the colour is golden-brown. Nowadays cairngorms are becoming much scarcer. Prob-ably the largest specimen on record is now preserved at Braemar Castle. It came from Ben Avon, and weighs about 50 lb.

Since 1954 the country round Loch Morlich, on the north-western slopes of the Cairngorms, has been designated the Glen More Forest Park. The area thus protected includes some 3,300 acres of pine and spruce woods, as well as 9,200 acres of mountain land. In addition, the Cairngorm Mountains as a whole now form the largest National Nature Reserve in Great Britain, covering no less than 58,882 acres in Aberdeenshire and Inverness-shire. Scotch pine, birch and juniper, as well as moorland plants, and in the corries and upon the mountain plateaux, reindeer moss and many rare Arctic-Alpine plants, are thus offered some protection; while measures are taken both to protect and to control the native fauna, which includes red and roe deer, wild cat, golden eagle, ptarmigan, dotterel, cross-bill (a bird of the pine woods) and Scottish crested tit, a species peculiar to Scotland, and now happily on the increase. These nature reserves are maintained in the national interest in such a way as to conserve, as far as possible, their native flora and fauna, and to make them accessible to all visitors who are prepared to respect their inhabitants, whether plants or animals. They are, of course, mercifully secured from what is euphemistically styled 'development'. Wardens are available at Aviemore and Braemar to give information and guidance to visitors, particularly to those who come bent on scientific research.

On Donside, the entry to the Highlands is usually placed in the Glen of Brux, between Callievar (1,747 feet) and Lord Arthur's Cairn (1,699 feet), which conducts us through from the Howe of Alford to the Kildrummy basin. But, owing to the characteristic Donside alternation of 'close gorge and open reach', there is a fine stretch of truly Highland scenery lower down, where the river, emerging from the Alford basin, forces its way through a narrow wooded gorge, picturesquely known as 'My Lord's Throat', between Bennachie and the Menaway range. The swart couchant mass of Bennachie, 'the sphinx of the Garioch', with its shapely 'Mither Tap', must be regarded as a bastion of the Highlands, thrust boldly forward into the howe of the Garioch. Although it is not the highest of the six summits of Bennachie, the 'Mither Tap' (1,698 feet) is by far the most conspicuous and the most beautiful; and celebrated as it has been in song and story, and in the works of famous artists, it has impressed itself indelibly upon the imagination of generations of Aberdeenshire folk, at home and abroad. The summit of the 'Mither Tap' is girt by the massive remains of one of the finest hill-forts in Scotland.

The Kildrummy basin, long famed for its corn-growing qualities, contains the majestic ruins of the famous castle (p. 101). This basin, and Strathdon generally, are noted for the frequency of earth-houses—weird underground galleries, roofed with great slabs of stone, and extending sometimes to a length of over 80 feet. They date from the first two or three centuries of our era: in one of them was found a denarius of the Emperor Nerva (A.D. 96–98). Earth-houses are always associated with the foundations of huts, to which they served as *souterrains*—though their exact purpose, or purposes, remain obscure. One Strathdon earth-house, at Glenkindie, has two chambers, shaped like the letter Y.

Strathdon, despite modern communications, still gives the impression of a pleasantly sequestered district; but it offers much variety of scenery and abundant historical and antiquarian interest. Boldly placed at the junction of the Water of Buchat with the Don stands the fine ruin of Glenbuchat Castle (p. 111); and three miles further up the strath is that splendid monument of Norman engineering, the Doune of Invernochty (p. 97). A beauty spot of Strathdon is Poldhulie Bridge, whose single lofty semi-circular arch spans a wooded gorge of the river. This bridge was built in 1715, the very year of the rising, by John Forbes of Inverernan, the recipient of the Earl of Mar's irate letter, already reproduced (p. 88). John Forbes himself bore his part manfully in the Rising, and died in Carlisle the night before he was due for execution.

From many points in upper Donside, fine southward views are obtained of the great bulk and fine outline of Morven (2,862 feet)—Byron's "Morven of Snow". Dominating as it does the Howe of Cromar, this is usually claimed as a Deeside hill, but in fact it forms part of the watershed betwixt both valleys. From Strathdon it is conveniently ascended by Glen Deskry. Being composed of serpentine, it is grassy rather than heath-clad; and, since it stands somewhat isolated from the westward summits, it commands a remarkable view, including the Cairngorms and the whole varied line of the Mounth from Lochnagar to its termination above Aberdeen.

The turnpike road ends at Corgarff, a lonely tower which, like Braemar, was reconditioned by the Government and garrisoned in connexion with the military road, of which more hereafter. Corgarff Castle, like the castle of Braemar, was burned in 1690; but, unlike its Deeside counterpart, had been reconstructed. During the 'Forty-five' it was held by the Jacobites, and was captured (2nd March, 1746) by a detachment of Government troops, after a remarkable two days' march from Aberdeen, through very deep snow. At an earlier epoch in its stormy history, Corgarff Castle was the scene, in November, 1571, of the frightful tragedy commemorated in the beautiful ballad of "Edom o' Gordon", when Margaret Campbell, the wife of the occupant, Forbes of Towie, was burned to death, with her family and servants, by a party of Gordons from Auchindoun (p. 105). The castle is under the guardianship of the Ministry of Public Building and Works. It is the remotest in Aberdeenshire, standing at a height of 1,416 feet, overlooking the south bank of the Don, here a slender, peaty stream. The situation of the castle is a striking one; and the tall, high-shouldered tower, guarded by its Hanoverian defences, presents an aspect of sturdy, repelling strength in perfect harmony with its surroundings. "Seen in summer, when the heather is awake and the sun shines on the fields that stretch upward to the foot of its loopholed curtain wall, the castle has an awe-inspiring aspect, a lone, stern, friendless appearance. But in winter it is gaunt and cold and forbidding, like some grim monster brooding over a desolation." Grimmest of all is its aspect in a blinding autumn rain, when the castle looks a scowling infamy, as if conscious of the horror and iniquity of which it has been the scene:

> O then outspoke her youngest son,
>   Sat on the nurse's knee,
> "Dear mother, gie owre your house," he says,
>   "For the reek it smithers me."
>
> "I would gie a' my gowd, my bairn,
>   Sae would I a' my fee,
> "For ae blast o' the westlin wind,
>   To blaw the reek frae thee,"
>
> "But I winna gie up my house, my dear,
>   To nae sik traitor as he:
> Cum weil, cum wae, my jewels fair,
>   Ye maun tak share wi' me."

Direct communication between Braemar and Corgarff is provided by the old military road, whose northward progress from Blairgowrie we have followed in the last chapter. The section with which we are at present concerned was built in 1753; and with one diversion to be noted, its course is followed by its modern successor. The military road crossed the Dee, as we have seen, by Invercauld Bridge. Descending the valley, it then turned north opposite Balmoral, and at Gairnshiel crossed the River Gairn by another military bridge, still in use and unaltered. The River Gairn, which joins the Dee above the western outlet of the Pass of Ballater, rises in Ben Avon; with a length of twenty miles, it is the longest tributary of the Dee. In its lower course the Gairn flows down a wide and roomy valley, once thickly peopled but now almost uninhabited. From Bridge of Gairn the military road strikes northward, and on the watershed reaches a height of 1,805 feet. The present descent on Donside is modern; the old road held north-westward along the south side of the river towards Corgarff. This portion is now used only as a footpath; but evidence of its former importance survives in the three small neglected military bridges crossing tributaries of the Don. The old bridge, by which it crossed the river below Corgarff Castle, was a hump-backed, one-arched structure like that still in use at Gairnshiel.

In 1754 the military road was continued northwards from Corgarff to Grantown on Spey, and finally to Fort George. This is the famous—and fearsome—Lecht Road, which, mounting the watershed to a height of 2,114 feet, descends by Glenconglas to Tomintoul in Strathavon (p. 192). This section of the road is accurately dated by the Well of the Lecht, with its inscription recording that in 1754 "five companies, the 33rd. Regiment, Right Honbl. Lord Chas Hay, Colonel, made the road from here to the Spey". Although the Lecht Road has been much improved, its bends and gradients still demand care from the motorist. In the early days of cars, sixty years ago, I well remember how many drivers stuck on the steep brae, with a gradient of one in four, behind the Allargue Arms Hotel in Corgarff, and had to be rescued by mine host with a cart and horse and a couple of chains! Looking south and west from the ascent, the traveller will enjoy magnificent views of Lochnagar and the Cairngorms.

As we have already noted, these great natural cross-country routes were in use long before the Hanoverian engineers arrived upon the scene. For example, we find King Robert II, during his hunting holiday at Kindrochit in 1384, paying a baker's bill incurred in remote Glen Conglas, a long narrow glen that joins the Avon below Tomintoul. The Well of the Lecht is at the point where the military road dips into Glen Conglas; but we may be pretty sure that neither Lord Charles Hay nor his men of the 33rd knew that, nearly four centuries earlier, they had been preceded in this remote solitude by the first Stewart King.

CHAPTER XI

THE NORTHERN STRATHS
AND THE GREAT GLEN

From the north-eastern flanks of the Central Highlands three well-known rivers—in order from east to west, the Spey, the Findhorn, and the Nairn—descend north-eastwards into the Moray Firth. Each differs in character from its neighbour; but all have much to offer in scenic and historical interest.

Glen Spey, as the upper part of the Spey valley is called, can hardly rank among the finest Highland scenery. From Dalwhinnie on the Great North Road, General Wade's road to Fort Augustus branches off to the left and runs northward to Laggan Bridge, an iron structure, whence the modern high road holds westward down Loch Laggan and Glen Spean to Fort William. Below Laggan Bridge, on the left or north bank of the river, is Cluny Castle, formerly the ancestral seat of Cluny Macpherson, since 1873 Chief of Clan Chattan. The locality is for ever associated with the memory of the Cluny Macpherson of the 'Forty-five', who after Culloden was hunted by the redcoats, with £1,000 on his head—yet, thanks to the devoted loyalty of his clansmen, he rarely required to seek a lurking place outside his own domains. Much of his time he spent in a cave high up on the brow of Craig Dhu—the Black Rock (2,350 feet)—from which it is said that he watched the burning of his castle by order of the Duke of Cumberland. According to tradition, the soldiers on the prowl for him used to cross a near-by burn by stepping stones, one of which was loose and plashed in the water when trod upon, so that the fugitive in his cave could count their number. Not until 1755 did he at length escape to France. The present castle which replaced that destroyed in 1746, is a quaint mixture of the 'Gothick' and classical styles. Built of granite, it has corbelled parapets and solid turrets with pointed stone helmets, but also Ionic pilasters and Venetian windows—the whole making up a charming *mélange*.

Alas! the many Jacobite relics which Cluny Castle once housed are now dispersed; but the famous Black Chanter and Green Banner are in safe-keeping at the Clan House in Newtonmore. The present Chief lives in Australia. For some time the castle was leased by Andrew Carnegie.

Wade's road to Fort Augustus ascends the head waters of the Spey as far as Mealgarbha, and then strikes northward over the famous Corrieyarrick Pass (p. 91), at a height of 2,507 feet, in order to descend lovely Glen Tarff upon Fort Augustus. Garva Bridge, or St. George's Bridge as Wade called it, where his road crosses the Spey, is a fine two-arched structure, 150 feet in length, completed in 1736. Here the river is already an obstreperous infant, brawling along in a rocky channel. At Mealgarbha, four miles further up, the driving road ends: and the Corrieyarrick Pass is now a mere mountain track, with Wade's little bridges over the burns now falling into ruin. Pennant in 1769 tells us that "people often perish on the summit of this hill, which is frequently visited during winter with dreadful storms of snow"; while in 1834 Anderson describes it in spine-chilling language:

> The whole stage being one continued hill, the traveller is obliged to dwell for hours on the dreariness of this forlorn region, and patiently to endure the cutting blasts, which he is sure to encounter towards the middle of his journey, when he gains the summit of the ridge, where snow posts, lining the road for miles, denote the horrors of a passage in winter, and make him thankful if he does not stand in need of their guidance.

Cattle and sheep were driven over the Pass as late as 1896 and 1899 respectively: but it is not surprising that Wade's road is now derelict, and that Fort Augustus today is reached by a good road along the west side of Loch Ness (p. 236).

An account has already been given of Strathspey as far as Aviemore, where the Great North Road turns off leftward in order to cross the Monadhliath to Inverness. We have now to explore the valley up to Aviemore from Craigellachie, where the Speyside Highlands may be said to begin.

Strathspey is probably the most populous valley in the Highlands. It owes this favour not only to its splendid scenery and fine dry, sunny climate, but to the facilities that it offers for mountain sports, and to the employment provided not only by tourism but also by forestry and distilling. As to the last mentioned industry, Strathspey is the principal whisky producing area in Scotland—a matter of great importance in the present state of the Highlands, and indeed of the national economy, since most of the whisky is exported to America, and is one of our greatest dollar-earners. Barley is therefore an important crop on Speyside. A remarkable feature of the Strath is the succession of attractive towns and villages, all laying themselves out for summer visitors: Rothes; Craigellachie; Aberlour; Grantown; Nethybridge; Carr Bridge; Boat of Garten; Aviemore; Kingussie; and Newtonmore.

Rothes is overlooked by a fragment of its high-perched thirteenth-century castle of the de Polloks, in which Edward I spent a night on 29th July, 1296, on his return march from Elgin. The King had come down by the Glen of Rothes, through which now run road and disused railway. This is the real Glen Rothes. Nothing can be sillier than to have applied this name to a synthetic modern town in Fife—particularly when the place now so miscalled possessed the fine old Scotch name of Auchmutie! Rothes, a distillery centre, is also in other respects a pleasant town, finely situated at the outlet of its glen, and commanding, across the Spey, a view of Ben Aigan (1,544 feet)—the first of the Speyside hills.

One of the sights of Speyside is the road bridge over the river at Craigellachie, by which the north-bound traveller passes from Banffshire into Moray. It is a graceful bridge of a single span, 150 feet long, between two pairs of embattled towers, built between 1812 and 1815 to the design of Telford. The bridge has recently shown alarming signs of weakness, necessitating urgent repairs. Here the river flows at the base of a precipitous gorge, feathered with pine and birch trees. At Craigellachie the Spey is joined on the right or Banffshire side by the River Fiddich. Its valley, of distilling fame, is also in its own right a beautiful Highland glen, and one teeming with historic interest. It contains the fine thirteenth-century parish church of Mortlach, still in use, occupying the site of a Celtic monastery founded in the second half of the sixth century by St. Moluag from Lismore; as well as the two notable castles of Balvenie and Auchindoun, described already (pp. 99, 105). Balvenie Castle and Mortlach Kirk stand on opposite sides of Dufftown, a distilling centre and holiday resort, but founded originally in the interest of the woollen industry. This is one of several examples which we shall encounter in Strathspey of towns deliberately laid down by an enlightened landowner. Dufftown, as its name indicates, was founded in 1817 by James Duff, fourth Earl of Fife, and with its central market square enclosing a lofty clock tower, and its gridiron of streets, at once proclaims itself to be a product of town-planning. It now contains about 1,550 inhabitants. Here the Water of Dullan joins the Fiddich on the right bank. The Dullan flows beneath the noble mountain of Ben Rinnes (2,755 feet) whose shapely cone dominates Glen Rinnes, as the valley of the Dullan is called. A feature of the view from the summit of its great granite 'nose'— for the name Rinnes means just that—is the superb prospect over the Moray Firth to the high summits of the Northern Highlands. From Glen Fiddich the ancient road, followed by Edward I, traverses the moorland wastes of the Cabrach to descend upon Donside at Kildrummy.

Returning to Speyside, we continue our ascent of the Strath, amid scenes of ever-increasing Highland splendour, with the grand panorama of the Cairngorms opening in front, and the broad masses of the Monadhliath on our right. On the left, for some eight miles or thereby, the Strath is bounded by the Hills of Cromdale, whose highest point is Creagan a'Chaise (2,367 feet). Broad, flat, and peaty, these hills are worth traversing for the sake of the views that they offer over the Spey valley. On their south-western skirts are the Haughs of Cromdale, where, on 1st May, 1690, the Government forces under Sir Thomas Livingstone defeated the Jacobites, and so brought to a mournful end the Rising so gloriously begun by 'Bonnie Dundee'.

The hills of Cromdale lie between Strathspey and that of its largest feeder, the pellucid River Avon—

> The Water of A'an it rins so clear
> 'Twould beguile a man o' a hunder year—

which enters the Spey at Inveravon, near Ballindalloch Castle (p. 116). The Avon is the Spey's longest tributary. Rising on Ben Macdhui, and traversing the Loch to which it gives its name, it has a total length of some thirty miles, passing on its way Tomintoul (p. 188)—another example of a planned village, and a most delightful one to boot. It was laid out, on the site of a poor Highland clachan, by the Duke of Gordon in 1779 after some years of discussion and planning; but for long it failed to 'catch on', and when Queen Victoria passed through it in 1860 she described it as "the most tumble-down, poor-looking place I ever saw". With its pure air, fine views, and excellent fishing, Tomintoul is now well established in popular favour. Most of the houses are built of red freestone, a fact unusual in the Highlands: but the village stands on a Middle Old Red outlier. A substantial proportion of the inhabitants are Roman Catholic; and this seems to be a genuine case where a community has preserved the ancient faith throughout the Reformation and the two centuries of persecution and scorn that followed. At 1,160 feet above sea-level, Tomintoul is the highest village in the Scottish Highlands—though it is exceeded in altitude by Wanlockhead (1,380 feet) in the Southern Uplands. Around Tomintoul the Forestry Commission have a large and promising afforestation scheme; but special care is taken to respect the rival claims of sheep-rearing and agriculture, while ski-ing is being actively developed.

To judge by a contemporary account, Mrs. Mackenzie, mine hostess of the 'best inn' at Tomintoul, the Sign of the Horns, in 1794, must have been a remarkable personage:

This heroine began her career of celebrity, in the accommodating disposition of an easy virtue, at the age of 14, in the year 1745. That year saw her in a regiment in Flanders, caressing and caressed. Superior to the little prejudices of her sex, she relinquished the first object of her affection, and attached herself to a noble personage high in the military department. After a campaign or two spent in acquiring a knowledge of man, and of the world, she then married, and made her husband enlist in the Royal Highlanders, at the commencement of the war in 1756. With him she navigated the Atlantic, and sallied forth on American ground, equally prepared to meet her friends, or encounter her enemies, in the fields of Venus or Mars, as occasion offered. At the conclusion of that war, she revisited her native country. After a variety of vicissitudes in Germany, France, Holland, England, Ireland, Scotland, America and the West Indies, her anchor is now moored on dry land in the village of Tomintoul. It might be imagined that such extremes of climate, such discordant modes of living, such ascents and declivities, so many rugged paths, so many severe brushes, as she must have experienced in her progress through life, would have impaired her health, especially when it is considered that she added 24 children to the general aggregate of births, besides some *homunculi* that stopped short in their passage.

Near its confluence with the Spey, the Avon is joined by the Water of Livet. Wherever whisky is liked, the name of Glen Livet is known. But the glen has other claims to distinction—fine scenery; the ruined castle of Blairfindy, bearing the date 1586; and the battle field of Balrinnes, where, on 3rd October, 1594, the Catholic insurgents, under the Earls of Huntly, Angus, and Erroll, though greatly outnumbered, inflicted a smart defeat upon the royal forces led by the Earl of Argyll. The insurgents were much aided by three brass cannon, brought up from Huntly's castle at Strathbogie. The story of the battle is told, from the Catholic standpoint, in a long ballad—or rather a narrative poem, for it is not in the true ballad style:

> This deed sae doughtilie was done,
>   As I heard true men tell,
> Upon a Thursday afternoon,
>   Sanct Francis' eve befell.

Overlooking the junction of the Livet with the Avon is the fine ruined keep of Castle Drumin. On the Crombie Burn, a head-stream of the Livet, is Scalan, where from about 1712 the priests of the ancient faith unobtrusively maintained a humble 'college' for the training of their theological students. In 1746 the thatched building was burned by orders of the Duke of Cumberland. In 1799 the college was transferred to Auchorthies on the Don above Inverurie; and finally, in 1829 to its present imposing quarters at Blairs on Lower Deeside.

Grantown-on-Spey, some twenty-four miles above Craigel-lachie, and 712 feet above sea-level, declares itself by its name to have been a foundation of the Grant family, now represented by the Countess of Seafield. Castle Grant, the ancient seat of this fine old clan, stands, forsaken and sadly neglected, about a mile and a half to the north. The town, which claims to be the capital of Strathspey, was founded in 1765 by Sir Ludovic Grant. His prospectus proposed that the place should be a centre of wool and linen manufactories, as well as of the timber trade and carpentry; but, as elsewhere on Speyside, Grantown, now a flourishing community of some 1,580 inhabitants, today thrives mainly on visitors, including winter sportsmen. Its spacious High Street, between an avenue of trees, and its substantial white granite buildings make a most agreeable first impression, which is heightened in due course by the lovely scenery and bracing air. Looking up the Strath, the Cairngorms and the Monadhliath make a fine show on either side of the noble river; the lower slopes around are clad with pine and birch; and every time you go out of doors your nostrils are greeted with the authentic 'tang' of the Highlands—that complicated, pleasing fragrance of birch, pine, peat, and wild flowers. The fine old three-arched bridge which carried the military road from Corgarff across the Spey on its way to Fort George bears an inscription testifying that it was built in the same year and by the same force that left their record on the Well of the Lecht. It has now been superseded by a concrete bridge with a single span of 240 feet. About six miles to the north-west, in the middle of the sombre Dava Moor, once studded with crofts but now abandoned to sheep and grouse, lies lonely Lochindorb, with its island castle (p. 100). Celebrated for its trout fishing, this lake is also, like Loch Avon, haunted by a water kelpie. From Grantown a road leads northward over Dava Moor to the lower Findhorn and so down to Forres, while another link connects Grantown with the Great North Road at Carr Bridge—passing on its way the interesting ruined castle of Muckerach, a Grant stronghold built in 1598.

Four miles above Grantown-on-Spey is Nethy Bridge, another of the Strathspey resorts, which, with Boat of Garten, about the same distance further on, form excellent centres for exploring the magnificent pine forest of Abernethy. Boat of Garten takes its name from the Ferry which once crossed the river at this point. In the neighbourhood of Nethy Bridge is Castle Roy (p. 101). About six miles further on we join the Great North Road at Kinveachie, below Aviemore (p. 149). The stretch of Speyside between Grantown and Aviemore is rich in prehistoric monuments—stone circles, standing stones, cup-marked boulders and burial cairns.

The Spey valley has a place of renown in the history of Highland music. It has given its name to the special form of reel known as a 'Strathspey', otherwise called a 'twasum dance', since only two persons are engaged; as also to the lively tune to which such a dance is performed. The 'Strathspey' is a slower and graver form of reel. By far the best known 'Strathspey' takes its name from

the farm of Tullochgorum, near Aviemore, where it is believed
to have been composed in the early eighteenth century. To this
tune the Rev. John Skinner, Episcopal minister at Longside in
Buchan, and one of the most distinguished of Scottish vernacular
poets, fitted a ballad—if so it may be called—which Burns declared
to be "the best Scotch song Scotland ever saw":

> What needs there be sae great a fraise
>   Wi' dringing dull Italian lays,
> I wadna gie our ain Strathspeys
>   For half a hunder score o' them;
> They're dowf and dowie at the best,
>   Dowf and dowie, dowf and dowie,
>   Dowf and dowie at the best,
>   Wi' a' their variorum.
> They're dowf and dowie at the best,
> Their allegros and a' the rest,
> They canna please a Scottish taste
>   Compar'd wi' Tullochgorum.

Lovers of the Spey contend with vehemence that its scenery is
superior to that of 'Royal Deeside'. Be this as it may, I for one
assert that nothing on Speyside quite equals the best scenery on
the Findhorn. No less a person than Benjamin Jowett, Master of
Balliol, maintained indeed that "The Findhorn!—it is the most
beautiful river in Great Britain."

The River Findhorn rises in the heart of the Monadhliath Mountains—the long range which we had on our left hand side as we
followed the Great North Road in its descent of Upper Strathspey.
The Grey Mountains—for such, you will remember, is the meaning of the Gaelic name—are formed of Moine schists and quartzites, with some granitic intrusions. They are a fine range, which
has been unaccountably neglected by visitors to the Central
Highlands. For some thirty miles it extends north-eastward along
the Spey valley from above Garva Bridge to abreast of Grantown.
The highest summit is Carn Mairg (3,087 feet). The great dark
heathery and grassy chain, with its partly wooded flanks, almost
nowhere achieves a spectacular skyline, and hard things have been
foolishly said about its 'vast and dreary wastes' and its 'irksome
solitudes'. Yet the hill walker, as distinct from the mountaineer,
will find much to gratify him, notably in the unexpected little

pastoral valleys, long known for their excellent cattle and sheep grazing; while the higher grounds are the haunt of the grouse, the eagle, the ptarmigan, the red deer, the mountain hare, the fox, and the wild cat. The deer-stalking and grouse shooting of the Monadhliath rank among the best in the Highlands. A traverse along the crest of these mountains brings a rich reward in the varying panorama of the giant Cairngorms across the valley of the Spey. Moreover, this despised mountain range embosoms Strathdearn, the cradle of the Findhorn, which rises in Cairn Mairg; and Strathdearn is one of the least known and loveliest of Central Highland glens.

In our pilgrimage along the Great North Road we have already encountered the Findhorn where the road crosses the river above Tomatin. Taking this charming little village, therefore, as our centre, we propose to make our very brief survey of the Findhorn, turning first leftwards up the glen, and thereafter in the opposite direction, so as to track the river down to the point where it may be thought to emerge from the Highlands. The name of the valley is Strathdearn; its middle portion is known as 'The Streens'.

Civil engineers will find much to admire in the two bridges which cross the Findhorn at Tomatin. The suspension bridge carrying the road, three quarters of a mile above the village, was the gift of two enlightened lairds. The railway bridge is a majestic structure, a viaduct rather than a bridge. It is 445 yards long and 142 feet in height, and is carried upon eight granite piers, with two abutment arches at either end, while on the western side the railway is continued towards the higher ground upon a further viaduct of nine arches. The fact that it is built on a curve adds to the impressiveness of the bridge.

The explorer who follows the Findhorn up to its source finds himself penetrating the very heart of the Monadhliath. Though the sides of the glen are steep, there is flat ground alongside the river; and it is here, interspersed with heath and juniper, that the rich pasture lands are found, to which allusion has already been made. Unfortunately the Monadhliath Mountains are notorious for their sudden, vehement downpours, so that the farmlands of Strathdearn are much liable to flooding. On the upper slopes, deer have long been replacing sheep—as in their day the sheep had replaced the summer cattle-grazing, and so brought the shielings to an end. Evidence of depopulation is thus all too apparent in the frequent larachs or ruined townships and homesteads which meet us in our ascent—alas! not that this phenomenon is in anyway peculiar to Strathdearn. Cultivation ceases, more or less, in the district known as 'the Coigs', from various places so called: Coignascallan, Coignafinternach, Coignashee, Coignafearn, and Coignavullin. The word 'coig' is an old measure or portion of land signifying a fifth. Below the Coigs there is a certain amount of plantation, notably around Glenmazaran. Hereabouts the farming in olden times was regarded as very poor; it was said that "in the Coigs of Strathdearn the peat stacks are bigger than the cornyard!" Above the Coigs we emerge upon an utter desolation, impressive by virtue of its sheer loneliness. Strips of bright green grass still margin the infant river, but the broad landscape is a wilderness of boulders, pebbles and gravel, with peat bogs upon the tablelands.

This is indeed a glacial landscape. No geologist who has viewed the Monadhliath uplands can fail to be struck with the evidence of the part that ice has played in forming this desolate landscape. Particularly notable are the huge banks of coarse gravel through which the young river has cut its channel. Not that the glaciation of the Monadhliath is in any way unusual in Scotland: but their broad flat surfaces, their easy accessibility, and the fact that, not being so high, they have suffered less from post-glacial erosion than have the Cairngorms, combine to make them a favourable field for the study of the relics of intense glaciation at what has been termed the High Plateau level of the Highlands.

Returning to Tomatin, we now consider briefly the lower reaches of Strathdearn. In general, the valley here presents the same succession of 'close gorge and open reach' which we noted as a characteristic of Donside. One of the finest of the gorges is found at Pollochaig. This forms the entrance to The Streens, and was justly described by Sir Thomas Dick Lauder as "one of the most romantic passes that can be imagined". Here the river forsakes the county of Inverness for Nairnshire. For several miles the river presents us with a perfect picture of an 'incised meander', winding its way between steep and often rocky banks garnished with alder, birch, and pine. At Drynachan we encounter an Old Red Sandstone bluff, an outlier from the main Moray Firth development of this formation. At Dulsie Bridge we emerge from The Streens in one of the masterpieces of Highland scenery.

The river makes its way through a narrow gorge between granite rocks of the most fantastic shapes amid which birch and pine trees find a precarious hold, with rowan, hazel and alder by the waterside. The stream itself forms a series of deep black pools, separated by seething rapids. This gorge is spanned by a single-arched bridge of 46 feet span, built to carry the military road on its way from Grantown-on-Spey to Fort George.

The same kind of scenery, in ever-varying picturesqueness, and much enhanced by noble forests, is continued down the river as far as Randolph's Leap, at which point the Findhorn emerges from the Highlands, and therefore from this narrative. To emphasize its emergence, at Daltulich Bridge, a little above, the river passes down from Nairnshire into Moray; while at Sluie, a little below, it enters the Old Red Sandstone; and, though there still remain to be enjoyed some of the characteristic gorge phenomena of that formation (p. 164), the general character of the scenery is now of a lowland cast. Randolph's Leap is one of the most famous beauty spots in Scotland. Here the river struggles through a rock gorge about 70 feet wide above, but narrowing to no more than 8 feet at water level. During the 'Muckle Spate' of 3rd-4th August, 1829, the river here rose about 50 feet, so as totally to submerge the gorge and inundate the haugh above. At Relugas—the former residence of Sir Thomas Dick Lauder—the Findhorn is joined from the right by its chief tributary, the Divie, which, rising in the Cromdale Hills, receives on its left bank the Dorback Burn, originating in historic Lochindorb.

In the 'good old days' Strathdearn, as a principal avenue between the Highlands and Laich o' Moray, was much afflicted by caterans —descending from the Monadhliath fastnesses—to such an extent that it is said the local practice was to eat the beef before the broth, for fear lest the pot should be robbed!

In addition to its marvellous and varied scenery, Strathdearn presents us with two ancient monuments of outstanding interest: the Princess Stone at Glenferness and the belfry tower at Ardclach.

The Princess Stone, now in a frail and weather-worn condition, stands, where it has stood perhaps for twelve centuries, on a small cairn of earth and stones within the grounds of Glenferness House. This is one of those mysterious slabs carved in relief with a cross and Pictish symbols, of which, doubtless due to the presence of easily worked freestone, there are many richly decorated examples in the Laich o' Moray; but it is unusual to find one in such a remote situation as Strathdearn. On its front, the stone displays an equal-armed Celtic cross with interlacing pattern; and, underneath the cross, spiral ornament, with at the base two men apparently embracing and kissing each other. On the reverse of the slab an upper panel is carved with interlaced and possibly zoomorphic subjects; while below are Pictish symbols: the so-called 'elephant', twice repeated; the crescent and V-rod; and a very splendid double-disc and Z-rod. In front of the upper 'elephant' is an archer on bended knee about to draw his bow, and below him a hound in full cry, presumably after the archer's quarry. This fine monument, in coarse freestone, is about 5 feet 6 inches high. When the purpose of such monuments was forgotten, idle legends were invented to explain them. "There is a tradition that an Irish prince, having fallen in love with a daughter of the King of Denmark, and both having come together across to this country, they were pursued and overtaken here, but rather than allow themselves to be taken, they rushed into the Findhorn and were drowned—the pillar being raised to mark their memory, at the spot where their bodies were taken out of the river."[1]

The little square belfry tower at Ardclach stands high above the parish church, and has plainly been designed for purposes of defence. It has a vaulted basement and an upper living room, well furnished with gunloops. It bears the date 1655, which is surprising, in view of the unusual degree of peace and order which Cromwell's government enforced in the Central Highlands. From its lofty stance the bell would be widely heard, not only to call parishioners to church but also in case of an alarm. Ardclach was regarded in some sort as a gateway to the Monadhliath Highlands; and it is not without significance that in 1699 a Report of the Committee anent the Peace of the Highlands proposes that a garrison should be posted here. There is no building quite like this in Scotland. It is now under the guardianship of the Ministry of Public Building and Works.

The Highland portion of Strathnairn is much less in area than the corresponding part of the Findhorn valley. It may be held to extend from the sources of River Nairn upon the western flanks of the Monadhliath, to the point where it is crossed by the Great

[1] For Pictish symbol-stones see Chap. VIII of my *The Ancient Stones of Scotland*.

Castle Urquhart and Loch Ness
(overleaf) Canisp and Suilven

North Road, which here at Craggie makes a deep narrow bend up the valley, between Faillie and Daviot. At Daviot the river passes out from the Moine Schists on to the Middle Old Red Sandstone. The part of the valley with which we are thus concerned, about eighteen miles in length, is wholly in Inverness-shire. Mostly the river flows in a narrow glen between bare heathery hills, the glen itself being often very rugged; but there are considerable plantations and much good livestock farmland along the riverside. While pleasant and varied throughout, and not lacking in grandeur in the upper levels, the scenery is in no way comparable with that of Strathdearn. From the uplands the views across the Moray Firth towards the Caithness mountains are particularly fine. As in the case of Findhorn, the Nairn has cut its way through thick glacial gravels, and there are fine displays of kames and moraines. The river sands have long been known to contain gold, but probably not in deposits rich enough to repay commercial exploitation.

Good roads lead up both sides of the river as far as Daviot, beyond which a road is continued up to the head of the valley and thereafter over the moorland to Loch Mhor, and thence to Fort Augustus, with right-hand branches to Inverfarigaig and Foyers on Loch Ness.

We pass finally to the Great Glen, the eastern side of which pertains to the Central Highlands. Most travellers traverse the Great Glen by the road on its western side and unquestionably this provides the most picturesque and varied scenery. But the eastern road is also very fine. It follows the line of Wade's road (built in 1733–4), clinging to the Glen as far as Foyers, then ascending the River Foyers to White Bridge, and so continuing south-westwards until it sweeps round to the right, through Stratherrick and past Loch Tarf, so as to join the Great Glen at Fort Augustus. From here the military road continued along the eastern shores of Loch Oich and Loch Lochy, diverging leftwards at Letterfinlay to cross the River Spean at High Bridge; whereas the modern road, bending still more to the east, crosses the river at Spean Bridge. From the Spean valley to Fort William the old road and new do not always coincide, the present highway crossing the old road several times.

It was by Wade's road that Thomas Pennant journeyed from

The Jacobite Memorial, Loch Shiel. The railway viaduct, built in 1906, was the first to be built in Britain of ferro-concrete

Mallaig

Inverness to Fort Augustus on the last day of August, 1769. He has left us his usual observant and careful description of the route. As the basic features of the scenery remain unchanged, it seems worth while to quote what he says:

Leave Inverness, and continue my journey west for some time by the riverside: have a fine view of the plain, the Tommin [Tomnahurich], the town and the distant hills. After a ride of about six miles reach Lough Ness, and enjoyed along its banks a most romantic and beautiful scenery, generally in woods of birch, or hazel, mixed with a few holly, whitethorn, aspen, ash and oak, but open enough in all parts to admit a sight of the water. Sometimes the road was straight for a considerable distance, and resembled a fine and regular avenue; in others it wound about the sides of the hills which overhung the lake: the road was frequently cut through the rock, which on one side formed a solid wall; on the other, a steep precipice. In many parts we were immersed in woods; in others, they opened and gave a view of the sides and tops of the vast mountains soaring above: some of these were naked, but in general covered with wood, except on the mere precipices, or where the grey rocks denied vegetation, or where the heath, now glowing with purple blossoms, covered the surface. The form of these hills was very various and irregular, either broken into frequent precipices, or towering into rounded summits clothed with trees; but not so close but to admit a sight of the sky between them. Thus, for many miles, there was no possibility of cultivation; yet this track was occupied by diminutive cattle, by sheep, or by goats: the last were pied, and lived most luxuriously on the tender branches of the trees. The wild animals that possessed this picturesque scene were stags and roes, black game and grouse; and on the summits, white hares and ptarmigans. Foxes are so numerous and voracious that the farmers are sometimes forced to house their sheep, as is done in France for fear of the wolves.

Pennant gives us a vivid portrayal of the Falls of Foyers, which in his day were a noble cascade, with a total descent, in two stages, of about 200 feet. In 1894–5 the spectacular character of the Falls was much abated by the use of their water-power in connexion with the aluminium works which led to the establishment of the smart and well-sited villages of Foyers and Glenlia. This was the first occasion on which hydro-electric power was brought into use in Scotland. Alas! after seventy-one years of varying luck—including a visit from a Nazi bomber in February, 1941—the aluminium factory was closed on 22nd February, 1967; and the two villages, which in their heyday housed something like six hundred folk, are now in process of becoming derelict.[1]

Wade's road crossed the rocky gorge of the Spean by High Bridge, one of whose lofty arches is now broken down. Here were fired the first shots in the 'Forty-five'. Close to the present Spean Bridge, upon a conspicuous site, is the Commando Memorial, a superb work by Scott Sutherland. This was unveiled in 1952 by Queen Elizabeth The Queen Mother.

Fort William is now a spacious, well laid out, and bustling town of some 2,700 inhabitants, depending for its prosperity upon the large aluminium factory and its great pulp-mill, powered with electricity generated by the Lochaber hydro-electric scheme, which has necessitated the driving of a tunnel, fifteen miles long, from Loch Treig through the northern skirts of Ben Nevis. The town derives its name from a fort, the successor of the medieval castle of Inverlochy (p. 100) first built in 1655 by General Monk, dismantled after the Restoration, and rebuilt for King William by General Mackay in 1690. The town which grew up in dependence upon the garrison was originally called Maryburgh, after William's Queen. Little of the fort now remains; but the entrance gate has been re-erected at Craig's cemetery. In modern times Fort William has become a favourite holiday centre, due to its railway communications; its situation at the base of the highest mountain in Britain; the magnificent Highland scenery around; and the neighbourhood of Glencoe, with its sad old memories and recent fame as a ski-ing centre. At Fort William is the West Highland Museum; and near the town in August takes place the annual Lochaber Gathering.

Ben Nevis (4,406 feet) though the highest, is by no means the most shapely of British mountains. Round-headed, broad-shouldered and hump-backed, in fact from not a few points of view it is positively ungainly—but always impressive by reason of its sheer enormous mass and the fact that, unlike the Cairngorms, it rises from sea-level. Nevertheless certain aspects of the Ben are truly grand, notably the stupendous north-eastern cortie; while Glen Nevis, which laps round its western and southern skirts, is as fine a Highland glen as any. As might be expected, the view from the summit is extensive, though impeded towards

[1] Since the above was written it is reported that the Hydro-Electric Board are considering a plan to establish a generating unit at Foyers.

the north-east by the great massif of the Cairngorms. The Inner
Hebrides of course bulk large in the westward prospect; beyond
them is visible the long broken line of the Outer Isles; and on a
clear day a glimpse may even be got of the Ulster hills.

Geologically, Ben Nevis is a mountain of the highest interest.
It is the ruin of a great volcano of the Old Red Sandstone. The
central portion of the Ben, including its summit, is a core of
volcanic rocks, agglomerates and lavas, 2,000 feet or more in
thickness, surrounded by two concentric belts of granite, into
the inner of which, while this was still viscous, the volcanic
materials, with the platform of schist upon which they were
ejected, have sunk body-bulk. As usual on Highland summits,
the scalp of the mountain is a naked wilderness of rock-waste.

In Glen Roy, to the north-east of Ben Nevis, are the famous
'Parallel Roads', long a mystery to the early geologists, and the
theme of mythological explanations among the native Highlanders. They are now known to be simply the beaches formed by
three successive levels of a glacial lake that occupied Glen Roy,
as its waters were released, by stages, owing to the gradual melting of the Lochaber ice sheet uncovering in turn three cols which
controlled the water-level. Similar terraces are found in Glen
Gloy and Glen Spean. Lady Prestwich, wife of the famous geologist, and herself an accomplished devotee of the noble science,
has given us a vivid word picture of these three terraces, extending for seven miles along both sides of Glen Roy, and maintaining
their faultless horizontality as they girdle each flank and fit into
each recess and hollow—their course being visible from a distance
by the contrast between their clothing of coarse grass or bent and
the purple heather of the hill-slopes above and below.

Between the more or less west-east line formed by Glen Roy
and the upper valley of the Spey; the noble Loch Ericht on the
east; the Moor of Rannoch and the Blackwater Reservoir on the
south; and the fjords of Loch Leven and Loch Linnhe on the
south-east, is the vast tangle of the Lochaber mountains, presenting in full splendour every variety of Central Highland scenery,
whether in mountain, glen, lake, moorland or forest. Little inhabited, almost devoid of roads and traversed only by the West
Highland Railway, this is emphatically a region to be explored
only by him who is "prepared to take his feet in his hands".
Crofts are few and far between, and the only hope for the future

of this vast sterile area would seem to be afforestation. Yet in the eighteenth century it is said that as much as 3,000 head of cattle were exported annually from Lochaber. According to Pennant, their sale brought a gross income of about £7,500; but of this sum rents claimed £3,000, and imported oatmeal about £4,000 —"so that", he concludes "the tenants must content themselves with a very scanty subsistence, without the prospect of saving the least against unforeseen accidents." Small wonder that this sage and observant traveller found:

The houses of the peasants in Lochaber are the most wretched that can be imagined; framed of upright poles, which are wattled; the roof is formed of boughs like a wigwam, and the whole is covered with sods; so that in this moist climate their cottages have a perpetual and much finer verdure than the rest of the country.

PART TWO

THE NORTHERN HIGHLANDS

CHAPTER XII

PHYSICAL CHARACTERS

To the north and west of the Great Glen lies the vast area of country generally referred to as the Northern Highlands. Not all this country, however, is of Highland character. Along the eastern coasts of Ross and Cromarty and Sutherland runs a strip of lowland which in the north-eastern knuckle of Scotland broadens out into the spacious and fertile plain of Caithness. The low altitude and soft aspect of this eastern tract is due to the fact that the rocks are mainly sediments belonging to the Old Red Sandstone and Jurassic systems. Not pertaining to the Highlands, they therefore form no part of our present survey. The huge wilderness of mountain and moorland, with which we are alone concerned, includes some of the most inaccessible and loneliest scenery in the British Islands. Since the Northern Highlands have always been scantily peopled, it is inevitable that they should offer less of human interest than the Central Highlands which have hitherto been our theme. Therefore they will be dealt with in more summary fashion than the more populous and storied country portrayed in the first part of this book. Nevertheless, in their geological structure, physical features, natural history, and recreational facilities, the Northern Highlands offer much of interest to the tourist, scientist or sportsman. In recent years the road system has been greatly improved; hotels, guest-houses and youth hostels have increased both in number and in quality; so that year by year the Northern Highlands attract more and more visitors, and few who have penetrated their fastnesses leave without a strong nostalgic desire to come back again.

In the Northern as in the Central Highlands, the governing feature of the scenery is provided by Drumalban, the *dorsum Britanniae*, of which I spoke in Chapter II. North of the Great Glen, Drumalban extends in a sinuous line from the cluster of heights over 2,000 feet in Ardgour, the district west of Loch

Linnhe, northwards to Ben Hope (3,040 feet) overlooking Loch Eriboll in the extreme north-western corner of Sutherland. On this 'spine of Britain' the highest peak in the Northern Highlands is Beinn Dearg (3,547 feet) near the head of Loch Broom in Wester Ross. Since Drumalban lies much nearer the western than the eastern coast, it follows that in the Northern as in the Central Highlands the longest rivers flow towards the North Sea, not the Atlantic. For the same reason it also follows that the westward streams, having a steeper and more rapid descent, are endowed with greater cutting power, so that in a number of cases they have worked their sources back until they have 'beheaded' the upper waters of rivers flowing eastward. The result has been to create breaches in Drumalban and its lateral spurs, which today afford the principal avenues of communication between the North Sea and the Atlantic. A notable example of this, in the northern part of our area, is the way in which the River Naver, flowing north-wards into the Atlantic Ocean at Bettyhill, has captured the head waters of the River Ullie, which descends south-eastward into the North Sea at Helmsdale. Loch Naver and Loch Choire, which once formed the sources of the Ullie, now send their waters north-wards to feed the River Naver. Through the low country which was the scene of capture now runs the road connecting Helmsdale with Bettyhill, via Kildonan, Kinbrace, Syre, and Skelpick.

Broadly speaking, the Northern Highlands may be considered, equally with the Central Highlands, as a dissected plateau, a high table-land whose general slope appears always to have been to-wards the east. The average present height of this plateau may be estimated as about 2,000 feet. The Atlantic shores afford us a superb example of a drowned coast-line. Its long sea-lochs are true fiords, valleys first deepened by glacial action and then drowned by the sea owing to a general submergence of the land on this side since the close of the Ice Age. As often on the western coasts, these sea-lochs exhibit a shallow area or barrier near their mouths, defining the old ice-basin, while inland they often reach great depths. So also do some of the freshwater lochs: for example, Loch Morar, south of Mallaig, reaches the astonishing depth of 1,015 feet. Beyond doubt this is the deepest lake in Britain, and it has been claimed as the "deepest known hollow on any part of the European plateau, except the submarine valley which skirts the southern part of Scandinavia".

Geologically considered, the Northern Highlands consist in the main of Moine Schists (see above p. 19), with, along the western seaboard, considerable inliers of Lewisian Gneiss, that very ancient deposit of which I have given some account in my previous volume of this series.[1] By an inlier, the geologist means an area of older rock exposed by the denudation of later deposits overlying it. It appears that the Moine Schists rest upon the Lewisian rocks unconformably, that is to say, upon their worn edges. If this is true, the fact points to a vast lapse of time between the deposition of the two series. Such Lewisian inliers may be well studied in the country between Loch Hourn and Loch Carron, where they form broad belts among the Moine Schists. The Moine Schists themselves are a complicated series of highly metamorphic rocks of banded aspect. About their origin and nature much is yet to learn; but many of them seem to have begun as pebbly, sandy, muddy or limy sediments. In Arisaig and Morar current bedding and ripple marking occur. Whether driven by the wind or urged forward by a river, the currents seem in general to have set in a northerly direction, perhaps in a shallow estuary. With the Moine Schists are associated igneous intrusions, both basic and acid. What seems to be the largest of these forms an area about 25 miles in length and 18 inches breadth, to the west and south of Strath Halladale. This may be roughly described as a granitic injection complex. On the south-west side of our area another extensive granitoid injection-complex occupies a large irregular tract between Loch Duich and Loch Linnhe, covering much of Knoydart, Morar, Arisaig, Moidart, and Morven.

Along the western coastlands the Lewisian Gneiss is overlain unconformably by Torridonian sandstone, showing that the gneiss had formed a submarine platform upon which the Torridonians were laid down. Before this platform was submerged, to receive the Torridonian deposits, it will have been a much denuded land surface, generally of low relief—the oldest land surface so far recognized in Britain. It is needless here to repeat what I have written about the Torridonian sandstone in my former book. Next in age to the Torridonians come the Cambrians, the oldest fossil-bearing formation so far on record in Britain. In considering

[1] *Portrait of Skye and the Outer Hebrides.*

the Cambrians we encounter one of the most astonishing geological phenomena to be found anywhere on the surface of our globe. This is the celebrated Moine Overthrust Plane, which extends in a sinuous line from Kyle of Lochalsh on the south-west to the eastern side of Loch Eriboll upon the northern coast. Along this mighty thrust-plane a series of vast crustal movements, complex and prolonged, have carried up the Moine Schists body-bulk westward over the much younger Torridonians and Cambrians—in some places to a distance of at least ten miles! Likewise the Torridonians have in some cases been carried or rolled over the Cambrians, which originally were laid down on top of them. This is well seen on Beinn Liath Mhor (3,034 feet) north of Achnashellach, where the upper part of the mountain, composed of dark red contorted Torridonians, overlies whitish Cambrian quartzites—truly a case of a mountain standing on its head! Within the zone of the thrust, masses of the Cambrian rocks have been detached, thrown up or down to any angle, or even turned upside down. It is difficult for the non-geological reader to understand how sometimes, under conditions of enormous and prolonged pressure or stress, solid rock masses can behave as if they were pliable, or even viscous.

The Cambrian rocks of the Northern Highlands comprise a long strip of greatly varying width, which extends from Loch Kishorn to Loch Eriboll, with a detached outlier extending inland from Durness, and another at Achiltibuie on the Coigach peninsula in Wester Ross. The rocks are partly arenaceous and partly calcareous. Of the latter, the most important is the Durness limestone. Much of this is dolomitic in character, with a high magnesian content. Dolomite is used as a refractory in making steel; but unfortunately, owing to its remoteness from the centres of manufacture, it does not seem economically possible to exploit the Durness limestones. As to age, they belong to the uppermost strata of the Cambrian series, and indeed are now often assigned to the base of the next great geological system, the Ordovician. They have yielded a large assemblage of molluscan fossils, as well as those strange crustaceans the trilobites, about which I have written in my former book. Unfortunately the lime in the Cambrian sea was deposited so slowly that many of the animal remains were partly decayed before they became covered up; so that the fossils are now mostly in poor condition.

The Northern Highlands also contain patches of much later sedimentary rocks: Old Red Sandstone at the Kyle of Tongue and east of Strathy Point, as well as here and there in central Sutherland; Triassic and Jurassic strata at Applecross and elsewhere: but these are mostly unfossiliferous, and of little general importance. Mention, however, must be made of the conspicuous twin peaks, Ben Griam Mhor (1,936 feet) and Ben Griam Beg (1,903 feet), fronting each other across a moorland loch in eastern Sutherland. These are masses of Old Red Sandstone resting upon the Moine Schists. The higher summit of the pair embodies the plug of a volcanic vent.

The ancient and complex suite of rocks of which I have been trying to give a brief sketch have been moulded into their present form—the Northern Highlands as we have them—by the grinding and scouring action of moving ice; first during the period when the whole area was shrouded in an icy mantle, and subsequently when the ice-sheet had disappeared and every glen had its own glacier. During the maximum period of the general ice-sheet it is probable that only Beinn Dearg (already mentioned), An Teallach (3,483 feet), above Little Loch Broom, and Ladhar Bheinn (3,343 feet), above Loch Hourn, thrust forth their dark peaks above the white wilderness, like the nunataks in Greenland today. This vast ice-sheet was not static. On the contrary it moved slowly outward, east and west, from an ice-shed which for some reason appears to have lain to the east of Drumalban. This fact, whatever the reason, seems to be proved from a study of the sources of the 'erratics' or transported boulders which the long vanished ice-sheet has left stranded on the mountains and moorlands. On the western side of the ice-shed, the striae or scratches engraved upon the bare rock-surfaces show that there were two movements, one towards the north-westward, and the other directly to the west; but which came first is still a matter of conjecture.

Apart from its effects upon the general topography, the principal traces left by the Ice Age in the Northern Highlands are the characteristic boulder clay and the fluvio-glacial sands or gravels. In the glens there are the usual lateral and terminal moraines, and the tourist with a geological eye will detect many 'hanging valleys' and innumerable glacial lakes.

Lastly, a word about the post-glacial raised beaches. In the

North Highlands the 100-foot raised beach has not so far been detected along many of the western sea-lochs, probably because at the time of the subsidence that gave this beach its origin, these valleys were still occupied by glaciers reaching out into the open sea. By contrast, the 50-foot raised beach is well developed in Loch Torridon and in Loch Morar, now a freshwater lake.

Such then is the solid framework of the Northern Highlands. How shall we endeavour to compile a general picture of the aspect of this remote country? Sterner it is, and infinitely lonelier, than the Central Highlands. The mountains seem more closely packed, and abodes of men are few and far between. Brown and tawny moorland, black bog, and bare grey rock surfaces set the general colour-tone; while the fantastic red Torridonian peaks, Coulbeg (2,523 feet) and Coulmore (2,786 feet), Suilven (2,399 feet), Canisp (2,779 feet), and Quinaig (2,653 feet) rising above their platforms of gneiss, and in some cases capped with white Cambrian quartzite, have an eerie grandeur which neither pencil nor camera will avail to capture. Looking upon such solemn scenes, we realize how the poet felt when he penned these lines:

> Now turn I to that God of old
> Who mocked not any of my ills,
> But gave my hungry hands to hold
> The large religion of the hills.

It is, however, among the fiords of the Atlantic seaboard that the scenery of the Northern Highlands reaches its climax. Although on a smaller scale, irresistibly it reminds one of the western coast of Norway: only upon the summits around there is no eternal snow. Also in our western fiords there is probably more fertile land, relatively speaking, than in Norway. Another difference, which indeed is true for the Northern Highlands as a whole, is the comparative absence of trees—though much is being done, mainly by the Forestry Commission, to remedy this want. Three National Parks have been formed: an area of 10,000 acres between Kinlochewe and Ben Eighe (3,302 feet); a much larger one (26,827 acres), known as Inverpolly, in the north-west corner of Ross and Cromarty, around Loch Sionascaig; and the smallest (3,000 acres) above Inchnadamph. Areas of native pinewood, all now carefully conserved, exist in a number of localities—for example in Glen

Moriston, Cluanie, Glengarry, Strathglass, and Loch Maree.

Three large counties, Inverness, Ross and Cromarty, and Sutherland, make up the Northern Highlands. To them should be added the mountainous south-western corner of Caithness, culminating in the twin summits of Morven (2,313 feet) and Scaraben (2,054 feet)—isolated and conspicuous peaks, visible far away across the Moray Firth, from the coastal tracts of Aberdeen and Banff, and themselves commanding an unrivalled view of the rich cornland of Caithness. Scaraben is a quartzite mass belonging to the Moine series; but Morven has been carved out of the Old Red Sandstone, and survives as a striking proof of the former great depth of this system over what is now the Caithness plain.

So far British Rail have graciously permitted the survival of their line from Tain to Lairg, and thence up the eastern coastal plain to Wick and Thurso: the line from Dingwall by Strathpeffer and Achnasheen over to the west coast at Kyle of Lochalsh; and the line from Fort William to Mallaig. The principal roads to the north and west start from the Great Glen at Invermoriston and Invergarry, uniting at the lower end of Loch Cluanie and proceeding then westward to Loch Duich, Dornie Ferry, and Kyle of Lochalsh; from Dingall to Ullapool; from Bonar Bridge at the head of the Dornoch Firth by Lairg to the north coast to Tongue, with leftward branches to Lochinver and Kinlochbervie; and from Helmsdale northward to connect with the east-west coastal road from Thurso. This road, rounding the northern fiords and cutting across the base of the Cape Wrath promontory, pursues its winding course down the western seaboard to Gairloch and Strome Ferry. Lastly must be mentioned the road connecting Banavie, above Fort William, with Mallaig. This is the most direct access to the motor-vessel service linking the mainland with the Outer Hebrides. Much is now doing to improve and extend this road system: but bridges are urgently required to replace the ferries at Kylesku and Tongue.

Owing to their remoteness, poverty of natural resources and sparse habitation, it cannot be expected that the North Highlands should offer a rich field for the antiquary. Yet the field is by no means barren: in fact, the huge area of ground which has never been broken up for cultivation has resulted in the preservation of large numbers of prehistoric monuments which, beyond doubt, would otherwise have perished. So on the solitary moorlands and in the sequestered glens we encounter burial cairns, stone circles, solitary standing stones, stone settings—that is to say, rows of earthfast stones set up for some purpose that eludes us—earth-houses or underground dwellings, hill-forts, and here and there a lake-dwelling. Above all we find the brochs, of which the two finest examples are Dun Troddan and Dun Telve at Glenelg, mentioned in my former volume of this series.[1] Another well-preserved broch in our area is Castle Cole, picturesquely situated on an isolated rock overhanging the gorge of the Black Water, about two miles above the point where it falls into the River Brora. A third fine example is Dun Dornadilla (p. 261) in Strath More below Ben Hope.

In addition to the two fine early castles of Mingary and Tioram, described in my former volume, the Northern Highlands boast one medieval stronghold of the first class in fame and magnitude. This is Castle Urquhart on Loch Ness, now under the guardian-ship of the Ministry of Public Building and Works. It occupies a commanding position upon a promontory jutting forth into the lake; and before the water level was raised six feet in the construc-tion of the Caledonian Canal, its aspect must have been even more imposing. Occupying the site of a vitrified fort, the castle began as a motte with a double bailey, the defences of which were re-fashioned in stone during the thirteenth and fourteenth centuries. Much of the existing buildings, however, including the gatehouse and the upper part of the keep, date from after the Chiefs of Grant got possession of the castle in 1509. It has played a great part in Scottish history from Edward I's invasions until the Jacobite Rising of 1689, after which it was blown up.

Half way down the Great Glen, and steeply overlooking Loch Oich, is the shattered ruin of Invergarry Castle, a stronghold of the Macdonalds which, when not yet fully built, was burned by Cromwell's troops during the Royalist rising of 1654, restored and again given to the flames in 1746 by the Duke of Cumber-land. The remainder of Northern Highland castles are of minor importance: but mention must be made of the remote ruined tower-house of Ardvreck, situated amid wildly desolate scenery at the head of Loch Assynt. Ardvreck Castle owes its niche in

[1] For a discussion of the brochs reference may also be made to Chap. IV of my book, *The Ancient Stones of Scotland*.

history to the fact that hither, in sore distress, came the fugitive Montrose, after his last defeat at Carbisdale in 1650—only to be betrayed by the owner, Neil Macleod of Assynt. Attempts have been made to whitewash his conduct, but Royalist reaction is forcefully expressed in Aytoun's well known *Lay*:

A traitor sold him to his foes;
  O deed of deathless shame!
I charge thee, boy, if e'er thou meet
  With one of Assynt's name—
Be it upon the mountain's side,
  Or yet within the glen,
Stand he in martial gear alone,
  Or backed by arméd men—
Face him, as thou wouldst face the man
  Who wronged thy sire's renown;
Remember of what blood thou art,
  And strike the caitiff down!

In a category by itself is Eilean Donan Castle, near Dornie in Wester Ross. This fortalice, renowned in West Highland history, stands on a small rocky tidal islet at the meeting of three fiords, Loch Duich, Loch Long, and Loch Alsh, and commands a superb view over gleaming water and shaggy mountain, culminating in the 'five Sisters' of Kintail. It is said to have been built by Alexander II as a springboard for his meditated attack upon the Norse kingdom of the Isles. Certainly it was in existence in the early fourteenth century, for in 1331 the Regent Randolph had fifty 'mysdoaris' executed there:

And the hevyddis[1] of thame all
Ware set wp apon the wall
Hey on heyght on Elandonane.

In 1503 the Earl of Huntly occupied the castle on behalf of James IV, who six years later granted it to John Mackenzie of Kintail. In 1539 it was unsuccessfully attacked by Donald Gorm of Sleat, but a second attempt resulted in the capture and burning of the castle. A seventeenth-century writer describes it as "composed of a strong and fair dungeon upon a rock with another tower compasd with a fair barmkin wall, with orchards and trees, all within ane yland of the lenth of twa pair of butts[2] almost round". The

---

[1] 'heads'.   [2] i.e. bow-shots.

castle met its doom during the Jacobite venture of 1719 (p. 229), when its Spanish garrison was bombarded into surrender by men-of-war of the Royal Navy; and thereafter it was blown up. All that remained was the shattered fragments of the "fair dungeon" and "barmkin wall", together with the stump of a heptagonal tower containing a well or cistern. Almost no architectural features survived in the bleak, lonely ruin; but between 1912 and 1931 the castle was wholly rebuilt, in such a way as to embody the ancient remnants, by Lieut.-Colonel John MacRae-Gilstrap of Bailliemore—at a cost, it is said, of a quarter of a million pounds! Practically all the existing architectural features are modern; but the reconstruction was both imaginative and scholarly, and the castle, now connected with the mainland by a stone bridge of three arches, makes a noble and highly picturesque appearance. It is now maintained as the shrine of Clan Macrae.

CHAPTER XIII

SAGA TIMES

The following are the tribes listed in Ptolemy's geography as seated in the Northern Highlands: in the south-west, over against Mull, the Cerones: north of them and opposite Skye, the Creones: along the remainder of the Atlantic coast as far as Cape Wrath, the Carnonacae and Carini: in the north-east, the Cornavii; and along the eastern coast, successively towards the south, the Smertae, Lugi, and Decantae.

In post-Roman times the Northern Highlands were divided between two of the seven provinces which made up the kingdom of the Picts. The Province of Cat covered the whole country from the Pentland Firth and the Atlantic Ocean to the Dornoch Firth. When the Norse settled in Cat, they called its north-eastern portion Caithness, which means the ness or promontory of Cat. To the rest of the Province they gave the name of Sutherland, the 'southern land' from the standpoint of the Norsemen. Hence the remarkable fact that the most northerly Scottish shire is today known as Sutherland. The remainder of the Northern Highlands, south of Strath Oykell and the Dornoch Firth, formed part of the old Pictish Province of Moravia. The name survives in the modern shire of Moray; but the old Pictish Province included the whole country between the Spey and the Dornoch Firth, as well as (beyond Drumalban) a part of what is now North Argyll (see above, p. 69).

At least as early as the eighth century, the Norsemen began to settle in Cat. The circumstances of this remarkable immigration belong to general Scottish history, and need not detain us here. The reader must not imagine that the native Pictish population were exterminated or driven out. Many of the men would survive; and, as always happens in such cases, the women would be preserved, and in due course would mingle their blood with that of the invaders. Hence arose a mixed breed, known as the Gall-gael, half Celtic and half Norse. Nor, as is now becoming clear, was Celtic Christianity obliterated. This is shown by Celtic dedications and holy places surviving throughout the period when the Norse overlords were still worshippers of Odin and Thor; as well as by Celtic sculptured stones (p. 266) dating from within the Norse occupation.

Today, the chief memorials of the Norse occupation of the Northern Highlands are found in the place names—most abundant, of course, in the coastal strips and lower portions of the valleys. And philologists tell us that the old Norse language has strongly influenced the Gaelic still spoken—alas! by ever dwindling numbers in our area.

The Norse power in Scotland reached its climax during the reign of the great Jarl Thorfinn Sigurdsson, 'Thorfinn the Mighty'. He was a contemporary of Macbeth, with whom it appears that he shared the kingdom. Under his rule were Caithness, Sutherland, Ross, Moray; and he seems likewise to have had a controlling interest in Buchan, Mar, the Mearns, and Angus, as well as the Hebrides. Not until Thorfinn's death in 1064 could Malcolm Canmore, who had defeated and slain Macbeth at Lumphanan in Aberdeenshire seven years previously, call himself undisputed master of Scotland south of the Great Glen. Jarl Thorfinn was largely of Gaelic blood. A vivid description of him is furnished by the *Orkneyinga Saga*; and it is clear that in personal aspect he little resembled the conventional blond Viking type. He is portrayed to us as the biggest and strongest of men, black-haired, sharp-featured, large-nosed, and beetle-browed. A figure of international renown, he visited Rome, probably along with Macbeth. After a long life of bloodshed, he died in his bed at Birsay in Orkney, and was buried in the Cathedral that he had built there, alongside his palace—the remains of both which buildings have been excavated in recent years. A distinguished Norse scholar has described Jarl Thorfinn as "a politician on a grand scale", whose "qualities of constructive statemanship rank equally high with those of the kings who in this period made the history of northern Europe".[1]

Some of the fear of the Norse invaders entertained by the Gaelic population of the Northern Highlands survived until the early

[1] W. Brögger, *Ancient Emigrants*, pp. 150-1.

part of last century—though usually, as elsewhere in Scotland, the Vikings are thought of, in popular legends, as Danes. This last fact may well be due to the celebrated History of Hector Boece, first published in Latin in 1527, and in a Scotch translation some ten years later. Boece's work contains many fantastic stories about the doings of the 'Danes' in Scotland, and thus has been responsible for a kind of spurious tradition, certainly in the eastern Lowlands. But in the remote Northern Highlands, and among the Gaelic peasantry, who can have had scant acquaintance, even at second-hand, with the legends related by Boece, it is difficult not to recognize in the continued fear of the Scandinavian intruders a genuine memory of the terror they had inspired. Thus about 1820, when English engineers were employed in making a survey of the Duke of Sutherland's estates, the rumour spread that they had been sent by the King of Denmark, prior to an invasion of the country! And when in 1846-7 the great Danish archaeologist Worsaae travelled through Scotland collecting material for his classic pioneer study, *An Account of the Danes and Norwegians in England, Scotland, and Ireland*, published in English in 1852, he encountered some comic experiences in north-west Sutherland:

Having employed myself in examining, among other things, the many so-called 'Danish' or Pictish towers[1] on the west and north-west coast of Sutherland, the common people were induced to believe that the Danes wished to regain possession of the country, and with that view intended to rebuild the ruined castles on the coasts. The report spread very rapidly, and was soon magnified into the news that the Danish fleet was lying outside the sunken rocks near the shore, and that I was merely sent before-hand to survey the country round about; nay, that I was actually the Danish King's son himself, and had secretly landed. This report, which preceded me very rapidly, had, among other effects, that of making the poorer classes avoid, with the greatest care, mentioning any traditions connected with defeats of the Danes, and especially with the killing of any Dane in the district, lest they should occasion a sanguinary vengeance when the Danish army landed. Their fears were carried so far that my guide was often stopped by the natives, who earnestly requested him in Gaelic not to lend a helping hand to the enemies of the country by showing them the way; nor would they let him go till he distinctly assured them that I was in possession of maps

[1] He means, of course, the brochs.

correctly indicating old castles in the district which he himself had not previously known. This, of course, did not contribute to allay their fears; and it is literally true that in several of the Gaelic villages, particularly near the firths of Lochinver and Kylesku, we saw on our departure old folks wring their hands in despair at the thought of the terrible misfortunes which the Danes would now bring on their hitherto peaceful country.

Upon the great Jarl Thorfinn's death his mainland territories, so the *Orkneyinga Saga* tells us, were lost, and men "sought for themselves the protection of those chiefs that were there native-born to the dominions". From this time onwards we find the Kings of Scotland making their presence more and more felt in the Northern Highlands. Earl Thorfinn's widow, Ingebjorg, became the first wife of Malcolm Canmore, an alliance which would materially strengthen the influence of the King of Scots north of the Great Glen. The result was a period of some thirty years of comparative peace in this area; nor does it seem to have been much affected by the famous Hebridean expedition of the Norwegian King, Magnus Barelegs, in 1098. King Duncan of Scotland, Macbeth's victim, had created his nephew Moddan ruler of Cat; and, although Moddan had perished at the hands of Jarl Thorfinn, it is clear that after the latter's death the descendants of Moddan succeeded in establishing themselves in Sutherland, where, from now onwards, Norse influence appears to have been on the wane. The foundation of the See of Caithness, including the whole eastern mainland north of the Dornoch Firth, by David I about the year 1128, was a landmark in the increasing dominance of the Anglo-Norman monarchy in these remote parts. Broken up into the feudal Earldoms of Caithness and Sutherland, the lands of the old Norse Jarldom of Cat were parcelled out among feudal tenants holding their lands by military service due to the Crown.

It was in the reign of the good King David that one of these feudal incomers, Freskin of Duffus in Moray, Freskyn the Fleming as he is often called—though there seems to be no contemporary evidence for his origin—obtained those vast grants of land in Moravia and Cat which established the greatness of his family, so that in due course they became the ancestors of the powerful baronial houses of Atholl, Moray and Sutherland, which play so large a part in later medieval Scotland.

About this time took place the grim episode of the Burning of Frakok—a story which has been rightly claimed as one of the most purely Sutherland tales in the whole of the *Orkneyinga Saga*. This was among the more lurid episodes in the colourful life of that formidable character, Swein Asleifsson, of Gairsay in the Orkneys—justly styled by Eric Linklater as "the Ultimate Viking".

Frakok was the younger daughter of Moddan, King Duncan's nephew whom he had made ruler of Cat. Her career, which to put it mildly was sensational, may be read at length in the *Saga*. She and her grandson, Olvir All-ill, otherwise the Unruly, had been responsible for the burning alive of Swein's father, Olaf. Determined to take vengeance on the guilty pair, Swein, after a circuitous journey to avoid suspicion, arrived from Atholl unexpectedly in Strathullie, which the Norse called Hjalmundal —now better known, tautologically, as Strath Helmsdale.[1] It was here that Olvir and his grandmother lived. By this time the lady, in the ungallant opinion of Earl Rognvald, the sainted (though far from saintly) founder of Kirkwall Cathedral, was "a good-for-nothing old hag". Though surprised, Olvir had time to turn out with his men; but worsted in the combat, escaped, and ultimately found refuge in the Hebrides. His grandmother was not so lucky, for Swein, having plundered the house, set it on fire, with Frakok and her *entourage* therein.

As near as can be calculated, this deed of violence took place in 1140. Horrible though it may strike my readers, the burning alive of one's enemies in their homes is all too common in the sagas: in fact, it forms the central theme of perhaps the finest of them all, the *Saga of Burnt Njal*.

The first feudal Earl of Ross, as distinct from Norse Jarls or Celtic Mormaers, of whom we have a distinct portrait in the history of those turbulent and obscure times, is Ferchard Macin-taggart, who was a prominent figure in the Northern Highlands during the first half of the thirteenth century. His name declares his Celtic origin; but the fact that he was the son of a priest— Mac-in-Taggart—implies no stigma, since he was the heir of line of the lay abbots of Applecross (of which more hereafter). In

---

[1] 'Strath' and 'dale' of course mean the same thing. The modern village of Helmsdale takes its name from the valley.

history he is celebrated as the founder of the Premonstratensian Abbey of Fearn, in Easter Ross. From him the later Earls of Ross were descended, until in the fourteenth century his line ended in a lady, Euphemia, who married an Aberdeenshire laird, Walter Leslie. Her subsequent decision to take the veil led to the famous quarrel over the Earldom of Ross which culminated in the 'Red Harlaw' (see *supra*, p. 77). Earl Ferchard was a distinguished soldier, who in 1235 conquered Galloway on behalf of Alexander II. His son, Earl William, conducted the wanton and cruel invasion of Skye in 1262, which was the immediate cause of the intervention of King Haakon IV of Norway, and the campaign and battle of Largs. To that memorable event, in so far as it affected the Atlantic coasts of the Northern Highlands, it is necessary now to turn—the more so as we possess so detailed and vivid a contemporary record in *Haakon Haakonsson's Saga*.

While King Haakon's mighty armada with its warlike host was assembling in the roadstead of Bergen, an advance party under two of his captains sailed over to the northern coast of Sutherland. At Durness they landed, and "stormed a castle that was there, but the men that were there fled away. After that they burned more than twenty hamlets"—a detail which shows that the north-western knuckle of Sutherland was well inhabited in 1263. The remains of this stronghold, known today as Seanachaisteal, the 'old castle', may still be seen upon a lofty promontory thrust forth into the sea about a mile north of Durness Church. On St. Lawrence's Day (10th August) the King himself with his whole fleet of "brine-deer"—to use the picturesque term of the Saga,[1] arrived off Cape Wrath, and anchored in Asleifarvik, in another manuscript called Halsayjarvik. The name still survives as Aulsherbeg, now anglicized into Oldshore, on the west side of Durness. To the local peasantry this great fleet must have been a splendid yet awe-inspiring sight, headed by the royal galley built of oak, with its thirty-seven rowers' benches and its great dragon head plated with gold. We catch the nautical enthusiasm of the saga writer as he bursts forth repeatedly into ecstatic song:

[1] The picture of the Norwegian galleys bounding from roller to roller like a herd of deer is imaginative and poetic in the highest degree.

Ruined crofts in Sutherland: the rehabilitation of a derelict area

The sides of his galleys
Bore shields bright as suns,
Both wave-wont and sail-wont
Were ships of that king.
  The host of the king
As it skimmed o'er the main
Was like unto lightning
That springs from the sea.

Widely different were the bedraggled galleys that cast anchor in Loch Eriboll on 27th October: yet still a formidable armament, sufficient to ensure the submission of some of the local notables, who promised to bring down cattle and in pledge left a hostage on board. The sequel, however, was unexpected:

It happened that day [28th October] that eleven men of the ship of Andrew Kusi went on land in a boat to fetch water. A little after it was heard that they called out. Then men rowed to them from the ships; and there two of them were taken up swimming much wounded, but nine were found on land all slain. And the Scots had come down on them, but they all ran to the boat, and it was high and dry, and they were all weaponless, and there was no defence. But as soon as the Scots saw that the boats were rowing up, they ran to the woods, but the Northmen took the bodies with them.

It is typical of Haakon Haakonsson that, despite this gross provocation, he dismissed the hostage unharmed. With this massacre on Loch Eriboll saga-times in the Northern Highlands may be regarded as reaching their close. As a final comment, it is interesting thus to learn that in 1263 there were woods around Loch Eriboll.

One of the puzzles in Scottish archaeology is the scarcity, in these northern and western regions which the Norsemen colonized and ruled so long, of relics of their presence—particularly grave-goods. So far as the Northern Islands and Caithness are concerned, part of the explanation doubtless lies in the fact that the settlers here were not Vikings as popularly imagined, but humble peasants from the western and southern coasts of Norway, whom over-population and other causes, part political and part economic, drove to seek a new life west-overseas. But on the far side of Scotland, as I have pointed out elsewhere, the Norse settlers were Vikings in good sooth, warriors and traders who often

Ben Loyal from the Kyle of Tongue

acquired wealth—vouched for by their richly-furnished graves.[1] Yet it is strange that no such graves have been found upon the eastern side of the Minch, on the long extended coast of Ross and Sutherland, which with its numerous fiords so closely resembled the land from which the Vikings came. Perhaps the explanation is in part due to the sterility of these tracts. As the Royal Commission on Ancient Monuments remarks about Sutherland, "its western half, from its mountainous and barren character, is extremely unfavourable to the support of human life, and it need occasion no surprise that comparatively few traces of the occupation of the prehistoric people are to be found in these infertile districts". Another possible reason for the dearth of evidence of Norse settlements on the western seaboard was advanced by Worsaae. Reviewing the evidence of place-names from Cape Wrath southwards, he finds that

. . . the real Norwegian population evidently ceased at Laxfjord. Norwegian names of place are scarcely to be found on the coasts of the Highlands to the south of Sutherland. The country there was so wild, rocky and remote, that foreign conquerors could only with the greatest difficulty have maintained a position against the Highlanders, who were always prepared to make sudden and dangerous attacks from the mountains in the interior. Aware of this, the Norwegians seem to have limited themselves, on the western shores of the Highlands, chiefly to the levying of provisions along the coast, and to the plundering of cattle and other property.

The late Professor Shetelig pointed out, at the first Viking Congress held in Lerwick in 1950, that such plundering of cattle was "an old Scandinavian habit justifying, to a certain degree, seafarers' provisioning on long voyages by 'strand-hogg', the word literally meaning: securing butcher's meat by killing other people's cattle on the shore".

---

[1] *The Ancient Stones of Scotland*, pp. 123–5; *Portrait of Skye and the Outer Hebrides*, pp. 16–17, 162.

CHAPTER XIV

THE NORTHERN CLANS

The long and turbulent Age of the Sagas was succeeded by an equally long, and certainly no less turbulent, Age of the Clans. We have seen how the Earldom of Ross originated in the territories of a Celtic magnate, Ferchard Macintaggart, who cast in his lot with the Anglo-Norman, feudalizing policy of the Scottish Crown; and how likewise the Earldom of Sutherland was held by the great family of de Moravia, the descendants of Freskin, Lord of Duffus. Early in the sixteenth century this Earldom passed by an heiress to a branch of the Huntly Gordons—then mounting steadily to that climax of power in Scotland north of the Mounth, which gained for the Earls of Huntly their proud title of 'Cock of the North'. To the south-east of the Gordon territories were the lands of the Frasers and the Grants, families whose chiefs became respectively, Lords Lovat (in the early fifteenth century) and Earls of Seafield (in 1811). Farther down the Great Glen the Camerons of Lochiel had as their neighbours on the western seaboard Macleans in Morvern, Campbells in Ardnamurchan, and Macdonalds in Moidart, as well as in Glengarry. On the western coast of Ross was firmly established the powerful clan Mackenzie, whose chief in 1609 became Lord Kintail, and Earl of Seaforth in 1623—a title taken from their conquests in Lewis, referred to in my former work. Finally may be mentioned the important Clan Mackay, located on the northern coast of Sutherland. The centre of their power lay in Strathnaver, apart from the eastern coastal strip, the most fertile tract in Sutherland. In 1628 the Chief of the Clan Mackay, Sir Donald, was created Lord Reay. A distinguished professional soldier, he served the Protestant cause under Gustavus Adolphus in the Thirty Years' War, but, returning to Britain in 1644, joined the Royalists, and, after being captured in the storming of Newcastle, was released from prison after Montrose's victory at Kilsyth. Disgusted, as it would seem, with both factions, he retired to Denmark, where he died in 1649. His career has seemed worth giving in outline, even in this short sketch, as illustrating the fact that even the remotest magnates in the Northern Highlands were in touch with the wider world of politics and war, not only in Britain but upon the Continent.

Just as happened in the Central Highlands, the feuds of the northern clans were caught up in the great national conflicts of the Reformation and the Civil Wars, and in the Jacobite risings. Those clans who clustered round the Gordons supported first Catholicism, and then the Stuart cause; while the satellites of Clan Campbell were Protestants and Covenanters. All this of course is broadly speaking. On both sides there were exceptions; and indeed, as I have pointed out already (p. 81), the half-hearted support of the Gordons was a prime cause of the failure of Montrose.

The Northern Highlands are for ever associated with the catastrophe of Montrose. His last campaign has indeed all the qualities of a Greek tragedy. The story is too well known to require more than the briefest outline. Unaware that he had been secretly betrayed by his royal master, Charles II, the 'Great Marquis' landed from Kirkwall at Thurso, on 12th April, 1650, and, after capturing Dunbeath Castle, marched southward along the coastal plain of Sutherland. But his Danish, German, and Orcadian levies had little heart for the cause; and, surprised (27th April) by a Covenanting force at Carbisdale on the Kyle of Sutherland, were easily dispersed. Montrose took to the moorland; and we have already told (p. 217) how at Ardvreck Castle in the far north-west he vainly cast himself upon the mercy of Neil Macleod of Assynt. A Cavalier historian, writing after the Restoration, laments in feeling tones "the end of one of the noblest gallantest persons that age saw amongst all the wars and broils in Christendom: a captain whose unexampled achievements have famed a history; and were its volume ten times bigger, it would yet be disproportionate to the due praises of this most matchless hero".

In Viscount Dundee's Rising of 1689 the Northern Highlands played little part; but his antagonist, General Hugh Mackay, deserves mention since he was the laird of Scourie, a small estate on the north-west coast of Sutherland. This is the Mackay country; but General Mackay was an exception to the rule, for in the main his clan were Royalists. He was a brave, competent and humane soldier, who at Killiecrankie, like Cope at Prestonpans, was the victim of a mode of war in which he had no experience, and of the inferior quality of the troops under his command. After a most distinguished military career in Britain and Ireland and on the Continent, he fell at the disastrous battle of Steinkirk (3rd August, 1692). At his graveside King William observed: "there he lies, and an honester man the world cannot produce". The Dutch troops said of him that he knew no fear but the fear of God. In his native Sutherland he was long remembered as *Shenlar Mor*, 'the great general'.

During the Fifteen, the combined influence—for very different motives—of the Earl of Sutherland, Duncan Forbes of Culloden, and the notorious Simon Fraser, Lord Lovat, in the main kept the northern clans quiet, though the Earl of Seaforth was able to force his way south to join Mar's army at Perth. In marked contrast to the affairs of 1689 and 1715, the next Jacobite movement, in 1719, was wholly played out in the north-west Highlands. In March, 1719, a handful of Jacobite leaders in exile, led by the Earl Marischal, his brother the future Field-marshal James Keith, the Earl of Seaforth, and the Marquess of Tullibardine, at the head of a small force of Spanish regular troops, disembarked from three frigates at Stornoway, and thence moved across to Gareloch. The expedition anchored under the walls of Eilean Donan Castle, where they established a hutted camp; and from there sent out the Fiery Cross, in the chilly cause of 'Old Mr. Melancholy'. The little force was soon augmented by about 1,300 clansmen: but almost immediately they were attacked in front and rear; for behind them three English frigates entered the Gareloch, while in front Major-General Joseph Wightman, advancing with speed from Inverness up Glenmoriston, brought the Jacobites to battle in Glenshiel (10th June, 1719). The result was a foregone conclusion: after a stiff resistence the Highlanders broke, and the Spanish levies, 274 in all, surrendered next day. As related already (p. 218) Eilean Donan Castle was first bombarded and then blown up. Trifling enough in itself, the battle of Glenshiel has a European content, in so far as the Jacobite venture was prompted by the tortuous policy of Cardinal Alberoni, under whose forceful rule Spain, for the last time in her long and glorious history, was able briefly to play the part of a Great

Power. Spain had declared war on Great Britain, and Alberoni's intervention was directed to rouse the Scottish Jacobites as a diversion in the Hanoverian Government's rear. Our sympathy remains for those hapless victims of power-politics, the Spanish troops thus thrown ashore in far Kintail. They could neither live without bread, so they complained, nor make hard marches through such a country. One is glad to learn that the poor fellows were allowed to keep their baggage. In surroundings unfamiliar and unfriendly and in a quarrel not their own, they had quitted themselves like men. Indeed their commander, Don Nicholas Bolano, had offered to make a further attack upon the enemy.

The Forty-five broke out in a much cooler atmosphere, so far as Jacobite enthusiasm was concerned, in the Northern Highlands. The landing of Prince Charles in Moidart, the hoisting of the standard in Glenfinnan, his march to the Corrieyarrick Pass, and subsequent dash upon Perth and Edinburgh are set forth elsewhere in the present volume. In his rear, the steadying influence of Duncan Forbes, despite the machinations of Lovat, kept the northern clans for the most part quiet; and the three garrisons of Fort Augustus, Fort William, and Fort George (at Inverness) held out during the most critical period, though Inverness and Fort Augustus both fell to Prince Charles after his retreat to the north in the spring of 1746. In March the Jacobites, from their headquarters at Inverness, moved northward against the Hanoverian forces, whose commander, Lord Loudoun, pusillanimously retired before them into Sutherland. The Duke of Perth, who commanded the Jacobite expedition, pursued him as far as the head of Loch Shin, but the approach of Cumberland's army from Aberdeen deprived this successful side-show of any permanent influence upon the disastrous course of the main campaign. The horrible proceedings of Cumberland's troops, particularly in Glenurquhart, Glenmoriston, and Lochaber, in the months that followed Culloden, have left an indelible scar upon Highland memories.

In another volume I have told the story of the hunt for Prince Charles in the Outer Hebrides and in Skye. On 4th July, 1746, the Wanderer embarked at Elgol, and was rowed across to Mallaig, which his little party reached early next morning. In the country round about they skulked for several days, amidst constant alarms and in no small peril. On the 10th they reached

Borrodale, where they found the laird, Angus Macdonald, asleep in a bothy, for his house had been burned. The Chief had with him only two clansmen. John Mackinnon of the Prince's party went into the bothy first, and put the question to Borrodale, had he heard anything of the Prince? "Since I see you," replied the Chief, "I expect to hear some news of him." "Well then, I have brought him here, and will commit him to your charge. I have done my duty: do you yours." "I am glad of it, and shall not fail to take care of him," was Borrodale's simple reply; "I shall lodge him so securely that all the forces in Britain shall not find him out." For some days thereafter they lurked in a cave. Meantime rumour had got abroad that the Prince had returned to the mainland; and soon the fugitives learned that troops and vessels had come into Loch Nevis, while in the country all around no less than twenty-seven camps, containing between 500 and 700 men, were deployed so as to draw a cordon all round Clanranald's country, from Loch Hourn to Loch Shiel. Here therefore was no place to stay. With no more than three companions the hunted Prince struck northward towards Loch Hourn. After some hair's-breadth escapes, and suffering much from hunger, dysentery, lice, and midges, they passed safely by Kinlochhourn and reached the head of Glen Shiel. At Corriedoe, north of Loch Cluanie, they met with the famous 'Seven Men of Glenmoriston', sworn Jacobites who since Culloden had lurked in the Northern Highlands, vowed to undying hostility to their Hanoverian persecutors. When they saw their hunted Prince they bound themselves by a second and even mightier oath: "that their backs should be to God and their faces to the Devil; that all the curses the Scriptures did pronounce might come upon them and all their posterity if they did not stand firm to help the Prince in the greatest dangers". Under their careful guidance the Wanderer, sleeping by night in caves or sheilings, was conducted eastward and northward to Glencannich (5th August) and then southward again to the Braes of Glenmoriston, which they reached on the 12th. Heading now southward, by the 21st they had reached Achnacarry, where the Prince took a grateful leave of the Seven Men of Glenmoriston. As a farewell gift he gave them twenty-four guineas, to be divided among them. Had they betrayed him to the Government, they would have shared £30,000.

A message now came in from Cameron of Locheil, urging the

Prince to join him in his hide-out in Badenoch. On Ben Alder, overlooking Loch Ericht, the Prince, after a wretched journey in appalling weather, duly met Locheil (30th August). Still lame from his wounds—both his ankles had been broken by grapeshot at Culloden—the gallant Cameron would have knelt before his Prince. "Oh no, my dear Locheil," said Charles Edward, clapping him on the shoulder. "You don't know who may be looking from the tops of younder hills." In Locheil's miserable hut the Wanderer enjoyed his first square meal since he had landed again on the mainland. There was mutton, beef sausages, bacon, butter, and cheese, with abundance of whisky. "Now, gentlemen," said Charles with feeling, "I live like a Prince!" Here they were joined by Cluny Macpherson, who judged it safer that the Prince should remove to his own refuge, two miles away—the celebrated Cluny's Cage, of which we have a vivid description, which despite its length must not be omitted:

> The habitation called the Cage, in the face of that mountain [Ben Alder] was within a small thick bush of wood. There were first some rows of trees laid down in order to level a floor for the habitation; and as the place was steep, this rais'd the lower side to equall height with the other; and these trees, in the way of jests [joists] or planks, were entirely levelled with earth and gravel. There were betwixt the trees, growing naturally on their own roots, some stakes fixed in the earth, which with the trees were interwoven with ropes made of heath and birch twigs all to the top of the Cage, it being of a round or rather oval shape, and the whole thatched and covered over with foge [moss]. This whole fabrick hung as it were by a large tree, which reclined from the one end all along the roof to the other, and which gave it the name of the Cage; and by chance there happen'd to be two stones at a small distance from other in the side next the precipice, resembling the pillars of a bosom chimney, and here was the fire placed. The smock had its vent out there, all along a very stonny platt of the rock, which and the smock were all together so much of a colour that any one could make no difference in the clearest day, the smock and stones by and through which it pass'd being of such true and real resemblance. The Cage was no larger than to contain six or seven persons, four of which number were frequently employed in playing at cards, one idle looking on, one becking [baking] and another firing bread and cooking.

In this "very romantic comical habitation" the Prince remained in comparative security and comfort, until word came that two

French ships had arrived in Loch nam Uamh to take him off. At one o'clock in the morning of the 13th September the Wanderer quitted the Cage. Travelling overnight by Glen Roy and across the River Lochy—an adventurous ferrying in a crazy boat—to Achnacarry and so along Loch Arkaig, on the 19th Charles Edward went aboard ship in the very same place where he had first set foot on the Scottish mainland, some fourteen months before— months shot with glory and crowned with tragedy.

The Northern Highlands shared in the sweeping changes that followed upon the Forty-five: the abolition of the heritable juris-dictions; the destruction of the clan system; the proscription of the tartans and the kilt; the slow erosion of an age-old Celtic culture; the scornful discouragement of the Gaelic tongue. But something must be said about an episode that has left abiding rancour in the glens of Sutherland, and among the descendants of those who sought a new life west-overseas: the 'Clearances' of the first half of the nineteenth century.

All the evidence makes it certain that by that time the popula-tion of the Northern and Western Highlands was grossly in excess of the means of subsistence. Since the Forty-five this prob-lem had been partly solved by emigration, voluntary, sometimes assisted by the landlords and tacksmen, who, in the general rise in their standard of living owing to the combined influence of peace and anglicization, were only too prone to demand higher rents than their native tenants were willing to pay. Much in-formation and wise comment on this matter will be found in Dr. Johnson's *Journey*. He first became aware of the problem through a conversation with his host at Anoch in Glenmoriston:

From him we first heard of the general dissatisfaction which is now driving the Highlanders into the other hemisphere; and when I asked him whether they would stay at home if they were well treated, he answered with indignation that no man willingly left his native country. Of the farm which he himself occupied the rent had, in twenty-five years, been advanced from five to twenty pounds, which he found himself so little able to pay that he would be glad to try his fortune in some other place. Yet he owned the reasonableness of raising the Highland rents to a certain degree, and declared himself willing to pay ten pounds for the ground which he had formerly had for five.

The penetrating mind of Johnson clearly saw the social evil of the mass emigration which was in full swing at the time of his famous tour. In the earlier stages, so he comments:

> Those who then left the country were generally the idle dependents on overburdened families, or men who had no property; and therefore carried away only themselves. In the present eagerness of emigration, families, and almost communities, go away together. Those who are considered as prosperous and wealthy sell their stock and carry away the money. Once none went away but the useless and poor; in some parts there is now reason to fear that none will stay but those who are too poor to remove themselves, and too useless to be removed at the cost of others.

An enormous impetus was given to this mass emigration by the general introduction, in the Northern Highlands, of sheep pasture. The problem of winter fodder had been solved by the turnip. It therefore became possible to breed a better and so more profitable sheep—the black faced Linton instead of the small, white-faced native breed. The economic pull was irresistible; and so over the great Highland estates, in the North as elsewhere, small holdings were combined, and their tenants dispossessed in favour of sheep. In Sutherland the evictions caused great hardship and were sometimes conducted with violence. Houses were pulled down, and it is even asserted that the pastures were burned in order to prevent the dispossessed tenantry from returning as 'squatters'. It is fair to add that in not a few cases villages were built to house the displaced tenantry, often by the side of a sea-loch, in the hope that the erstwhile farmers might augment their living by fishing. In this way, and in building roads and bridges, the Marquess of Stafford, who in 1785 had married the Countess of Sutherland, spent about £60,000 of his own money—in those days a vast sum—between 1811 and 1833. Also it is fair to add that all the violence was not committed by the lairds and factors.

However we may judge the pros and cons of the argument, the Sutherland clearances remain a great human tragedy, the piteous memorials of which may yet be seen, in many a long-silent glen, in the ruined crofts and villages, now submerged in nettles. Nor did the clearances solve the economic problem of the Highlands. Overgrazing by the sheep led in due course to a reduction in their numbers, and so many acres of pasture land were abandoned to the stealthy encroachment of bracken. Lowland farmers, using turnips and rotation grasses, were able to support their sheep upon a smaller acreage. Free trade led to the competition of foreign wool and mutton. And so in due course over thousands of acres the tall deer replaced the lowly sheep; the hill shepherd, who had ousted the crofter, in his turn withdrew in favour of the gamekeeper and the gillie; and the depopulation of the Highlands continued as before. But now, upon many a mountain and moor, the forest finds a place beside the deer; and so a new hope dawns.

CHAPTER XV

THE ROADS TO THE WEST

In recent years the road along the west side of Loch Ness has borne a phenomenal amount of summer traffic owing to the droves of tourists hopefully questing the 'Loch Ness Monster'. One is apt to forget how long this quest has now been going on. Away back in 1932, when I was engaged in making a survey of Castle Urquhart, the Drumnadrochit Hotel was crowded with press reporters from far and near, including the correspondent of a Japanese newspaper—all patiently waiting for a glimpse of the Monster! Nor must we forget how ancient is the pedigree of the creature itself. It first appears on record in the sixth century, apparently at the time of St. Columba's famous visit to the Pictish King, Brude MacMaelchon, in his capital at Inverness: for Adamnan, the Saint's biographer, tells us how one of his monks had a miraculous escape from the ravening jaws of an *aquatilis bestia* in the River Ness! Let us hear the story in his own words:

When the blessed man [Columba] was sojourning for some days in the province of the Picts, he was obliged to cross the River Ness; and when he had come to the bank, he sees some of the inhabitants burying an unfortunate fellow whom, as those who were burying him related, a little while before some aquatic monster seized and savagely bit while he was swimming, and whose hapless body some men, coming up though too late in a boat, rescued by means of hooks which they threw out. The blessed man, however, hearing these things, orders one of his companions to swim out and bring him from over the water a coble that was beached on the other bank. And hearing and obeying the command of the holy and illustrious man, Lugne Mocumin without delay takes off his clothes, except his tunic, and casts himself into the water. But the monster, which was lying in the river bed, and whose appetite was rather whetted for more prey than sated with what it already had, perceiving the surface of the water disturbed by the swimmer, suddenly comes up and moves towards the man as he swam in mid stream, and with a great roar rushes on him with open mouth, while all who were there, barbarians as well as brethren, were greatly terror-struck. The blessed man, seeing it, after making the salutary sign of the cross in the empty air with his holy hand upraised, and invoking the name of God, commanded the furious monster, saying: "Go thou no further, nor touch the man; go back at once!" Then, on hearing this word of the saint, the monster was terrified, and fled away more quickly than if it had been dragged off by ropes, though it had approached Lugne as he swam so closely that between man and monster there was no more than the length of one punt-pole. Then the brethren greatly marvelling, seeing the monster had gone back, and that their comrade Lugne had returned to them in the boat, untouched and unharmed, glorified God in the blessed man. And even the barbarous heathens who were there present, constrained by the greatness of the miracle which they themselves had seen, magnified the God of the Christians.

The learned commentators upon this veracious story have pointed out that it is a habit of aquatic monsters in Celtic mythology to emit fearful roarings. So it is to be hoped that the indomitable watchers who each summer establish their station on a position overlooking the Loch, have included among their scientific equipment a tape recorder. But it is remarkable that in these days, when our newspapers are full of reports of marvellous appearances on the sky—'flying saucers'; 'cigar-shaped craft with port-holes and a blue halo giving out strange electrical noises'; 'white balls with four spikes'; 'bright fiery crosses'; and all the rest—public interest persists in a mere terrestial marvel like the Loch Ness Monster.

With or without the Monster as an additional lure, the road along the west bank of Loch Ness deserves all the attention that it gets from the tourist fraternity. In recent years it has been greatly improved; and work seems never to stop, as the impatient motorist, unmindful that all is designed for his own advantage, is apt to forget. Anyhow, impatience is a vice in the Highlands, which can only be enjoyed at leisure. At times the road seems barely to find room for itself between quarried cliffs and the gleaming loch, fringed usually with boulder beaches, varied by strips of purest sand; while on the landward side the cliffs and slopes are gracefully clad with birch, rowan, oak coppice, and alder. A dozen miles south of Inverness opens the noble alcove of Urquhart Bay, terminated at the far end by the fine sandstone promontory of Strone (Gaelic *sron*, a nose) crowned by the vast ruin of Castle Urquhart (see p. 216), thrust forth into the loch like a clenched fist. Glen Urquhart, which opens on the right, is large, roomy, and well-wooded. Its river is the Enrick, which midway in its descent forms a fine little lake—Loch Meiklie. From the head of Glen Urquhart a road continues over into Strath Glass, Glen Affric, and Glen Cannich. All three are Highland valleys of great beauty, each with its own distinctive variant of mountain, moorland, forest, and water. In Glen Cannich Loch Mullardoch and Loch Lungard have been combined for hydro-electric purposes; though Loch Affric, the loveliest of them all, has not been enlarged. But the most sensitive skill has been employed to reduce the scenic damage; and many will concede that—leaving altogether aside the immense public boon conferred by electricity—in these great dams of granite and concrete, and the large tranquil sheets of water which they impound, a new beauty, austere it may be and graver, has replaced the old. Nor should a tribute be withheld from the designers of the power-houses, which teach us how modern functional architecture can be adapted to Highland scenery—in total contrast to the unfeeling crudity of the Strathspey Hotel at Aviemore!

At Invermoriston, some thirteen miles farther down Loch Ness from Castle Urquhart, we turn aside up Glen Moriston. This is now *par excellence* the 'Road to the Isles'. Though the engineers seem always busy on it, it appears as little as ever capable of carrying the immense burden of summer traffic. Few more beautiful and more varied feasts of scenery are presented in Scotland than the fifty-six-miles run from Invermoriston to Kyle of Lochalsh. Moreover, it is a road steeped in Jacobite history. Here also we find that the landscape has been altered, though not greatly impaired, by hydro-electric works. At Dundreggan is a large dam, and farther up the lovely Loch Cluanie has been extended, and the road on its north side has been replaced at a higher level. Two considerable streams, Doe on the north side and Loyne on the south, pay tribute to the River Moriston about midway in its course. Near the confluence to the Doe a simple roadside monument, recently repaired, commemorates the heroic self-sacrifice of Roderick Mackenzie. The son of an Edinburgh jeweller, and an ardent Jacobite, he became one of Charles Edward's bodyguard, and men often remarked upon his personal likeness to the Prince. About the end of August, 1746, the royal fugitive was lurking in a cave at Corriedoe, a couple of miles or thereby up the Doe, watched over by the Seven Men of Glenmoriston. The garrison at Fort Augustus were aware that he was somewhere in the neighbourhood; and a party was sent out in search of him. Instead, they encountered Roderick Mackenzie, who was likewise lurking in Glenmoriston. Taking him for the Prince, they made to seize him. Instead of flying, the young man offered stout resistance, and in the end was shot down. With his dying breath he murmured, "you have slain your Prince". His bleeding head was carried back in triumph to Fort Augustus by the redcoats, who doubtless thought with rapture of the £30,000 awaiting them. But Cumberland, who was then at the Fort, had his doubts. So the grisly relic was taken to London to be identified by the Prince's valet, Richard Morison, then lying under sentence of death in Carlisle. But by the time the valet could be brought from Carlisle, the head was beyond recognition. It is satisfactory to end this gruesome story by saying that, in acknowledgment of his 'services', Morison was reprieved.

The lower part of Glen Moriston is richly wooded, but the upper part becomes progressively wilder, until at a height of 889 feet the saddle is gained at Cluanie.

Somewhere before the Loch is reached, on Wednesday, 1st September, 1773, a famous book was conceived. Let Samuel Johnson tell us the story in his own words:

> As the day advanced towards noon, we entered a narrow valley, not very flowery, but sufficiently verdant. Our guides told us that the horses could not travel all day without rest or meat, and in-treated us to stop here, because no grass would be found in any other place. The request was reasonable and the argument cogent. We therefore willingly dismounted and diverted ourselves as the place gave us opportunity.
>
> I sat down on a bank, such as a writer of romance might have delighted to feign. I had indeed no trees to whisper over my head, but a clear rivulet streamed at my feet. The day was calm, the air soft, and all was rudeness, silence and solitude. Before me, and on either side, were high hills, which, by hindering the eye from ranging, forced the mind to find entertainment for itself. Whether I spent the hour well I know not; for here I first conceived the thought of this narration.

Beyond Loch Cluanie the long descent begins into "the dark Alpine defile" of Glen Shiel. Hereabouts the scenery is extremely grand, the road conducting us through a narrow glen between two chains of stern and barren mountains: on the north Carn Fuaralach (3,241 feet) and Sgurr a Bhealaich Dearg (3,378 feet); and on the south Maol Cheann Dearg (3,342 feet), Sgurr an Lochain (3,282 feet), Sgurr Beag (2,926 feet) and Creag nan Damh (3,012 feet). At the head of Glen Shiel we pass, on the right hand, the battlefield of 1719 (p. 229). As we descend towards Loch Duich, the country opens out; and, northward and backward, the views are increasingly dominated by the Five Sisters of Kintail. Nowhere, perhaps, in northern Scotland can the characteristic scenery of the Moine Schists be seen to better advantage than in Kintail. To borrow again the eloquent pen of Sir Archibald Geikie:

The gnarled and twisted mica-schists and fine-grained gneisses tower into some of the most conspicuous heights in the west of Inverness-shire. Perhaps the defile of Glen Shiel, with its encircling group of lofty naked hills, may be taken as one of the best examples of the more savage and rugged forms which these rocks assume. Masses of bare rocks piled upon each other give a corrugated outline to the steep acclivities which, deeply cleft by the gullies of the mountain torrents and scooped into many a dark corry, sweep upwards into an array of broken serrated ridges from which rise the peaks of Glenelg and Kintail.

From Shiel Bridge our road, now rapidly descending, sweeps round the broad upper end and along the north side of Loch Duich—as fine a fiord as any in Scotland—till it brings us to Dornie Ferry: no longer now a ferry, but a handsome stone bridge which carries the road over Loch Long, a narrow and winding northward branch of Loch Alsh, its southward branch being Loch Duich. The meeting of the three lochs is dominated by Eilean Donan Castle (p. 217). Here we are on the Atlantic seaboard, and another ten miles brings us to Kyle of Lochalsh, the springboard of Skye. On the way we skirt the National Trust's estate at Balmacara. This comprises some 8,000 acres of crofting country. The mansion is now used as a residential school for crofters' children, in which special training is provided in crofting economy and agriculture.

The Faraid Peninsula, north of Durness, looking towards Cape Wrath

From Killilan at the head of Loch Long, or from Morvich in the north-eastern alcove of Loch Duich, the hardy walker can make his way over moorland and through forests to the celebrated Falls of Glomach. The water comes down in a single drop of about 300 feet, below which there is a second fall of some 50 feet: but, if one takes in the steep cataract above the falls proper, the entire descent has been computed at 750 feet. Except in times of spate, the lack of volume abates from the grandeur of the spectacle.

We now return to Invermoriston, and resume our journey up Loch Ness. The head of the Loch is found, half a dozen miles farther on, at Fort Augustus.

The Gaelic name of this celebrated place is *Cill Chuimin*, Cummein's Church. St. Cummein was the seventh Abbot of Iona, over which monastery he presided from 637 until 669. He was the author of the first book known to have been written in Scotland, a tract on the miracles of St. Columba, which was transcribed, body-bulk as it would seem, by his successor St. Adamnan into his own more famous work. Not far from Fort Augustus is his *suidhe* or seat. Such terms must surely indicate the personal presence of the Abbot, and forms a useful proof that Columba's successors at Iona continued to use the Great Glen as a natural avenue of approach to the heartland of the northern Picts.

In 1719 the Hanoverian Government began to erect, towards the root of the promontory between the rivers Oich and Tarf, a fortified barrack on the same design as the one built about the same time at Ruthven in Badenoch (p. 117). A portion of this barrack survives behind the present Lovat Arms Hotel. But in 1729–42 General Wade, feeling that something more defensible was required in this strategically important situation, midway along the Great Glen, replaced the barracks by a regularly constructed fort upon a site on the very edge of the promontory, overlooking Loch Ness—upon which, like his predecessor Monk in Cromwell's time, he placed a galley, fitted up either for rowing or for sailing, and capable of transporting fifty or sixty men. This galley, so he reported in 1725, "will be of the greatest use in conveying provisions and ammunition from Inverness to the barrack at Killyhuimen,[1] where four companies of foot have been

[1] Note the accurate phonetic transcription of the Gaelic *Cill Chuimein*.

A Speyside distillery
The chair-lift on Cairngorm

quartered since the beginning of last October". Upon his new fort Wade bestowed the name of Fort Augustus, in honour of his king's third son, William Augustus, afterwards destined justly to earn undying hatred, in Scotland and far beyond, as the 'Butcher Cumberland'. Fort Augustus was devised by Wade as the military lynch-pin and administrative centre of the garrisons established in the Highlands. Therefore it was designed upon the most up-to-date pattern of mid-eighteenth century military engineering, and must in Scotland have been surpassed only by the much larger and more elaborate Fort George, built after the Forty-five. A square enclosure, flanked by acutely pointed bastions, was surrounded by handsome administrative and barrack buildings. Each bastion enclosed a low drum tower with a conical helmet. On the old plans they look very formidable, but only one—labelled 'magazine'—served a strictly defensive purpose; the other three were respectively the girnel, the well-house, and—the 'necessary house'.

The history of war abounds with examples of 'impregnable' fortresses which, on being attacked, collapsed like a house of cards. Such, on 1st March, 1746, was the fate of Fort Augustus. Besieged for no more than three days by the Jacobites, it capitulated after a lucky shot had blown up the magazine, whose position in one of the bastions must strike the layman as unduly exposed. Be this as it may, the unfortunate commandant was court-martialled and dismissed the service. Thereafter the victorious Jacobites destroyed the Fort: so that it was not therein, but in a hut erected by the soldiery, that Cumberland inspected the gory head of Roderick Mackenzie. Subsequently Fort Augustus was restored, with a new moat and glacis. As thus refashioned, it provided accommodation for one field officer, four captains, twelve subalterns, and 280 rank and file, with four six-pounder guns. It continued to house a garrison (latterly much reduced) until 1854. Dr. Johnson thus describes his reception there, after dark on 30th August, 1773:

Mr. Trapaud, the governor, treated us with that courtesy which is so closely connected with the military character. He came out to meet us beyond the gates, and apologised that, at so late an hour, the rules of a garrison suffered him to give us entrance only at the postern.

Boswell, more specific (as usual) in such matters, records that their supper included fricassee of muirfowl, and comments with gusto of thus encountering "all the conveniences of civilised life in the midst of rude mountains".

In 1867 the Government sold Fort Augustus to Lord Lovat; and in 1876 his son handed it over to the English congregation of the Order of St. Benedict. Some of the first monks came from the *Schottenkloster* at Regensburg. This happy association, however, is not quite so appropriate as it may seem to the unwary reader, for when the 'Scotch monastery' at Regensburg was founded, *Scotus* meant, as it had meant in St. Columba's time, an Irishman; and the *Schottenkloster* at Regensburg was in fact an Irish foundation—though Scottish medieval fabulists appropriated the founder as a Scotsman from Dunkeld. Dating from about 1090, the monastery of St. James at Regensburg was the earliest Irish Benedictine house in Germany, and the church, still in use though the monastery was closed down in 1862, is famous for its *Schottentor*, one of the great masterpieces of German Romanesque sculpture. Considerable remains of the Hanoverian fort are embodied in the beautiful buildings of Fort Augustus Abbey, which was opened in 1878. Repeatedly enlarged, the Abbey, which is also a first-rate higher school for Roman Catholic boys, now forms a stately and extensive pile, with its two soaring towers, all embowered in a gracious pleasance, fronted by the broad crystal current of the River Oich, and set against a sombre back-cloth of hills, whose lower slopes are gracefully wooded.

About seven miles farther along the Great Glen we come to Invergarry, with its power-station, and the gaunt upstanding ruin of its castle (p. 216) overlooking Loch Oich. Here another mountain road ascends the River Garry, passing in succession along the north banks of Loch Garry and Loch Quoich, finally to come down upon the Atlantic at Kinlochhourn. Glengarry has suffered more than usual from the demands of hydro-electric power. Loch Garry is now twice its former length, and Loch Quoich has been enlarged by damming it and raising the water-level. There are few more majestic sights in Britain than this Loch Quoich dam, which measures 1,000 feet in length and 122 feet in height. No one should grudge these beneficent interferences with Dame Nature; and anyhow, Glen Garry is still wonderfully beautiful. A useful modern cross-country road now connects Loch

Garry, *via* Glen Loyne, with the road (already described) leading up Glen Moriston to Loch Cluanie and Glenshiel, and so over to Loch Duich on the western seaboard. Loch Loyne has likewise been involved in the hydro-electric power scheme. What led the engineers to put these famous highland lochs into harness was, first of all, the fact that the catchment area of Loch Quoich has one of the highest annual rainfalls (about 200 inches) in the Northern Highlands. This, combined with the steep gradients and the presence of convenient cross-valleys, makes the whole area ideal for the exploitation of water as a source of power. Since the last War, therefore, the whole western side of the Great Glen has become "one vast hydro-electricity producing area, utilizing, at last, the basic natural resource of this region, water, and exporting it in a practical form".[1]

Towards the upper end of Loch Oich the visitor will come across a startling roadside monument, displaying seven decapitated human heads perched on the top of a pyramid, resting upon a square base which bears a pompous inscription, in English, Gaelic, French, and Latin, commemorating, as an example of "the swift course of feudal justice", the slaughter of seven brothers, kinsmen of the young chief of Keppoch and his brother. The seven had murdered both the young men on their return from France after their father's death. The murderers had acted upon the pattern set by the husbandmen of the vineyard—"This is the heir; come, let us kill him, that the inheritance may be ours." There was, however, little of "feudal justice" in the manner in which their crime was punished. In fact, it is more truly described, on the same inscription, as an "ample and summary vengeance". According to the story, the family bard, who organized the slaying of the murderers, washed their severed heads in a well near the spot before presenting them as an agreeable trophy to the Chief of Glengarry. Ever since then, the well (which still exists under the modern road) has been known as Tobar-nan-Ceann, 'the well of the heads'. This gruesome event is supposed to have taken place in 1663, though the inscription places it "early in the sixteenth century". The monument was erected in 1812 by Colonel Alister Ranaldson Macdonnel of Glengarry. The last chief of his clan to possess his ancestral estate, he was an enthusiast for his own conception of Highland history. Up till

[1] A. C. O'Dell and K. Walton, *The Highlands and Islands of Scotland*, p. 251.

his death in a drowning accident in 1828, he always went abroad at the head of a body of retainers in full Highland costume, who were regularly posted as sentinels outside his quarters! He is said to have provided his friend Sir Walter Scott with the character of Fergus MacIvor in *Waverley*.

At Laggan Bridge the road crosses the Caledonian Canal to join the old military road down the east side of the Great Glen (pp. 201–2). Beyond this point, there is no road along the western shore of Loch Lochy. From the Wade road, a long mile west of Spean Bridge, a branch diverges westward, crosses the River Lochy at Gairlochy Inn and on the opposite side joins the road from Banavie (opposite Fort William) along the right bank of the river up to Clunes, whence it holds westward to Loch Arkaig. This fine lake, thirteen miles in length, is too seldom visited, for the road along its north bank steadily worsens till it comes to a stop at the upper end of the loch.

At the foot of Loch Arkaig is Achnacarry Castle, the seat of Cameron of Locheil. This is the modern castellated successor of the older mansion destroyed by Cumberland in 1746. Part of the ruins of the former building may still be seen beside its successor: it was built, after the Restoration of 1660, by the famous Sir Ewen Cameron (p. 83). The modern castle was erected by stages between 1802 and 1837, from designs by Gillespie Graham. The policies are noted for their fine avenue of beech trees, said to have been planted in 1745. During the Second World War, Achnacarry became a centre for the training of the Commandos.

Probably the last occasion when the power of pit and gallows was exercised in Scotland took place about 1754, therefore well after the abolition of heritable jurisdiction, when a cattle thief, caught *in flagrante delicto*, was summarily hanged, without any pretence of a trial, upon the *crochadh* or gallows tree at Achnacarry; and this in spite of the fact that the estate was then under forfeiture. No one of course can defend such summary justice. But it is well to remember some wise thoughts of Samuel Johnson upon the subject of heritable jurisdiction:

> Mountainous regions are sometimes so remote from the seat of government, and so difficult of access, that they are very little under the influence of the sovereign, or within the reach of national justice. Law is nothing without power; and the sentence of a distant court could not be easily executed, nor perhaps very safely promulgated,

among men ignorantly proud and habitually violent, unconnected with the general system, and accustomed to reverence only their own lords. It has therefore become necessary to erect many particular jurisdictions, and commit the punishment of crimes, and the decision of right, to the proprietors of country who could enforce their own decrees. It immediately appears that such judges will be often ignorant, and often partial; but in the immaturity of political establishments no better expedient could be found. As government advances towards perfection, provincial jurisdiction is perhaps in every empire gradually abolished.

To the north, across the sluggish River Arkaig, and well above the right hand side of the road, is a cave said to have lent its shelter to Prince Charles in April, 1746, during his westward flight from Culloden. To reach it, the Prince had to cross the river "up to his haunches" in the water. The throat of the glen, shadowed by umbrageous trees, is known as the Dark Mile, and the scenery here has, not unfairly, been compared with the Trossachs. Both banks of the river, and the lower margins of the loch, are beautifully wooded with pine and oak, but above the upper part is bare and desolate, and the mountain track through Glen Pean, by which the Fugitive made his way over to Loch Morar, is as wild a piece of scenery as anything of the kind in the Northern Highlands. At the head of the glen, Prince Charles with two companions obtained a night's rest in the cottage of one of Lochiel's clansmen, Donald Cameron. He arrived so exhausted that he fell asleep as one of his little party was unbuttoning his spatterdashes.

Near the lower end of Loch Arkaig a wooded islet encloses an old chapel site, the ancestral burial place of the Camerons of Lochiel. At Kinlocharkaig, the head of the loch, a barrack, the ruins of which still remain, was erected after the Forty-five: but it is said that the garrison was withdrawn after about six months.

Returning to Banavie, we now take another 'road to the isles'. It is also the railroad; for the vital line from Fort William to Mallaig has so far been spared by the London-based demolitionists of our Scottish railway system.

Near the Church of Kilmallie a lofty obelisk attracts attention. This was erected to the memory of John Cameron, eldest son of Sir Ewen Cameron of Fassifern, who commanded the 92nd Highlanders, and at their head fell on the field of Quatre Bras. The inscription is said to have been composed by Sir Walter Scott, but it seems much too pompous to be a product of his pen. From hereabouts the views of Ben Nevis, seen across the Great Glen, are particularly grand. Railway and road now closely hug the northern bank of Loch Eil, the north-western continuation of Loch Linnhe. It is a fine example of a West Highland fiord, about eight miles long. About half way along the loch is the pleasant white-harled house of Fassifern. The central part of the building is the house in which Prince Charles slept on the third night (23rd August) after the raising of the standard in Glen Finnan. The day before, "in our camp at Kinlocheil", the Prince, somewhat reluctantly, had replied to the Government's proclamation of a reward of £30,000 for his apprehension, by a counter-proclamation offering the same amount for the person of the "Elector of Hanover". It is said that the Prince, with a fine contempt, had at first proposed a reward of only £30! John Cameron of Fassifern, although a brother of Locheil, did not support the Rising, and had left his house before the Prince took possession. These were exalted days for the Young Adventurer. One of his adherents noted afterwards that "he had never seen the Prince more cheerful at any time, and in higher spirits". Yet already the practical difficulties of his audacious undertaking were making themselves evident; for during this time his little army of 1,400 men had nothing to eat but "beef roasted on the heath, without even bread or salt".

Between Kinlocheil and Glen Finnan road and railway traverse, unexpectedly, some four or five miles of lush meadowland. On entering Glen Finnan, rail and road part company, the former bearing to the right, and crossing the glen by a fine stone aqueduct. As we approach the head of Loch Shiel, the eye is caught by a lofty monument upon which many who are not Jacobites will look with deep emotion. It marks the place where, on Monday, 19th August, 1745, a day of mist and rain, the royal standard of King James the Eighth was raised by his gallant son, Prince Charles Edward Stuart. The monument consists of a tapering round tower 65 feet in height, rising within an enclosure of smooth green sward surrounded by a low wall. It was erected in 1815 by the owner of the ground, Alexander Macdonald of Glenaladale, whose ancestor had supported the rising from the outset, and despite three severe wounds sustained at Culloden, had helped the Prince in his hunted wanderings after that day of disaster. A later addition to the monument, crowning the tower, is the statue of a young Highland chief—not, as is often asserted, intended for a portrait of Prince Charles. The sculptor was John Greenshields. Inscriptions in Gaelic, Latin, and English commemorate both the occasion and the founder, who died before the monument was finished: "traveller, if you wish to celebrate the deeds of former days, pay homage here now!" Since 1938 the monument has been in the care of the National Trust for Scotland, which also possesses a restrictive agreement covering twenty-eight acres of ground, in order to secure the unspoiled beauty and (one may fitly add) the sanctity of the site.

At the foot of Loch Shiel is Eilean Fhionain, St. Finan's Isle, an ancient burial place of the Macdonalds, the heart of whose country we are now traversing. Here, on the altar slab of the ruined chapel, unprotected save by its sanctity, rests St. Finan's Bell, a Celtic missionary hand-bell similar to that at Loch Inch (p. 149). As late as the last century it was reported that "when a funeral takes place, the bell is brought down to the landing place to await its arrival, and carried in front of the procession to the graveyard". Loch Shiel is eighteen miles in length, but nowhere more than a mile in breadth. It forms the boundary between the counties of Argyll and Inverness. Roadless on either bank, the lake is traversed daily (except on Sundays), and in the evening again during the season, by a small steamer, plying between Glenfinnan and Acharacle at the root of Ardnamurchan. From Acharacle the River Shiel makes its short winding way to the Atlantic half way along the south side of Loch Moidart. That indomitable traveller, Queen Victoria, in 1873 penetrated to the remote fastnesses of Loch Shiel, and the description she has penned of it could not be bettered:

> As we suddenly came upon Loch Shiel from the narrow glen, lit up by bright sunshine, with the fine long loch and the rugged mountains, which are about 3,000 feet high, rising all round, no habitation or building to be seen except the house of Glenaladale, which used to be an inn, and a large picturesque Catholic church, reminding one, from its elevated position to the right and above the house, of churches and convents abroad. I thought I never saw a lovelier or more romantic sight, or one which told its history so well. What a

scene it must have been in 1745! and here was *I*, the descendant of the Stuarts and of the very king whom Prince Charles sought to overthrow, sitting and walking about quite privately and peaceably.

From Glen Finnan road and railway traverse a narrow, uninteresting glen, and then pass along Loch Eilt—the road preferring the north side, while the railway, coming later, perforce had to take the south. Both road and rail touch the Atlantic at the head of Loch nan Uamh: a melancholy place, for here, on the little beach at Borrodale, on the 15th August, 1745, Prince Charles, full of ardour and high expectation, landed on the mainland; and here, on 19th September, 1746, a defeated and hunted man, he stepped aboard the French vessel *L'Heureux*, sent to take him back whence he had come. Borrodale House, where the Prince slept under his first roof on the Scottish mainland, still remains in some part as he found it, though the place was set on fire after Culloden, by Captain John Ferguson, "that most abominable officer of the Royal Navy". It is now a long, low, white-harled comely house of a type common in the North-west Highlands.

Road and railway now turn north to Arisaig on Loch nan Ceall; and finally, after a journey of some forty-five miles, the terminus of both is found at Mallaig, whence the motor vessels sail forth to Skye and the Outer Isles. The bright little town, with its huddle of white-harled or painted houses looking down upon the harbour, is a busy place during the herring season, while in summer it is a centre for pleasure cruises.

Something must here be said about the famous 'white sands' of Morar, which encompass the little embayment where the troubled River Morar, descending from the lake of the same name (p. 210), enters the sea about three miles south of Mallaig. Low rocks and heathery braes, fringed with birch wood, front this beautiful, gleaming beach, while the pure white sand, extending out beneath the clear sea water, gives the latter a hue of the loveliest green. Loch Morar itself now forms a reservoir for the Hydro-electric Board, and there is an underground power-station close by the roadside. The Reformation never penetrated to this sequestered coast. Here, at Buorblach, in the days of persecution that followed the Forty-five, a humble seminary was established, almost furtively, for the training of priests. It is now represented, on a different site, by a chapel doubly dedicated to Our Lady of Perpetual Succour and to St. Cummein, the first biographer of

Columba (p. 241). On an islet in Loch Morar that venerable old scamp, Simon Fraser, Lord Lovat, was captured in June, 1746, after he had lurked there for twelve days, subsisting on oatmeal and water. His captors found the old man in a hollow tree, with his legs swathed in flannel. Impudent to the last, he died on Tower Hill with Horace's famous line upon his lips: *Dulce et decorum est pro patria mori!* Never was noble verse more shamefully soiled in the speaking.

The next great Road to the West is likewise used by road and rail. From Dingwall on the east coast it holds by Strathpeffer, Garve, the head of Loch Luichart, Strath Bran, Achnasheen and Achnashellach—a pair of lovely names!—and so down to the Atlantic at the head of Loch Carron, and along the latter to Kyle of Lochalsh, the stepping stone to Skye. The total length may be computed at just over eighty miles.

The lower part of this route is dominated from the right by the vast mass and noble outline of Ben Wyvis (3,429 feet)—a major landmark all round the inner portion of the Moray Firth. Itself one of the loftiest in the Northern Highlands, this broad-based, high-shouldered mountain commands attention by reason of its forward position overlooking an immense area of land and sea. It is a huge mass of pelitic schist belonging to the Moine series, rising in proud isolation between the deep clefts of Strath Garve and Loch Glas. From its summit, after a toilsome ascent, the visitor who has luck with the weather will be rewarded by a marvellous view. Before him to east and north is spread out the whole of the Moray Firth, with its varied coast-line extending in the one direction beyond Lossiemouth and in the other to the Ord of Caithness. Conspicuous among the sea of mountains are Ben Rinnes, the Cairngorms, and Morven of Caithness. Even in the height of summer, snow lingers in the corries of Ben Wyvis; and a tale, similar to that about the King's Tablecloth on Beinn a' Bhuird (p. 37), is told how the mountain is held from the Crown on condition that its owner shall provide his liege, upon demand, with a snowball on any day of the year!

At the foot of Ben Wyvis nestles the attractive little pleasure resort of Strathpeffer, once a spa whose chalybeate and sulphuret-ted waters, springing up from fetid Old Red Sandstone shales, were held in high esteem as a cure for a variety of ailments, real or fancied. Of more permanent value, perhaps, are the sheltered position, the pure climate, and the lush beauty of the surroundings; so that Strathpeffer still fairly maintains its popularity as a holiday centre, well equipped with the usual facilities for rest or recreation. In the neighbourhood are two places of high antiquarian interest. One is the vitrified fort of Knockfarrel, first described by John Williams in his pioneer essay on these enigmatic structures, published in 1777. Williams, a mining engineer, cut a carefully conducted section through the rampart, which must rank as probably the earliest piece of scientific excavation in Scotland.[1] The other antiquity near Strathpeffer is Castle Leod, a tall, turreted and many-windowed mansion bearing the date 1616. It stands amid finely timbered grounds. Castle Leod was one of the seats of the Earls of Cromarty. In this sheltered valley trees attain great height and girth. It is recorded that, about the middle of last century, a wind-blown chestnut tree was found to be 18 feet in girth at breast height.

Above Strathpeffer we enter sterner scenery. Here also the Hydro-electric Board has left its mark upon the transverse valley, from this part onward known as Strath Bran; for Loch Luichart and Loch Culen and Loch Achanalt are now harnessed and enlarged. Indeed the two last mentioned are now become one. All around us is a wild and barren mountain solitude, a bleak glacial landscape, closed in ahead by the giant peaks that keep their silent watch over the approaches to Loch Torridon. Railway and road, however, bear leftward at Achnasheen, and hereabouts, at a height of over 630 feet, between Moruisg (3,026 feet) on the south and Beinn Fionn (3,060 feet) on the north, we cross Drumalban. The corries of Moruisg are a temptation to the rock climber. At Achnashellach we join the River Carron, flowing westward towards the Atlantic, and begin the long descent first towards and then down Loch Carron. With every mile the scenery becomes softer and more green, with belts of timber and fields waving with corn. Road and rail now part company, the road taking the north side of the long fiord, while the railway keeps to the south. At Jeantown on Loch Carron a road branches off to the right, heading for Shieldaig on Loch Torridon. The narrowest part of Loch Carron provides an opportunity for the traveller

[1] For vitrified forts reference may be permitted to my work, *The Ancient Stones of Scotland*, pp. 75–6.

by road to cross at Strome Ferry, whence road and rail continue past the lovely village of Plockton to reach the terminus at Kyle of Lochalsh. 'Tumultuous' is the only word that can be used to describe the aspect of this most attractive townlet. The houses seem almost to have been tumbled about amid a complex of green braes and sombre rocks, all overlooking the railway station and the jetty whence the ferry boats ply busily to Kyleakin in Skye, the mountains of which loom grandly before us across the narrow strait.

Loch Carron is as striking an example of a sea-loch as can be studied in the Northern Highlands. It is gradually being shortened by the detritus brought down yearly by the impetuous River Carron. Along both sides of it the 25- and 50-foot raised beaches are well displayed, while below Strome Ferry we encounter also the 100-foot beach—a rare phenomenon on the western coast. Here the three beaches have been described as "grassy platforms, like lines of great fortifications".

The road from Jeantown to Shieldaig, mentioned above, provides the only landward access to Applecross, one of the remotest places in Wester Ross. It is reached from Tornapress by a difficult mountain track, known as Bealach nam Bo, the Pass of the Cattle. This is a route safe to use only in summer, for during much of the winter it is liable to be swept by furious gales or blocked by snow. Hairpin bends and stiff gradients—in one place as much as 1 in 4—add to the hazards encountered by the motorist. The summit is reached at 2,054 feet. From this vantage point a magnificent forward view is enjoyed of the Cuillins in Skye; while all around us are deployed the spectacular mountains of Wester Ross.

Applecross is a much corrupted version of the Gaelic Aporcrossan, the meaning of which is uncertain. This remote inaccessible village is one of the most famous early Celtic religious sites in the Northern Highlands. Hither in 673 from Bangor in Ulster, came St. Maelrubha. At Applecross he planted his monastery, and from this base he and his undaunted monks carried their missionary efforts widely throughout northern and eastern Pictland, as well as in the Hebrides. One of the greatest and most attractive figures in the evangelization of Scotland, St. Maelrubha died at Applecross on 21st April, 722:

In Alba in shining purity
Having relinquished all happiness
Went from us to his mother
Our brother Maelrubha.

His monastery at Applecross was enclosed by a famous *comraich* or sanctuary, marked out by stone girth crosses, of which the stump of one still remains. In the old churchyard still remains a Celtic cross-slab, though of a much later date than St. Maelrubha.

Long after the great missionary's death, his veneration, at Applecross and elsewhere in the neighbourhood, became associated with the "abominable and heathenish practice"—so the Presbytery of Dingwall described it in 1656—of sacrificing bulls to his memory on 27th August, his day in the Scottish Calendars, owing to a confusion with St. Rufus of Capua. The sacrifice was supposed to bring back health to the "sick and valetudinary". It is of course just another instance of the common phenomenon, familiar to all students of comparative religion, that when a higher form of faith prevails it has to come to terms with, and absorb within itself, many practices belonging to the worship which it displaces. In my former book I have told how, in a similar fashion, the cult of the sea-god Shony was fused into the veneration of St. Moluag at Eoropie in Lewis. One would greatly like to know more about the worship of bulls at Applecross. Some have sought to connect it with the bulls carved on stone which have been found in nine localities within the bounds of ancient Pictland—notably at Burghead, where no less than thirty are on record. Is it possible that among the Picts there was a cult of Mithraism, that soldier's faith which in the third century—or so at least some have contended—seemed almost to be an equal competitor with Christianity among military and influential society in the Roman Empire?

Applecross is of much interest not only to the historian but to the geologist: for, as I have mentioned already (p. 213), its little bay has been formed out of a patch of Jurassic rocks, evidently once continuous with those opposite on Raasay Island and Broadford Bay. These Applecross deposits consist of limestones overlaid by calcareous shales and sandstones. They have yielded a suite of fossils typical of their period.

The superb scenery of the mountain route from Strathpeffer

to Kyle of Lochalsh has been recognized by the railway authorities, who provide an observation coach on their morning train. Also, the railway line is a triumph of engineering, upon which it is obvious, even to the layman, than an infinity of expertise—science, skill and labour—has been expended, not to speak of the large amount of capital that has been, from first to last, sunk in the undertaking. Let not the distant politicians and unimaginative bureaucrats who control the destinies of Scotland wantonly cast aside this great national asset. With the galloping inflation of motorized transport that bids fair to strangle our road communications, the time will surely come when it will be found cheaper to resuscitate our railways, under wiser conditions of management and use, than to spend uncounted millions in driving *Autobahnen* through the intractable Highlands.

From Strathpeffer as far as Garve the route we have been following is classed as a trunk road. Thereafter, though a major line of communication, and a good road besides, it is not so accounted; while the trunk road is continued north-westward from Garve and along Loch Glascarnoch (an artificial creation for hydro-electric purposes), thence crossing Drumalban to the south of Ben Derg (3,547 feet) and so descending upon Loch Broom to Ullapool, a total distance from Garve of about thirty-three miles. A notable bit of scenery on this road is the deep canon of Corrieshalloch. Otherwise the landscape tends to be monotonous. Corrieshalloch, with thirty-five acres round about, is now the property of the National Trust. The gorge, through which the River Droma hurries in a series of cataracts, is about a mile long and 200 feet deep. The Falls of Measach, as they are called, are well seen from a suspension bridge (for foot passengers only) which has been thrown across the gorge; there is also an observation post lower down the river. The total descent of the Falls is reckoned at about 150 feet.

Ullapool began, in 1788, as one of those fishing villages founded by the British Fishing Society, with a view in this case, to re-establishing the inland population displaced by the earliest 'clearances'. It is now much more of a holiday resort than a fishing port; for the long haul by road hindered the transport of catches to the eastern markets. The neat white-harled houses, regularly deployed along the low promontory between Loch Broom and the mouth of Glen Achall, make a pleasant appearance; and if the fishing vessels are not now so much in evidence, yet the bay during the season is alive with small pleasure craft. There is a fine and safe beach, and the little town is sheltered from the cold eastern winds by the Braes of Ullapool. Since 1958, a plant for the exploitation of the local dolomite (p. 212) has been working in the town.

A sad memorial of "old unhappy far-off times" is 'Destitution Road', a mountain road, forty-five miles in length, which was made in 1851 as a relief project during the potato famine. In recent times this road has been greatly improved. It winds round from the Falls of Measach north by west along Little Loch Broom and over the root of Rhuda Mhor peninsula to Aultbea, with a later continuation southward to Gairloch. By this road splendid views are obtained of An Teallach, with its twin summits (3,483 feet and 3,474 feet). This is one of the most notable of Ross-shire mountains—a mass of red Torridonian sandstone capped by white Cambrian quartzite.

Also by the Aultbea road access may be gained to Inverewe, with its astounding garden, containing a collection, unsurpassed in Scotland, of tropical and sub-tropical plants. The garden was begun by Osgood Mackenzie, who bought the estate in 1862. The very soil had to be transported in creels to fill up hollows and crevices in what had been the bare surfaces of red Torridonian rock, or beds of black and acid peat. Moreover, before anything could be put in the soil, a shelter belt of Corsican pine and Scotch fir had to be planted. Birch, oak, mountain ash, larch, beech, and Douglas firs followed in due course; and protection at a lower level was furnished by thick rhododendron hedges. In 1932 the garden, with a substantial endowment, was given by his daughter, Mrs. Sawyer, to the National Trust; and since then the Trust, which now owns 2,125 acres hereabouts, has received help, to the tune of £10,000, from the Pilgrim Trust. It is completely beyond my competence, and moreover far outwith the scale of this book, to compile even the briefest account of the rare and exotic contents and manifold splendours of this unique garden. Reference may therefore be made to the excellent Guide Book written by the late Mrs. Sawyer, and published by the National Trust. The garden, which yearly attracts about 100,000 visitors, is best seen in May and June, though the herbaceous borders make a glorious display in August.

At Achnasheen another important road branches to the right, and makes north-westward through the mountain wilderness to the head of Loch Maree, ultimately reaching Gairloch, after a journey of thirty miles. About 10,507 acres of land on the west side of Loch Maree were in 1951 designated a nature reserve— the first in Britain. This action was taken in the first instance for the purpose of preserving one of the most important remnants of the ancient Caledonian pine forest. The Loch itself is one of the grandest in Scotland. There can be little doubt that once it was a fiord, a continuation of Loch Ewe. A subsidence of 35 or 40 feet would again convert it into an arm of the sea. Loch Maree measures twelve miles long, reaches a maximum breadth of barely three miles, and at its greatest is said to be 360 feet deep. It is ensconced between two splendid mountains, Ben Slioch (3,217 feet) in the north and Ben Eighe (3,309 feet) on the south. Ben Eighe indeed is more a range than a single summit. For a large part of the year its three main peaks are snow-clad, but even in high summer, when the sun shines on their gleaming white frontlets of quartzite, they give the impression of being capped in snow. By contrast, Ben Slioch, a mass of Torridonian sandstone founded upon gneiss, rises sheer from the shore of the loch as one vast bulk with a serrated outline. The finest scenery in the immediate neighbourhood of the Loch is to be found on the northern side, and is thus well seen from our road, which follows the southern bank. In its broadest part, near the lower end, the loch is studded with wooded islets. One of these, Eilean Ma-Ruibhe, with its ruined chapel of St. Maelrubha, gives the clue to the name of the Loch, which thus commemorates the famous Celtic missionary of the eighth century (p. 252). In the early seventeenth century the shores of Loch Maree were densely wooded with pine, oak, birch, ash, elm, and holly, which supplied material for the largest iron-smelting works in the Highlands. The site of these, on the north side of the lake, still bears the name of Furnace.

CHAPTER XVI

THE NORTHWARD ROADS;
AND THE ATLANTIC COASTS

We have now briefly to consider the three roads that lead from Lairg or Invershin respectively north-westward up Strath Oykell, and so across to Loch Assynt, Loch Inver, Scourie and the far north-west; north-westward by Loch Shin to Laxford Bridge; and due northward to Tongue. This group of roads, with their coastwise connecting links, serve the wildest, most inaccessible and least inhabited area of the British mainland. When we cross the Oykell, which flows into the Dornoch Firth, we leave Ross behind us, and now enter Sutherland, the northmost county in Scotland (excluding Orkney and Shetland). It would irk the reader were I to attempt even an outline portrait of so vast and desolate a tract. Yet, though the human interest may seem muted, the scenic and natural interests remain sublime.

The road towards Loch Assynt is remarkable for the way in which it brings successively into view the extraordinary group of isolated mountains, of red Torridonian sandstone capped, on some of them, by Cambrian quartzite: Quinag (2,653 feet); Canisp (2,779 feet); Suilven (2,399 feet); Stack Polly (2,009 feet); Coulmore (2,786 feet); and Coulbeg (2,523 feet): while to the far right is Ben More of Assynt (3,273 feet), which is the highest peak in Sutherland, forming part of Drumalban. Ben More is composed of crumpled Lewisian gneiss, with a cap of Cambrian quartzite: but the whole mass of the mountain has been thrust westward over Cambrian rocks, which crop out (much disordered) to the west in the little Glen Traligill. The most remarkable of the group is Suilven, whose abrupt sugar-loaf profile is positively startling. Of these mountains Dr. John MacCulloch in 1819 observed that they seem as if they had tumbled down from the clouds; having nothing to do with the country or each other, either in shape, materials, position or character, and which look very much as if they were wondering how they got there. Which of them all is the most rocky and useless is probably known to the sheep; human organs distinguish little but stone; black precipices when the storm and rain are drifting by, and, when the sun shines, cold bright summits that seem to rival the snow. . . . To almost all but shepherds, Suil Veinn is inaccessible: one of our sailors, well used to climbing, reached the summit with difficulty, and had much more in descending. Sheep scramble about it in search of the grass that grows in the intervals of the rocks; but so perilous is this trade to them that this mountain, with its pasture, which, notwithstanding its rocky aspect, is considerable, is a negative possession, causing a deduction of fifteen or twenty pounds a year from the value of the farm to which it belongs, instead of adding to its rent.

At the head of Loch Assynt is Inchnadamph, one of the most famous archaeological sites in Scotland. I see little profit in trying to tell the same story twice: so I may be permitted to reproduce what I have written elsewhere:[1]

What are probably the earliest traces of human presence in Scotland were found in 1926 in a group of four limestone caves some 200 feet above the present level of a brisk little burn at Inchnadamph, in remote and wild north-western Sutherland. These caves appear to have been filled with gravel by a marginal stream of melt-water, flowing alongside a glacier which then filled the valley to a height of 200 feet above its existing floor. In the caves were found the bones of Arctic animals, including the reindeer (which indeed survived in northern Scotland until the twelfth century), the cave bear, the Arctic lemming, the lynx, and the Arctic fox. Some of the reindeer antlers had been cut or scratched by man, whose presence was also revealed by burnt hearth-stones, bones burnt or split to extract the marrow, and charcoal. The high antiquity of the bones was shown by their state of fossilization—that is to say, by the degree to which the animal matter had perished or become mineralised. One at least of the caves had been occupied up to a comparatively recent time. In another, associated with the bones of a bear, were found two skeletons which clearly had been interred—but, of course, not necessarily at the time of the earliest occupation of the cave.

[1] *The Ancient Stones of Scotland*, p. 36.

It is computed that the occupation of these caves by paleolithic man must have taken place not less than 11,000 years ago.

A little below Inchnadamph, on a promontory jutting forth into Loch Assynt, stands Ardvreck Castle, of sombre fame (p. 217). Higher up is the ruin of Eddrachalder, or Calda House, a seventeenth-century mansion built about 1660 by the third Earl of Seaforth. Most unusually in old Scottish domestic architecture, Eddrachalder is built as a double tenement, with a midrib wall and twin gables at either end. "The traveller is surprised in passing through this wild region, where the ruins of ancient castles are almost unknown, to come suddenly on two such specimens, standing close together."

Loch Assynt itself exhibits all the grandeur of utter desolation. The road skirts its northern bank, and descends to the Atlantic at Lochinver, once a noted station for the herring fleets. From here the practised climber, undeterred by the experience of Mac-Culloch's sailor, may set his course for the ascent of Suilven—a mountain which, again to quote this lively writer, "fills the eye and the imagination".

Since 1956 an area above Inchnadamph, to the extent of about 3,000 acres, has been designated a Nature Reserve. While the overpowering interest here is geological, the area is also of most importance to botanists; for here, as seldom elsewhere in Scotland is found the arctic-alpine downy willow (*Salix lapponum*) as well as other rare plants. This is a land of many streams and lochans; and the springs of Assynt have long been famed for the abundance, purity, and coldness of their water.

A second road from Lairg conducts us along Loch Shin and so across Drumalban to the Atlantic at Loch Laxford, a distance of thirty-seven miles. From the head of this loch coastal roads conduct left and right, respectively to Scourie and Durness. Beyond Scourie the road continues southward in a devious course, crossing the Ferry between Kyle Strome and Unapool, and eventually joining the Lochinver Road below the head of Loch Assynt. The other road is likewise continued along the north coast of Sutherland and Caithness to Thurso and John o'Groat's.

Loch Shin is the largest sheet of fresh water in Sutherland. It is seventeen miles in length and half a mile in greatest breadth. The Hydro-electric Board have converted it into a gigantic reservoir, and by damming it have raised its level by 30 feet. A tunnel brings in to its head the water of Glen Cassley from the south, while another tunnel conducts the water from the foot of Loch Shin to the generating station at Inveran, five miles south of Lairg. Though the loch has a high reputation among anglers, it is not in itself one of the most beautiful lakes in the Northern Highlands. From its upper end, however, fine views are obtained of Ben More of Assynt. Farther on the road skirts the little Loch Stack, whose name sounds sweet in the ears of the angling fraternity. It is overhung on the west by the rugged mass of Ben Stack (2,364 feet), another of those extraordinary Sutherland mountains, consisting of Lewisian gneiss capped by Cambrian quartzite. In his remarkable pioneer book on the 'geognosy' of Sutherland, published in 1839, Mr. R. J. H. Cunningham gave the first detailed description of Ben Stack:

This singularly shaped conical mountain, rises abruptly above a rugged, but when viewed from a sufficient height, only hilly tract of gneiss country. The last named rock, dipping at an angle of 8°, forms the entire hill, with the exception of the summit, which is composed of that quartz-conglomerate so often found to pass into, and alternate with the quartz-rock. It is of very limited extent, occurring only over a length and breadth of a few hundred yards. Its position relative to the gneiss is . . . almost horizontal.

From another passage in his treatise, it appears that Cunningham had glimpsed, though only glimpsed, what, half a century afterwards, and after much controversy, has proved to be the truth, namely the colossal overthrusting that in large tracts of the northwest Highlands has actually carried older over newer rocks (see p. 212):

The instances in which both the quartz and the gneiss were found much disturbed, I did not consider sufficiently demonstrative of the inferiority of the mechanically produced quartz to the crystalline and chemically aggregated gneiss, for the very causes of these disturbances might, as has been found in other countries, have so acted as to make the oldest strata appear the highest in the order of sequence.[1]

[1] *Geognosy of Sutherlandshire*, p. 28. Like all early geologists, Cunningham of course did not realize that many gneisses are, in fact, altered sediments.

Loch Laxford is really a double name: Laxford means the salmon fiord, and this name was given to it by the Norsemen: subsequently with the decline of Norse predominance, the Gaelic prefix 'Loch' was added.

Scourie is famous as the family estate and birthplace of that devoted servant of King William, General Mackay (p. 228). Situated in a verdant alcove, this attractive little village, with its safe bathing and its facilities for exploring the superb rocky coast and the bird-sanctuary on Handa Island, is now coming into favour as a holiday resort. The improvement of the roads now in progress should enhance its prosperity. Handa Island, a mass of Torridonian sandstone, is worth visiting, not only for the sea-birds, and for its geology, but for the superb view it offers of the mainland mountains. Around Scourie itself the rocks belong to the Lewisian series and include belts of ultra-basic character, in places rich in garnets.

The third road from Lairg holds almost due north to the coast at Tongue, a distance of about thirty-seven miles. This is a rugged and desolate route, leading up Strath Tirry to its summit at Crask, at a height of 828 feet, whence there is a gradual descent down Strath Bagastie. The road is dominated on the right hand side by the imposing ribbed mass of Ben Clibreck (3,154 feet), while farther over and to the left is Ben Loyal (2,504 feet). The arduous ascent of Ben Clibreck—which is said to be in the exact centre of Sutherland—is worth making for the view it enjoys of the Northern Highlands, the northern coast, and the Orkneys. In the eighteenth century a cave on its side was the resort of a notorious cattle thief. Unlike its neighbours, Ben Loyal is an intrusive mass of syenite—a granite without quartz. This is a somewhat rare rock in Britain. With its four craggy peaks, Ben Loyal is not the least remarkable of the Sutherland mountains.

In Strath More, on the southern flank of Ben Hope, the tourist who has penetrated thus far is surprised to find one of the best preserved brochs in Scotland. Dun Dornadilla, for such is its picturesque name, still stands in places to a height of 22 feet, and its impressiveness is enhanced by its commanding situation and magnificent background. In the eighteenth century it was visited by those indefatigable travellers, Pococke, Pennant, and Cordiner. The last topographer, who had a pretty gift of writing, thus eloquently describes the scene as it struck him on 28th June, 1776:

> This venerable ruin dignifies the banks of a pleasant river which divides the dale. The verdure of the valley, not without rising corn, became a cheering scene in so dreary a wilderness; a solitary hamlet near the best-cultivated spot mingled a rural softness with the vast wilderness of the rest of the prospect. Projecting rocks, shagged with bushes, and frowning with vast length of shadows along the sides of hills of immeasurable extent; many cascades in deep-worn channels, rushing down among them, murmur their wild music to the winds and the echoing rocks; for now no plaintive bard sits listening "by the tree of the rustling leaf". Picturesque and lofty mountains terminate the view; the head of one immensely high in air, bending over its precipitous sides, seems nodding to its fall, and threatens the dale with its ruins. On every side the scenery is such as gives Dun Dornadilla a situation distinguishedly romantic, magnificently wild.

Strath More, which is served by an indifferent road branching off at Altnaharra, descends upon Loch Hope. Throughout its course the steep-walled strath is overhung by the great metamorphic mass of Ben Hope (3,040 feet), the northern terminus of Drumalban— the spine of Scotland, which we have followed, or at intervals traversed, from its southern beginning in Ben Lomond. Ben Hope is likewise the most northern 'three-thousander' in Scotland. Some of its admirers have claimed that its western front, with its grand escarpments "perhaps presents the most picturesque mountain outline in the kingdom". When Cordiner went to see Dun Dornadilla, he approached it from the north, traversing Ben Hope by the saddle between its two main summits. He tells us that this was the usual route for lightly burdened travellers between Tongue and Lairg, the lower paths being avoided because of the numerous streams, lochans, and treacherous bogs. By far the ablest writer among eighteenth-century tourists in the Highlands, Cordiner has left us a most detailed and vivid account of his traverse across Ben Hope. His eloquent narrative clearly shows how the romantic craze for Highland scenery was not started by Wordsworth and Scott. Upon all counts, his description is so remarkable that I think it proper to present it (somewhat abridged) to my readers. Cordiner was accompanied by two Highlanders who could speak English; and the party rode upon Orkney shelties:

For some time the ascent was perfectly easy; but the paths were to be sought (for scarce any two chose the same) amidst large masses of rock which projected from the soil; round stones and hillocks covered with heath filled the intermediate spaces. The ruggedness continued to increase as we approached the steeper parts of the mountain. The ponies wandered through with much seeming unconcern; but the danger of being thrown, on such road, was considerable. On showing an inclination to dismount, the guides told me "that I had better keep on horseback while the ways were good, because by and by I should be under the necessity of walking". There was but little comfort in this admonition; however, I trusted that they were exaggerating, for it was not easy to conceive in what manner the face of the earth could be more horridly rugged. But ere we had advanced an hour, I found their observation had been pertinent and just; their declaration became perfectly realised; there remained no more possibility of riding.

The vast chasms dug out by the winter torrents pouring down the steeps were so frequent and irregular that no art could avoid them: in many places the soil was entirely washed away, and left the rocky mountain bare; in other places it was stagnated in a soft and boggy state, where one might plunge to an immeasurable depth. Where the slope at any time was more level, and free of rock and bogs, the heath was rank and scraggy, and every part of the progress occasioned new fatigue. The ponies, left to themselves, followed us with great dexterity, and kept regular pace with us, whether we struggled through the brake or had occasion to jump and climb.

Sometimes the ascents were so very steep, and the ground precipitous, that we were obliged to make large sweeps, by traversing, to gain upon the hills. This toil, however, was not altogether void of entertainment; here, picturesque and moss-grown rocks overhung our way; there, passed the yawning gloom of some horrid chasm; or, from the higher eminences, looked down on the surrounding world, astonished at the greatness of the scene. About noon we arrived at a level, where there were green herbs and coarse grass, and rested that the horses might feed. It is a flat plot in the bosom of the mountain, sheltered round, except where it opens to the south-east. The day was pretty calm, and the sky clear; the air felt warm, though evidently purer. The superior distinctness of vision was exceedingly pleasant.

Soon as they thought the ponies sufficiently rested, we renewed our journey up the mountain, and got into the clouds which were hovering round its top. At first the mist only obscured our view, but felt chilly as we advanced. When we began to open the horizon beyond, sudden gusts of wind came down between the cliffs into which the summit of the mountain is divided; and the clouds were tossed about into eddies by the squalls, until they fell in showers of mingled sleet and rain. It became intensely cold. The current of air, loaded with these embryo-snows, was extremely penetrating. We quickened our pace to get beyond the highest part of our route, and soon found the difficulty of surmounting Ben Hope was over, and that we got into a milder climate again.

The Rev. Charles Cordiner, whom I have just quoted at some length, was the Episcopal minister at Banff. So far as I know, his book, which takes the form of a series of letters to Pennant, was the first treatise specifically devoted to the antiquities and scenery of the Northern Highlands. A feature of the work is the excellent illustrations, engraved from his own drawings. It is pleasant to add his opinion of the reception he had from the inhabitants of what was then an unfrequented and little known region: "The hospitality of these coasts appears no less romantic than the scenery. The being a stranger seems to be a title to every office of friendship, and to the most distinguished marks of attention and civility." Sixteen years earlier Bishop Pococke had met with a similar reception: "The people," he writes from Tongue, "are in general extremely hospitable, charitable, civil, polite, and sensible."

Tongue is one of those pretty localities to which the programme of road improvement now in progress in Sutherland offers a chance of development as a holiday resort. Hard things have been justly said about the ducal house of Sutherland in connexion with the 'clearances'; but it is not always acknowledged that there is another side to the medal. The road from Tongue westward to Loch Eriboll was made at the expense of the then Duke, who indeed built no less than eighty miles of good roads throughout north-western Sutherland since his purchase of the old Reay estates in 1829. This particular road, where it crosses A'Mhoine, a desolate soggy moorland, presented the road makers of those days with a formidable problem of construction:

> The foundation was formed with bundles of coppice wood, laid in courses across one another. A layer of turf was next placed over these, and the whole being covered with gravel forms a road of the best description. Great ditches and numerous smaller drains are excavated in different parts on either side to contain the moss water.

[The rivers Halladale, Naver and Hope were] crossed by a large flat boat, which is moved from one side of the river to the other by means of a windlass and chain, attached underneath to the boats, and connected also with the banks. These boats admit a carriage, without the horses being unharnessed; and the largest is capable of conveying 200 passengers, and of carrying seven or eight tons' weight at a time.

During the Forty-five, when the Jacobite army was encamped at Inverness, prior to Culloden, the Kyle of Tongue was the scene of a brisk little event. The Jacobites had captured H.M.S. *Hazard* and re-christened it "Prince Charles". Pursued by naval vessels, it ran ashore at Tongue and was there recaptured, with valuable stores and £12,000 in cash. Prince Charles sent a force of 1,500 men under the Earl of Cromartie to recover the money, of which he was then in sore need; but the expedition was attacked and made prisoners by the Earl of Sutherland and Lord Reay.

At Altnaharra our road touches the head of Loch Naver, whence a branch holds to the right along the north side of the loch and so down Strathnaver to the northern coast at Bettyhill. Loch Naver, a lonely sheet of water in an open and fertile but desolate valley, is famous, like the river of the same name flowing out of it, for its salmon fishing. Strathnaver is for ever associated with the Clearances. Prior to 1820 it supported some 1,200 folk: but in 1834 a topographer could write in these terms:

Now, for twenty-four miles, not a house is to be seen except shepherds' dwellings at measured distances. One cannot but regret the absence of living beings in such a scene, and of the want of those little hamlets usually seen in most highland glens, and by the sides of clear mountain rivulets. Where are these? Wormwood and a little raised turf alone mark the places where they stood; the down of the thistle comes blowing from the sod over the roof-tree, the fires are quenched, and the owners are far from the land of their fathers.

At the foot of Strathnaver on the northern seaboard is Bettyhill, so named after Elizabeth, Countess of Sutherland in her own right, who in 1785 married George Granville Leveson Gower. Her husband in 1833 was created Duke of Sutherland, whence his wife is usually known as the Duchess-Countess. Owner of great wealth, between 1812 and his death, in the year that he received his dukedom, he built 450 miles of road and 134 bridges in Sutherland: yet this is forgotten, while his memory is still loaded with the reproach of the Clearances. Originally a fishing port, Bettyhill is one of those places in Sutherland for which new prospects are being opened by the improvement of roads and the consequent development of tourism. The little bay is flanked by high dunes, and possesses a good sandy beach. The recent appearance of a caravan park must surely be regarded as a sign of the times.

My readers will not have forgotten how, in the sequestered Central Highland valley of Strathdearn, we encountered at Glenferness the Princess Stone, an outstanding example of the monumental art of the Celtic Church in Scotland. It is with even greater astonishment and delight that, in the old parish graveyard of Farr, within a mile of Bettyhill, we come across another superb example. The Farr stone measures 7 feet 6 inches in height. It displays a noble Celtic cross, standing on a long shaft provided with the characteristic 'armpits' and enclosed with a 'glory' or halo. The central boss displays a triple escaping spiral; there are similar spirals on the inner portions of the arms and crosshead, while the extremities bear panels of key-pattern. The shaft is carved with interlaced work. Interlaced work is likewise carried round the 'tumulus' or arched base of the cross: within this are carved a couple of birds with their necks entwined, so that each is pecking the other's back. In addition to this richly decorated, cross, the whole surface of the slab is highly ornamented. Above and below the cross are elaborate panels of key-pattern, and the four spandrels between the wheel of the cross and the edges of the slab are filled up with interlacing work, passing down, on the sides of the cross-shaft into a most ingenious arrangement of triple spirals. The edges and back of the cross appear to be undecorated.

Here, then, on the remote northern coast of Sutherland, we are confronted with one of the finest examples of Celtic Christian art in Scotland. There is no reason to doubt that it stands where it has stood since it was set up, in all probability about the middle of the ninth century, by an unknown craftsman in memory of a person or persons, likewise unknown. One thing at least is certain, that the stone was erected to the glory of Almighty God. But what shall we think of the Celtic Church, and the community that it served in remote Strathnaver, which could command the services of a mason-craftsman able to conceive such a masterpiece, and to execute it, not in kindly freestone, but in untractable Highland schist? And that at a period, mark you, when Strathnaver was under Norse dominion! Questions of profound importance, not to be discussed in the present context, are posed by the Farr Stone.

The church of Farr, dating from 1774, is now converted into a museum.

This is the country of Rob Donn, the celebrated Gaelic poet, who stands for the Northern Highlands as Duncan Ban MacIntyre does for the Central Highlands. His full name was Robert Calder Mackay, and he was born at Alltnacaillach, hard by Dun Dornadilla. He is a good example of what I have previously termed (p. 57) an illiterate culture. His mother, though apparently quite uneducated, had a wide and refined acquaintance with Gaelic music and poetry. Rob himself never learned to read, and earned his living as a cowherd and drover. In that capacity he entered the service of Lord Reay, but was dismissed owing to his inveterate addiction to deer-poaching. For a time he obtained other employment; but after a short time of service in the Highland Fencibles he was recalled to his former post by the indulgence of Lord Reay. He died on 5th August, 1778, and is buried in the kirkyard of Durness, where a granite obelisk, with inscriptions in Gaelic, English, Latin, and Greek, was erected by public subscription in 1829 to preserve his memory. Among those who 'have the Gaelic' no such memorial is necessary, for his fame is widely spread wherever the ancient tongue is spoken. His poems, in the Sutherland dialect of Gaelic, were published, with a Life, in 1830; and next year an English translation of some of them appeared in the *Quarterly Review*, accompanied by a memoir from the pen of Sir Walter Scott. As in the case of Duncan Ban Macintyre, many of Rob Donn's poems have a strong satirical, indeed caustic flavour. It is said that he was much in demand at weddings, merely because of the fear that, if uninvited, he would lampoon the happy couple and the guests! In general, Gaelic scholars, while acknowledging the excellence of Rob Donn's compositions, seem to regard him as inferior in poetic genius to Duncan Ban Macintyre.

The old parish church of Durness, now in ruins, was built in 1619. The re-establishment of episcopacy led, in the short interval between the accession of James VI to the English throne and the outbreak in 1639 of the wars of religion, to a distinct revival of ecclesiastical architecture in Scotland, which had fallen into squalor since the Reformation. The most interesting example of this all-too-brief renaissance is the well known parish church of Dairsie in Fife, built in 1621 by Archbishop Spottiswood. It is indeed surprising to find, in the remotest parish of the Scottish mainland, another illustration of what has been described as the Archbishop's "vast project—even that of covering Scotland in the seventeenth century with such church edifices and services as England has retained". Durness church has crow-stepped gables, a dignified, simple belfry, and in its north transept—the only one—a Gothic window with two pointed arches and a transom. The pre-Reformation font still remains. In addition to Rob Donn's monument, the churchyard contains a tombstone with the following remarkable inscription:

DONALD MACMURCHOV HIER LYIS LO
VAS IL TO HIS FREIND, VAR TO HIS FO
TRVE TO HIS MAISTER IN VEIRD AND VO 1623[1]

Pococke, who penetrated to this remote district, varies his dull factual narrative by the following account of how the peasantry fared in 1760:

The people here live very hardly, principally on milk, curds, whey, and a little oatmeal, especially when they are at the shiels in the mountains, that is, the cabins or huts in which they live when they go to the mountains with their cattle during the months of June, July and August. Their best food is oat or barley cakes. A porridge made of oatmeal, kail, and sometimes a piece of salt meat in it, is the top fare; except that by the sea they have plenty of fish in summer, and yet they will hardly be at the pains of catching it but in very fine weather. They are mostly well-bodied men, of great activity, and go the Highland trot with wonderful expedition. . . . When they were in vassalage they paid their rent in cattle to the landlord for the land they held, and for the cattle's sustenance he gave them what corn they wanted, and they were obliged to work whenever he required them. Of grain they have only barley and oats, with both of which they make cakes. They are not yet come into the use of potatoes, but are making a small beginning: in the middle and south parts of Scotland they are in plenty.

[1] var, worse: veird, prosperity.

Something must now be said about the coastal scenery of the Northern Highlands. Beyond doubt this offers the most superb fiord landscapes in the British Islands: and the visual splendour is enhanced by the geological interest. From points such as Kilchoan in Ardnamurchan, Arisaig, Mallaig, Kyle of Lochalsh, Torridon or Shieldaig, Gairloch, Poolewe, Ullapool, Kylestrom, Scourie and Kinlochvervie, the intricacies of the western coast-line can be explored by boat, if the visitor has time on his hands. But the only way to obtain a real picture of the whole tremendous sea-front is by a cruise; and this, alas! is an opportunity available to very few, for there is no one regular service of vessels plying along the entire coast. The northern coast can be similarly explored, in a local sense, from Durness, Tongue, Bettyhill, and Portskerra on the border of Caithness.

Of Ardnamurchan I have written in detail in *Portrait of Skye and the Outer Hebrides*, so that no detailed account is required here; but a few extra particulars may be supplied. This extraordinary peninsula, which since 1156 formed the political division between the Northern and Southern Hebrides, is, as more fully explained in my former work, mainly composed of the dissected roots of a vast Eocene volcano; but the eastern part of the peninsula is composed of Moine schist, while along the coasts are an interesting suite of Mesozoic rocks, some of them rich in well-preserved fossils. The name Ardnamurchan has been thought to signify 'the cape of sea-wickedness', in allusion to acts of piracy and wrecking perpetrated on its inhospitable shores. One such violent deed on the Ardnamurchan coast is in fact detailed for us in Adamnan's *Life of St. Columba*, and the story is conveniently summarized in my former work. Another name of Ardnamurchan, Sorcha, is found in the sixteenth-century *Book of the Dean of Lismore*, and is thought to signify high or mountainous. It occurs in the poem of Ossian about Fainesoluis, daughter of the King of Tiree, who is pursued by Daire Borb ("the Fierce") a son of the ruler of Ardnamurchan. The hunted maid seeks protection from Fingal:

> Then did the King of noblest mien
> Ask of the maid of fairest face
> "Whence is it thou hast come, fair maid?
> Give us now in brief thy tale."

Hearing about her sad case, Fingal grants his protection. Hard in pursuit of the maiden arrives Daire the Fierce, a gigantic figure, well mounted and fully armed. He seizes the maid, and, although single handed, furiously besets the followers of Fingal. In the end he is attacked by Oscar, Fingal's son, and the redoubted champion, Gaul, son of Morni. First Oscar kills his horse, and then Daire himself, after a fierce struggle, is slain by Gaul. And thus is vindicated the fame of Fingal as "the generous friend of all distressed". Or, as the hero-king himself says to Oscar in Macpherson's epic: "my arm was the support of the injured; and the weak rested behind the lightning of my steel".

At Strontian,[1] near the head of Loch Sunart, Arruindle Wood, being an area of some 283 acres of naturally regenerated oak trees, in 1961 was designated a Forest Nature Reserve. Strontian is otherwise notable for the remarkable suite of minerals yielded by its igneous rock. One of these, strontianite, takes its name from the locality. From it the element strontium, discovered in 1787, is extracted. Since the early eighteenth century the lead ores of Strontian have been intermittently worked, but production for the time being has ceased. Their exploitation led in 1723 to a remarkable development, when the locality was purchased by a Peeblesshire laird, Sir Alexander Murray of Stanhope, who established there a mining village which he designated New York—one must presume in hopeful rivalry with the famous American city! To his new foundation he brought some five hundred mine workers, most of whom were English. Their intrusion was furiously resented by the Celtic natives, who destroyed their houses. Later the mines were acquired by the York Buildings Company; but the new owners were no more successful here than elsewhere, and nothing now remains of the Scottish New York. Strontium is a metallic element, and is used for various industrial purposes, such as the refining of sugar and the production of a red colour in fireworks.

Glenelg, and its satellite Glenbeg, the latter with its two famous brochs, have also been dealt with in my former book. From the *hinterland*, Glenelg is approached over the famous Mam Rattachan Pass, across which Johnson and Boswell in 1773 rode over to Skye. The steep and devious ascent, with several hairpin bends, reaches the summit at 1,116 feet. This point marks the boundary

[1] The accent is on the second vowel.

between Inverness and Ross. "Upon one of the precipices," says Johnson, "my horse, weary with the steepness of the rise, staggered a little, and I called in haste to the Highlander to hold him. This was the only moment of my journey in which I thought myself endangered." Modern plantations have obscured the fine views formerly obtained in traversing this pass.

It is extraordinarily difficult to present a generalized description of the coastal scenery of the Northern Highlands. As I have said already, the long narrow fiords, like those of Norway, are simply drowned valleys, created by land subsidence in post glacial times. Between them are imposing frontlets of cliff, ravaged into a fantastic sequence of gullies, caves, pinnacles, stacks, and skerries by the ceaseless battering of the Atlantic waves. Naturally the effects produced by this age-long, unrelenting assault will vary according to the rocks that are its victims. Thus the Lewisian Gneiss produces the distinctive coastal scenery found in Assynt, and particularly in the stupendous 300-foot precipices of Cape Wrath. The contorted bedding and varied composition of the gneiss, with its bands of pale quartz and felspar alternating with dark hornblende biotite and the numerous joints by which it is intersected; the intrusive veins of granite and pegmatite that traverse it in all directions; combine to offer a resistance very unequal indeed to the titanic oceanic battery. Nowhere is this more strikingly seen than at and around Cape Wrath. Here the remorseless waves have sought out and exploited every weakness of the rock structure. They have forced apart and enlarged the natural jointing; they have shied away from the stubborn veins of granite and pegmatite; they have dislodged entire masses, rolled them backward and forward until they were reduced to pebbles and boulders: and, using these as battering missiles like a medieval trebuchet or mangonel, they have hammered the obdurate rock faces amid an age-long uproar, by which, in times of tempest, even the hoarse scream of uncounted thousands of sea-fowl is rendered inaudible.

Widely different is the effect of the oceanic siege upon the red Torridonian sandstones. More homogeneous in composition, these broad, well-bedded, usually horizontal, and very resistant masses tend to dissect into frontages more uniform and less confused: the cliffs thus are apt to be mural in aspect. As seen from a little distance out at sea, a striking effect is produced where the low tumbled irregular masses of gneiss are seen to be overlaid by the lofty Torridonian escarpments, and crowned in the background by the astonishing isolated peaks of Stack Polly, Coul Beg, Coul More, Suilven and Canisp. This is well seen as you sail into Loch Inver from Soyea Isle. If the sky be clear and the sun in the right quarter, the colour contrast between the gray gneiss, the red Torridonian, and the white caps of Cambrian quartzite is unforgettable.

A third type of scenery is provided by the Durness limestone. As is well known, limestone is a soluble rock. Thus the River Dionard, which empties itself into the Kyle of Durness, has dissolved the base of the rocks on either side, so that their upper parts overhang the stream in a singular fashion. Along the coast itself, the limestone has been similarly dissolved into a series of caverns, of which the most famous is the Cave of Smoo, which can only be explored by boat. The limestone here is horizontally bedded. The cave is entered through an arch 53 feet in height. This admits the visitor to the first cavern, 200 feet by 110 feet. A central pier helps to support the roof. A second compartment, entered from the first, measures about 70 feet by 30 feet. This compartment has two openings in its vault. The first affords a glimpse of the sky, which seems curiously remote and unreal. Down the second opening a cataract plunges with ceaseless thunder into the lake, having an estimated fall of about 80 feet. Finally a difficult access is obtained to a third and totally dark compartment, or rather a subterranean cleft, about 120 feet long, 8 feet wide, varying in height from 12 to 40 feet, and ending in a deep black pool. This long passage is filled with fantastic stalactites: but unfortunately these are mostly a dingy brown in colour. Many writers, from Pococke onwards, have sought to portray this astonishing multiple cavern, which probably is without its like on the British coast. The most graphic and detailed description will be found in the diary of Sir Walter Scott, who on 19th August, 1814, thoroughly explored the cave, at the cost of some hardship, and not without risk to himself and his party.

St. Benedict's Abbey, incorporating Fort Augustus

Glen Glass and Ben Wyvis

TODAY AND TOMORROW

At the close of Chapter 12 we had a glimpse of the wretched life endured by many Highlanders in the 'good old days'. The reader who has followed me thus far will have had it constantly borne in upon him that today the Highland scene is changing very rapidly. Without any doubt, by the time this book appears in print it will already be out of date in not a few particulars. What then can we forecast about the future of the Highlands and the way of life of their inhabitants?

It has been contended in this book that the racial, historical, social, and economic differences between Lowlands and Highlands have tended to be overstressed. In the same way, the problems that beset the Highlands today, the fears and hopes of those who care for the mountains and the moorlands and the glens, and for the folk who win a living among them, differ in kind rather than in degree from the problems facing Scotland as a whole. Only they are hardened by the remoteness of the Highlands and their lack of natural resources.

Undoubtedly the main problem is that of continued decline in population. This takes the form not merely of outright emigration from the Highlands, which can be easily assessed in terms of statistics, but of a steady migration of the people within the area, from the glens and the moorlands to the towns and villages. Of this it is not nearly so easy to obtain numerical particulars. But the fact that the people are forsaking the hill country, whether to congregate in the towns that border it, or to migrate into the Lowlands, or to desert Scotland altogether, is not in doubt. Many are the schemes and large the moneys which successive British Governments have devised and made available to arrest the decay of the Highlands.

Of these the most promising undoubtedly is the Highlands and

The Farr stone

Tongue

Islands Development Board, set up in 1964 and provided with sufficient financial resources to help existing undertakings and to sponsor new ones. It is most unfortunate that certain proposals of the Board have resulted in acute controversy and personal animosities; also that ministerial statements have aroused a doubt whether the Board will have a free hand to spend money in a big way on well-conceived projects. The most ambitious of these proposals aims to construct a vast industrial complex, forming a continuous linear city, with a total population of 300,000, all round the inner alcove of the Moray Firth from Nairn to Tain, and using the harbour facilities provided by the great landlocked basin at Invergordon—a natural harbour which proved its value as a naval base during the two World Wars. The intention appears to be that this town should be based mainly upon the petro-chemical and fertilizing industries. Obviously this proposed new city or urban agglomerate would exert a profound economic and social influence upon the whole of the Scottish Highlands. Some consideration of the project is therefore necessary here.

Many people doubt the long-term prospects of such a town. The future of the petro-chemical industries, their eventual location in a world where the centres of production are situated in politically unstable countries and therefore liable to change, the cut-throat international competition and the remoteness of Invergordon from the main British markets—all these considerations have aroused misgivings as to the feasibility of the project. To what extent would it contribute to arresting Highland depopulation? Rather would it not tempt the Highlanders still more to desert their boundaries and flock down into the Moray Firth alcove? Would not the prospect of high wages and cheap urban satisfactions tempt workers away from agriculture, forestry, and the small-scale industries already established in the Highlands? Conversely, would the new urban agglomerate come to be manned mainly by imported technicians, *entrepreneurs* and tycoons, to the still further weakening of the Highland way of life and culture? This misgiving, in itself a very real one, has not been allayed by certain pronouncements of the Chairman of the Board which suggest a doubt in his mind as to the future of what may be described as Scotland's Celtic heritage. Should it not rather be the purpose of the Board—so it is contended—to help the Highlanders to stay within their own territory, and to maintain, as far as possible, their ancient language, *ethos* and institutions? Such critics take the view that the Board's aim should be to promote or help small-scale industries within the Highland area, rather than to establish such a manufacturing colossus on its rim.

Another line of objection is found in the assumption that much of the enormous capital required for such a venture would have to be provided from America. Would the foreign investors always retain their interest in this peripheral Scottish enterprise? In the event of a slump in the petro-chemical industries, how high would Invergordon rank in the priority of survival?

These and other pertinent questions are being asked by many anxious friends of the Highlands who cannot be dismissed as mere captious critics. An even more strongly urged objection—though one more restricted in its scope—is found in the fact that the proposed Invergordon scheme will entail the sacrifice, in the interests of 'development', of a large area of the very best farmland in Scotland: indeed, is claimed, in all Britain. In these days when the production of food, food, and still more food is being urged from all sides in view of the 'population explosion' of our times, there are many who cannot reconcile themselves to such a sacrifice, and who contend with vehemence that with modern means of transport, piping, and storage, together with the possibility of future revolutionary developments in this field, the necessary industrial sites should be sought on the higher grounds overlooking the Invergordon basin.

The establishment of oil-production platforms at Nigg, following the discovery of North Sea oil, has already altered conditions in this area. Some local tradesmen and former agricultural workers have been trained and are employed in this work, while many skilled workers come from other areas.

On the other side, it is urged upon the Board's behalf that the ground is essential to the project, and that food production must be sacrificed in favour of what is asserted to be the wider national interest. The project, it is further claimed, will not only play an important part in augmenting the British economy, but will also be of benefit to the Highlands themselves. Depopulation of the Highlands, so it is urged, cannot now be arrested, therefore why not replace the vanished emigrants by a new population centre in the North? Of this 'linear city' Invergordon would be the industrial hub and Inverness the commercial and cultural focus.

And a Highland University at Inverness, furnished with financial resources far exceeding anything hitherto imagined, would form a potent centre for the promotion of Celtic studies and the maintenance of the Gaelic language.

If the proposed plans for the development of oil production platforms at Loch Kishorn, Wester Ross, are carried out, no doubt some local labour will be employed, but skilled workers from outside may alter the former way of life.

Meantime let us consider the other projects, on a more modest scale, which are being promoted for the rehabilitation of the Highlands. Despite all that improved methods of farming can do, poor soil, unfavourable climate, and remoteness from the main centre of consumption, do not encourage a hope for any great increase of agricultural production in our area. Much more favourable are the prospects for forestry; and here the Highland Board and the Forestry Commission are working fruitfully hand-in-hand. No one who travels through the Highlands today can fail to be pleased by the thriving plantations with which, to an ever increasing degree, the hill-slopes are coming to be clad. Mostly the plantations are coniferous, yielding the so-called 'soft woods': pine, spruce, larch, and Douglas fir. The broad leaved trees, yielding hardwood, such as oak, ash, beech, and sycamore, have been planted chiefly for reasons of amenity, particularly round the mansion houses, and also as wind-breaks. It can now be claimed that the activities of the Forestry Commission, and of the larger landowners working under covenant, are making a substantial contribution to the economy of the Highland area. It is not too much to say that there are many thousands of acres in the Central Highlands where afforestation offers the only possible land use. Unfortunately in a number of areas the interests of the forester clash with those of the sheep farmer. Yet, as an arrestment of depopulation, forestry employs about ten times as many workers as hill-sheep farming. Socially, also, it is more desirable, since foresters tend to live in communities. The neat forest villages, often built of timber, are now becoming quite a feature of the Highlands. As to private plantations, whether carried out under the grant-aided scheme known as 'dedication of woodlands', or by the landowner entirely out of his own resources, these are a hopeful augury for the survival of not a few of our great historic demesnes; for forestry is essentially a long-term investment, grounded upon confidence in the future. "Aye be sticking in a tree", recommended the Laird of Dumbiedykes: "it will be growing when ye're sleeping." About seventy years must elapse before a stand of hardwood is mature for felling: but of course a good interim profit is yielded by the thinnings, made generally after the twentieth and twenty-fifth years. Thinning may amount in the end to about two-fifths of a stand. In general, it is the practice in the Highlands to sell trees marked for thinning to a timber merchant, who undertakes to fell and extract them. In spite of the development of substitute materials, there will probably always be a large demand for timber—though a declining coal industry is likely to require fewer pit props, and the shrinkage of our railways will reduce the demand for sleepers, while there will be fewer telegraph poles as the wires go underground.

In the foregoing chapters much has been written in their place about the great hydro-electric power schemes which since the First World War are increasingly transforming the Highland scene. Of these perhaps the most spectacular, the Ben Cruachan scheme, opened in 1965 by H.M. The Queen, was said at the time to be the second largest in the world. The power-station, which has a capacity of 400,000 kilowatts, is housed in the very granitic bowels of the vast mountain. Water is pumped from Loch Awe up to a reservoir at a height of 1,315 feet in the corrie between the summit of Cruachan Ben and its eastern neighbour Ben Vourie. This reservoir is pent up by a dam no less than 1,037 feet long; while additional water is supplied by the damming of Loch Nant, between Loch Awe and Loch Etive, from which also an underground channel carries water to a subsidiary station lower down on the west bank of the first mentioned loch.

In 1943, as a result of the Hydro-electric Development (Scotland) Act, driven through Parliament by the greatest Secretary of State for Scotland of our time, the late Thomas Johnston, the North of Scotland Hydro-electric Board was called into being. It now has authority over all the power stations and systems north of the Tay-Clyde line. No one with any imagination can fail to anticipate the tremendous changes which this development of hydro-electricity, bringing heat, light, and power to the town and clachan, mansion-house and farm and croft, is bound to effect upon the Highland scene before the present century is out. It may be increased, but surely will never, in the foreseeable future, be superseded by the development of atomic power. Indeed it may well be that the two systems could work in harness; the surplus capacity of the nuclear power-stations at off-peak times being used to pump back used water into the reservoirs of the hydro-electric plants. One thing that the hydro-electricity should help forward is what many observers think may come to provide a more suitable alternative to the building of a mammoth industrial complex on the eastern margin of the Highlands—namely the encouragement among the haughs and glens of small-scale indus-tries, particularly those based on raw materials forthcoming in the Highlands. For example, we may mention the various sub-stances produced by processing wood, as exemplified by the pulp-mill at Fort William; exploitation of the native limestones for agriculture, building, cement production; paper-making; manu-facture of rock-wool and so forth; distilling—were only the penal taxation lightened; the utilization of the vast Highland peat mosses: not to speak of the innumerable minor arts and crafts, not specially dependent upon a local raw material, at which Highland minds and eyes and hands are good. There are those who believe, perhaps optimistically, that many forms of consumer goods could be profitably manufactured in the Central Highlands, where distances are not too great from likely markets.

However benevolent his intentions may be, the financier or industrialist meditating an enterprise in the Highlands must al-ways be prepared for the rebuffs that may spring from a certain perverse streak in the Highland character. It is as if a gifted race, who for too long have felt that they have been pushed to the wall, who cherish memories of long and heartless oppression and neglect, are now prone to resist innovation for its own sake. In the eighteenth century this spirit sometimes made his tenantry resist a laird, even against the threat of eviction, when he strove to persuade them to grow those new-fangled vegetables, potatoes, and turnips, which alone could guarantee their bestial and them-selves against starvation in the winter. I remember, nearly half a century ago, the late Dr. Thomas Ross, the distinguished auth-ority on Scottish architecture, at a time when he himself was well stricken in years, telling me how as a boy he stood by his father, a Perthshire farmer, watching for their first time a railway train steaming along below them. Said the father: "And what the better wull the Cairse o' Gowrie be for thae fleerin' deevils!"

But when all is said and done, so long as human nature remains unaltered, the main sources of revenue in the Highlands must continue to be: sport and tourism. Although the exaggerated rentals paid for deer and grouse moors before the last war, and for angling reaches, are now a thing of the past, there is no doubt that these pursuits bring each year a very large revenue into the Highlands, besides providing much direct and indirect employment. Nothing can be sillier, or more completely based upon political prejudice, than to accuse Highland landowners of possessing a 'grouse and gillie' complex. The rent of many a Highland moor helps to preserve from extinction an ancient demesne, crippled by punitive taxation. Indeed not a few proprietors are nowadays opening their mansions to paying guests during the shooting season. A curious, and significant, development of the post-war years is the growth in popularity of grouse moors as against deer forests. This appears to be primarily due to economic considerations. The grouse season is longer, it provides sport for more guns, and grouse moors can be easily worked by syndicates, at a much less cost per head.

Today, Highland sports are developing in many novel ways, suitable for those whose purses do not rise to a gun in a syndicate. It almost begins to look as if the wheel had come full circle. For generations, owing to economic pressure, every glen in the Highlands has had the same sad tale to tell of rural depopulation, which has cleared the fine men and women out of them and congested our cities with a landless ex-peasantry who have lost their tangy rustic culture and undergone a process of urban barbarization. Today we are witnessing, during the summer months, a converse explosion into the countryside of the vast populations herded in the towns, on the part of thousands wearied by the monotony of office and industrial routine, cloyed with the synthetic and mindless pleasures purveyed by dance-hall, cinema, television, and bingo. Out into the country they throng in their multitudes, camping, hill-walking, mountaineering, pony-trekking, boating, water-ski-ing—and in winter, ski-ing and snow-tramping. The more our slow-moving nation edges its way forward to a sensible policy of 'staggered' holidays, the longer and more numerous will be this annual invasion of the country by the towns.

Alongside sport, we must look for a great extension of tourism. The grandeur, beauty and variety of our Highland scenery, its richness in historical and literary associations, the number and different character of its ancient monuments, all will combine to allure more and more visitors from home and abroad. In particular, much more should be done, in Britain as a whole, for the preservation, even if only as a tourist asset, of our ancient monuments—our prehistoric cairns and standing stones and sculptured crosses, our churches and our castles, our ancient manor-houses large and small, and all the rest of our historic heritage. It angers me when I think upon the £140,000 spent on a portrait of Wellington—there are plenty of them in Britain—or upon the £800,000 provided for a Leonardo cartoon of whose existence in London few were aware. There is no relevancy (save mere metropolitan prestige) in this drawing being required in Britain; it could as properly have been anywhere else. Skilful reproductions are available for the ordinary student; with modern transport, the connoisseur could as easily visit it, say in America. On the other hand, our ancient and historic monuments belong to us alone. They are not to be seen elsewhere. There can never be any more of them. Their number is always being reduced, by one cause or another. And yet the provision made for their maintenance by the state remains pitifully inadequate. Almost literally, from Land's End to the Mucle Flugga there are scores upon scores of worth-while monuments vainly waiting for protection. When once this country has got its priorities aright, when irrelevant or nostalgic overseas commitments have at last been discarded, is it not too much to hope for the better care of our fast-dwindling national heritage?

Obviously all the above is going to pose vast problems for the Highland economy. New and well-equipped hotels, youth-hostels, camping sites, ski-huts, large scale lay-bys for motor transport of all kinds, a great extension of provision for 'bed and breakfast', with the necessary facilities—all this and much more will be necessary. There must be a huge increase in the number of that splendid old institution, the village or roadside shop—for the travelling van will never cope with the needs of multitudes who hardly know where they may be sleeping each succeeding night. Facilities for rational recreation must be available for those who are not always on the move. An enormous expansion and improvement in our roads will be necessary. In view of the appalling carnage that is certain to ensue, urgent consideration will require to be given to re-opening, under different conditions, of some of the railway lines closed down by purblind officials blinking at the Highlands from distant London. And an improvement in air-transport, despite the obvious limitations imposed by the mountains, must be diligently sought.

Along some such lines, in my submission, lies our main hope for the future of the Highlands. Clearly serious dangers lurk ahead—dangers to the Highland scene and to the Highland way of life. The town dweller must be educated to respect the country-side and those who make their homes in it. The young mountaineer must be warned that the great bens sometimes hit back hard at those who violate their sanctuaries, and that a climbing accident involves not only its victims in death or suffering, but his rescuers in risk and hardship. Heaviest of all rests the responsi-bility upon those who devise the many new buildings and instal-lations of all kinds which must arise amid the Highland scene. I have already animadverted on what has been suffered to happen at Aviemore: and others besides Macdonalds will fail to relish the idea of a camping and caravan site at Achnacon in Glencoe— right in the middle of the main scene of the massacre of 1692.

The policy which I have thus sketched out for the Scottish Highlands of course represents my own views only. Other pro-posals will no doubt be forthcoming. Whatever plans may be adopted, their carrying out is bound to require a long period of years. In the process, the Highlands as we know them will greatly change. Much of their peace and solitude will vanish for ever. It is the price that must be paid for economic survival. But the Highlands are large; and there will still be ample room for those who wish to escape from "the madding crowd", and who love to enjoy in loneliness "the large religion of the hills".

INDEX OF PLACES